Diane Macdonald
5, CarrieBlair
Cresent
Edderton
By Tain
Ross-Shire
Scotland.

New World of Knowledge

World History

New World of Knowledge

World History

Compiled and edited by Kenneth Bailey

Collins

Glasgow and London

Designed by Peter Sullivan, Charles Gould

Written by Richard Wright, Kenneth Bailey

Illustrated by Fred Anderson, Rupert Brown, Sheridan Davies, Gerry Embleton, Andrew Farmer, Terry Gabbey, The Garden Studio, John Glover, Charles Gould, Harry Green, John Grimwade, Harry Holland, Richard Hook, John Hutchinson, David Johnson, Angus McBride, David Nash, Peter North, Kenneth Ody, Anthony Roberts, Bill Robertshaw, Eddie Scott-Jones, Bill Stallion, George Thompson, Carol Wheeler, Maurice Wilson

First published 1973

Published by William Collins Sons and Company Limited, Glasgow and London

© 1973 William Collins Sons and Company Limited

Filmset by Typesetting Services Ltd, Glasgow

Printed in Great Britain

ISBN 0 00 106102 X

Acknowledgements
Photographs are reproduced by permission of the following: pages 69 and 95, Victoria and Albert Museum, London, Crown Copyright; page 138, from the collection of His Grace the Duke of Bedford, Woburn Abbey, Bedfordshire, England.

Contents

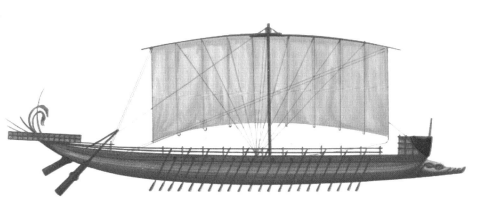

The Ancient World

Man is a late arrival on the planet earth, which had existed for many millions of years before anything like a human being appeared. How man rose from simple savage beginnings to be the controller of the complicated society in which we live today is a wonderful story. No primitive man could have imagined, as he scraped a bare living with his meagre resources, that his descendants would one day be able to place one of his kind on the moon as an advance spy of future plans.

The technical knowledge, huge reserves of wealth, and daring imagination required for space travel, are proof of man's success in mastering his home, the earth. This progress has never been smooth. Despite the advances of modern sciences, there are still many tribes living as simple savages in lonely places today. Many great civilisations have swiftly risen to supreme power, accomplished marvellous things, and then been destroyed. But always the adventurous, restless spirit of man built new marvels from the ashes of defeat.

Stone Age Man

Our first knowledge of man is not gained from books but from the bones and few possessions he left behind in caves and burial places. Man has always been a tool-making animal and the long period before the discovery of metal is known as the Stone Age. Bone and flint provided the cutting edges of his tools. Perhaps the most gallant struggle of mankind for survival was fought out in those distant days, when the murderous ice crept south from the Arctic, driving all life before it. The man who discovered fire was the saviour of that age.

By the end of the Stone Age, man the hunter had become man the farmer with a settled way of life. His food supply was reasonably certain and his home gave him adequate shelter and some comfort. Having mastered the crafts of the weaver and the potter, he had all the clothes and utensils he needed for basic living. A large part of the world's population lives no better now than early man did thousands of years before Christ.

Early Civilisation

Yet in certain favoured areas, civilisation was born and great empires came into being. In every case a great river valley was the cradle of the civilisation. Assyria and Babylon grew up in the Tigris–Euphrates basin, and Egypt on the banks of the Nile. Further east, there were two more civilisations of great size and splendour on the Indus of north-west India and on the Yellow River of China. In these fertile river valleys it was easy to grow good crops.

The food supply was certain and only a part of the population was needed to raise the harvest. Subdivision of labour took place and the specialist was born, the man or woman who could become an expert by concentrating on one job. Thus the craftsman was released from the plough and the hoe. In very privileged areas, the best craftsmen could specialise and become artists. In this way life soon became rich and varied. Surplus wealth meant larger taxes and grander projects for ambitious rulers.

Religion and Magic

Right from the start man was more than a machine merely working to keep himself alive. There is early evidence of art allied to magic and religion. Life was very unsure at first and man had little power to overcome a hostile environment. The unleashed forces of nature seen in storm, flood and earthquake terrified him with their blind power. He needed help and assurance and among the earliest peoples the priest soon became important. He was a mixture of doctor, magician, scientist and politician, and all early knowledge was in the hands of the priestly caste. Temples and tombs are the first truly impressive buildings of the early civilisations.

The concentration of many people in one area meant that better organisation was needed. All of the early civilisations were in warm lands and irrigation was practised to guard the precious life-giving water. Mining is a highly technical process and probably has led to more inventions by mankind than any other trade.

All these activities required political organisation to enable large bodies of men to work together. The small towns became cities and the cities became nations. Eventually the more powerful ones became empires with many weaker countries under their

control. It was these mighty empires which built the wonders of the ancient world. Their power was absolute, and slavery was the normal fate of those defeated in war.

However, all these civilisations gave birth to great religions which used their healing power to offset man's savagery in war and to teach him a better way of life than selfishness and greed. When the lead in civilisation passed to Europe, a new dimension was added to mankind's understanding. The ordinary man had no individual value in the East but in Greece he acquired his true position and dignity. The idea that all men were important was born in the free democracy of Greece. The rule of law was established by the Romans. Although there was still slavery and suffering, the birth of conscience and a feeling of responsibility for others had begun.

The Arch of Constantine in Rome

Man the Hunter

The geography of the land and the nature of man's environment have shaped the course of his history. All animals must learn to live within their environment—the natural conditions of landscape and climate in which they find themselves—in order to survive. Early man had exactly the same problems to face and overcome as other animals.

One reason for man's success on earth has been his ability not only to live in the environment as it is, but to impose his will upon it and if necessary change it to his needs. He overcomes cold by making clothes, building shelters and warming himself before fire. He feeds himself by growing crops and domesticating and slaughtering animals. He makes tools and weapons to aid his efforts.

Man the Tool-maker

Early man has been called 'tool-maker' and 'handy' man, references to the fact that he has been able to make things and use them as extensions of his hands. In this way he is unique. Other animals in the wild, notably apes, may pick up stones and sticks and seem to employ them to some purpose. But it is doubtful if any animal other than man makes conscious use of objects in the sense that thought leads to action.

When considering the early history of man it is only possible to do so from the point where he already possesses some form of social and

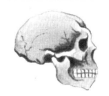 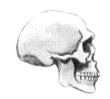 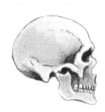

Three skulls which show the different structure of heads of prehistoric, primitive and modern man.

On the left is that of Peking Man, also known as *Homo erectus* because of his upright posture;

in the centre is that of an Australian aborigine; and on the right is the skull of a modern man.

cultural life, however primitive. How he arrived at that point—living in groups with other human beings, sheltering in caves, hunting animals, making clothes and using fire—can only be guessed at.

His use of tools and weapons may be described in three successive phases—selective, adaptive and inventive. First, he selects a natural object which can be used for some purpose as it exists (such as a stone for crushing things). Then he adapts a natural object so that it can be used more effectively (such as the flaking of a piece of flint to make a better cutting edge). And lastly, he invents for a particular purpose an object which does not exist in nature (such as a bow to propel a dart or arrow).

Although it is now generally accepted that man is related to the apes and monkeys it is not possible to say when man as a distinct creature began. It is likely that he first developed in central Africa. Southern apeman lived there probably as far back as two million years ago. Recent discoveries in Africa at the Olduvai Gorge in

Tanzania have led scientists to believe that a more advanced creature than Southern apeman also lived there about 1,800,000 years ago. Crude pebble tools and very primitive stone structures have been found at Olduvai.

A date about two million years ago may sound a long way off but within the general time-scale of the age of the earth it is relatively near. The age of the earth is nowadays reckoned to be about 6,000 million years, more than 3,000 times the probable age of Southern apeman and nearly a million times the whole period of man's recorded history.

The Ice Ages

Until about 10,000 years ago large areas of the northern hemisphere were in the grip of great sheets of ice. In prehistoric times there were four great Ice Ages, and on each occasion the ice spread downwards from the north polar regions and retreated again, at times covering almost one-third of the earth's surface.

The whole period of the Ice Ages lasted for tens of thousands of years and greatly affected the conditions of existence for primitive man and all animal and plant life. During the Ice Ages, perhaps about 50,000 years ago, man was fully developed as a hunting animal, instead of being simply a food-gatherer.

Knowledge of the kind of communal life led by early man comes mainly from studying the behaviour of those primitive societies which still exist, and the way in which groups of higher animals live together. When man became a hunter he would certainly have been grouped into family units, with these groups probably coming together to form loose-knit tribes.

The basic condition of a hunting existence was its restlessness. Man was constantly on the move and such 'homes' as he had would have been very temporary affairs, making use of natural shelter. Since there was no way of storing the meat of an animal

Some of the most remarkable cave paintings are those from the Tassili rock shelters in North Africa, drawn by Stone Age people as long ago as 5000 B.C. Animal fat was burned in a sandstone lamp (right) to provide light in the caves.

once it was slaughtered, fresh supplies were an almost day-to-day requirement. This meant that man shifted his ground to keep pace with the movement of the game he hunted. In some cases he travelled hundreds of miles following such animals as reindeer and buffalo.

It has been argued that the life of a hunter is the one most natural to man since he was conditioned to it for thousands of years. The monotony of civilised existence, which began with the first farming communities, is something to which he will never grow entirely accustomed. Hunting for wild animals was the principal occupation of men. Women would probably have spent much of their time gathering wild plants, berries and roots.

The Domestic Life

Like most animal mothers, women would also have had the task of rearing babies and looking after young children, although the ties between children and parents were much looser than in modern society. Women became more domesticated as social life developed, cooking food and making clothing. It has often been said that one of man's most important discoveries was the control of fire. Whereas fire was eventually used for the purposes of cooking, the other benefits it gave to man, such as warmth and protection against wild animals, came first.

Clothing of some sort was worn from very early times. Although the natural thing is to assume that it was adopted as a protection against cold and other hazards of a wild life, some anthropologists (scientists who study human origins) hold the view that man first began to cover his body as a means of display—that the earliest garments, in fact, were ornamental.

Most of the tools and weapons which early man fashioned were made from stone and for this reason the era in which he lived is known as the Stone Age. Since this era spread over a very long time, during which man made great strides along the path of basic discovery, it is usually split into Old and New Stone Ages, or to give them their scientific names, the Palaeolithic (from the Greek words for old and stone) and Neolithic (meaning new and stone). It was in the Neolithic, or New Stone Age, that man made the advance from hunter to farmer.

Prehistoric man hunted the woolly mammoth for food. The huge animal was sometimes lured into swampy ground or trapped in man-made pits before being killed with primitive spears.

Man the Farmer

The spread of farming communities, or the Neolithic revolution as it has been called, took place over a long period of time. When taking a rapid glance at man's progress through history it is all too easy to see events as a series of clear-cut and decisive steps forward. This is true even of comparatively recent history, when one talks of the Dark Ages, the Renaissance, or the Age of Exploration, as if each of these existed within a separate compartment with clearly defined doors marked entrance and exit. Nothing, of course, could be further from the truth. All developments are gradual and the pace at which things happened in the ancient world differed from place to place.

The main area for the successful growth of the first farming communities was a limited region of south-west Asia. This is a part of the world where all the major advances of early man seem to have been made. Here people came together to farm the land and look after domesticated animals.

One of the chief requirements for this kind of life was a favourable climate, an orderly succession of seasons with adequate rainfall in winter and warm summers. As the Ice Ages came to an end and the cold conditions receded northwards this requirement was met at its best in south-west Asia.

In other parts of the world conditions were not so good. Most of Africa varied between the extremes of the hot, dry Saharan deserts to the dank, tropical jungles of the interior. Europe was a mass of forestland. Not a great deal is known about primitive life in the Americas, but an agricultural society developed there in what must have been similar conditions to those in Asia: quite independently, most experts believe, from the Old World.

The New Stone Age

To get a clearer idea of the development of people in the New Stone Age it helps to remember that while man was enjoying the changed conditions of life in a small area of Eurasia, the people of Europe were still in a primitive state, some 4,000 years behind their Asian cousins. Other people in widely different parts of the world are still living in a Stone Age environment.

It seems likely that the two aspects of a settled agricultural life—the

cultivation of crops and the domestication of animals—happened at the same time. It is only possible to guess how it happened. Perhaps people began to clear ground around wild plants which they knew were good to eat and saw how they prospered and seeded themselves. Another clue can be seen in the custom among primitive peoples of making offerings to the

At Khirokitia in Cyprus the remains of an early farming community have been dug up. Here, about 5500 B.C., there was a small town of beehive huts built with mud bricks and plaster.

dead. Wild grain was sometimes scattered around them and this could have put forth new growth which led to an understanding of the process of seed dispersal.

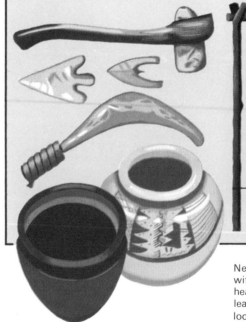

New Stone Age man used stone-headed axes with bone handles, flint knives and arrow heads. Later he made pots from clay and learned how to weave using a primitive loom built on a framework of sticks.

The domestication of animals probably began when wild animals were captured and kept in some kind of simple enclosure until they were needed as food and could be slaughtered. It would be a logical step to feed captive wild animals and look after them over longer and longer periods. Sooner or later breeding would have taken place naturally and all the advantages of herding animals become apparent.

Before man could settle into any

kind of communal village life it was necessary that there should be a surplus of food beyond his immediate requirements. Only when people were released from the necessity of the daily hunt for food could they begin the process we call civilisation. By this time man had speech and the means of communicating his thoughts and desires to his fellows. He was able to make quite complex tools, had mastered the gift of fire, wore clothes and built simple shelters. His creative talents in woodwork and pottery and the use of metals improved. The basic inventions of the lever, the wedge and, most important of all, the wheel, had been made.

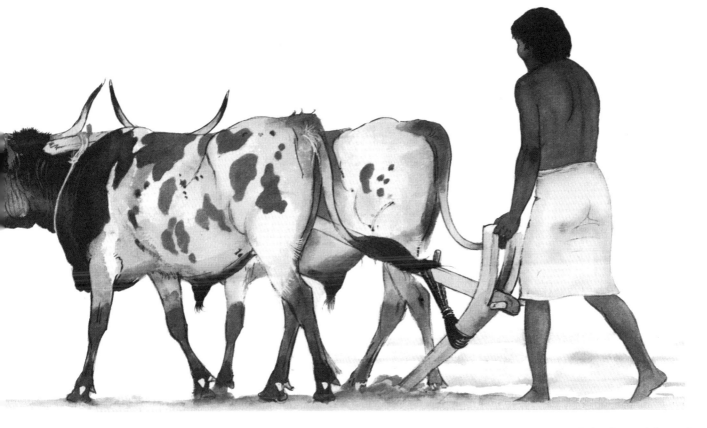

Villages and Towns

The many discoveries of Stone Age sites in Asia and Europe have enabled archaeologists to build up a fairly complete picture of early communal life. More and more places are being uncovered in modern times, particularly in Asia Minor, and the method of identifying the age of objects by what is known as Carbon-14 dating has brought greater accuracy to the dates of antiquity.

Carbon-14 dating is a technique scientists have discovered based on the fact that all living matter absorbs a substance called radio-carbon. When the living matter dies it no longer absorbs radio-carbon and the amount it contains is fixed. This amount gradually fades away from the dead matter at a known rate and by testing the amount of radioactivity left in an object, even if it is thousands of years since it died, its date can be assessed.

Jericho, near the Dead Sea in the Jordan valley, is one of the oldest known towns in the world. Carbon-14 dating has placed the lowest level of its buildings at about 7800 B.C. Both here and at Jarmo in the Kurdish hills near the River Tigris, another of the oldest sites to have been revealed, the houses were built partly of stone and partly of a mixture of clay, water and chopped straw. The famous walls of Jericho enclosed a town which covered about eight acres.

Local materials always played their part in determining the nature and shape of a building and different types of houses evolved which have in many cases remained characteristic of a district. From the very beginning there is plenty of evidence to suggest that man decorated the interior of his home and created basic articles of furniture of the kind that have served the same function ever since.

Some of the most remarkable houses of all are those excavated at Khirokitia in Cyprus. About fifty of them have been found, but it is believed that there were more than a thousand, which implies the existence of a small town with a population of several thousands. The houses were bee-hive shaped, built of mud and straw on stone foundations. Each had a central hearth and a hole in the domed roof to allow the smoke of fire to escape. The most interesting thing about them is the partial upper floor supported by limestone pillars and built on a wooden frame covered with brushwood and mud. The floor was reached by steps and was probably used as a sleeping area.

Crops and Animals

The most important plants to the early farmers were cereal crops: wheat, barley and millet in the Old World and maize in the Americas. It probably took hundreds of years to arrive at good cultivated plants from the wild originals. At the beginning all plants could be regarded as weeds, until the primitive farmer had selected and tamed a species to serve his needs. It is interesting to note that at first rye and oats existed only as weeds and were not cultivated for thousands of years. Maize is believed to be native to the Americas and was not known in the Old World until after the time of Columbus in the fifteenth century.

Root vegetables and wild fruits had

The population of the world in 3000 B.C. may have been about 100 million people. Today it is estimated to be about 3,700 million, which gives an average density throughout the world of about 70 people per square mile of land. The density in big towns is much greater. As this chart illustrates, the same area which supported one man in primitive times may now be occupied by several hundred people.

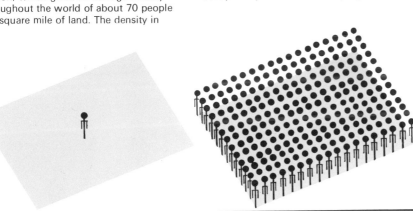

The first boat was probably a fallen tree trunk. Later, in the New Stone Age, man learned to make dugouts using tools and fire.

sites it is not likely that the animals were used for transport until much later in man's history.

Tools and Weapons
The basic tool for cultivating was the hoe or digging stick. Sickles were also widely used, the earliest consisting of flint knives set in straight bones or within the curved antler-bone of a deer. Weapons were few in early Neolithic times since society was essentially a peaceful one. The earliest weapons, of course, cannot be distinguished from implements used when hunting animals. The bow and arrow is very ancient, and so is the sling. Later there were maces, clubs and battle-axes.

Arts and Crafts
One of the most significant inventions of early man was that of pottery. There were early attempts at making pottery at Khirokitia but these were soon abandoned. Painted pottery with its characteristic red-on-cream design dates from about 5500 B.C. in southern Turkey. The making of pottery has enormous significance for the archaeologist, since it is through its remains

that so much of the history of the ancient world has been charted.

Early people were never satisfied with the simply functional, and the beauty of design, colouring and shape of pottery tells its own story of man's artistic achievement through the ages. Vessels were also made of wood, stone and ivory, though of course few wooden objects have survived.

Basketry and textiles date from about 6500 B.C. The first baskets were made by what is called the coiled technique. A core of material was woven into a long continuous strip which was then coiled layer by layer upon itself and stitched together to form the shape of the container. Spinning and weaving are also very old crafts. The earliest fragment of textile comes from Egypt and there are images of looms on Egyptian pottery dating from about 4400 B.C.

There is little evidence of the style of dress worn by Neolithic people, although since the invention of weaving it is probable that linen was used for clothes. Leather, furs and grass were also used to make garments. Naturally, the actual materials differed according to the climate of the land in which people lived. It was common for both men and women to wear necklaces, anklets and bracelets as ornaments, and all kinds of trinkets were popular.

The first earthenware pots were probably made by building up rolls of clay one on top of the other and then smoothing down the sides before the pot was hardened by fire. Basket-making is a very old craft and was practised by most primitive people.

been gathered and eaten by prehistoric man for thousands of years. It is difficult to establish when man began to cultivate them deliberately or when the improved varieties we know today first came to be developed. Crab apples, cherries, walnuts and olives grew wild, and there were wild peas and beans which formed an important part of diet and had the advantage of being easily dried and stored.

The first domestic animals—goats, sheep, cattle and pigs—all lived wild in the same area of Eurasia where farming began. It has been suggested that after the Ice Ages animals started to group together in areas where water was obtainable. Pushed nearer to man because of the surrounding desert areas, it is possible that animals began to benefit from the waste products of early farming activities. They stayed around to gather the husks of grain and stubble which man left behind.

It would have been a simple step for man to have captured and tamed some of these animals. Sheep and goats were the first to be domesticated; cattle are believed to have descended from the wild aurochs of southern Russia, and pigs from the common wild boar which roamed over large areas of Europe, Asia and Africa. Although the bones of horses have been found on New Stone Age

Apart from the dog, the first animal to be domesticated was probably the goat, kept at first for its milk. Later it was joined by cattle and sheep, which gave milk and meat.

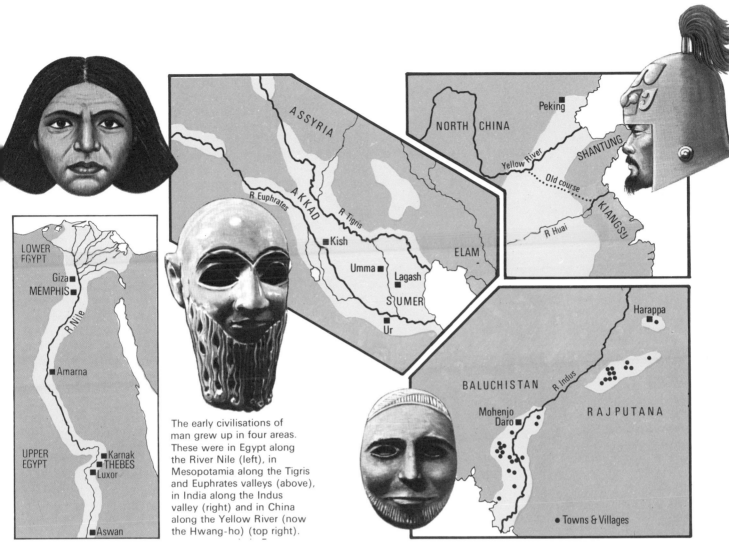

The early civilisations of man grew up in four areas. These were in Egypt along the River Nile (left), in Mesopotamia along the Tigris and Euphrates valleys (above), in India along the Indus valley (right) and in China along the Yellow River (now the Hwang-ho) (top right).

Early Civilisations

The first civilisations based on an urban society, that is people living together in towns, grew up in four main areas of the world. The earliest was probably that in Mesopotamia, centred on the valley of the Tigris and Euphrates rivers. Almost as old, and having links with Mesopotamia, is the civilisation of Egypt in the Nile valley. The recorded history of both begins some time between 4000 and 3500 B.C. Although each had existed for a long period before then, we know virtually nothing about them.

India and China

The third civilisation was in the north-west of India and is known by the name of the Indus Valley. Beyond the fact that the people of the cities there, Mohenjo-daro and Harappa, were foreign to the land in which they lived, not much can be said about them with any certainty. Again there are links with Mesopotamia and these early settlers in India may have been Sumerians.

Finally, there is the ancient Chinese civilisation which came into being in the area of the Yellow River in northern China. Here there are no written documents which can take China's history back before about 1400 B.C., although traditionally the Shang Dynasty was founded in 1766 B.C. But society had reached a high level by that time and quite obviously it had been in existence for many years.

One of the things that all four of these civilisations have in common is the fact that each grew up around a river. It is easy to see that a river formed a focal point for early people. There was water and fish—an important part of the diet—and a highway for the transport of materials over long distances. Logs, rafts and boats had all been used by men since Palaeolithic times.

Surrounding the rivers in each place were deserts or barren plains. This meant that people congregated in narrow strips of land along the river banks. Here the ground on either side of the water was enriched by flooding. It was easier to clear and cultivate than the dense forestland which enveloped such great rivers as the Amazon and the Mississippi in the Americas.

There was also greater protection for people from wild animals in cleared strips of land alongside water. Since hunting became more difficult and there was less natural growth for food-gathering, man needed to develop his skill as a farmer in order to live. And all the early civilisations were based on highly organised food-producing societies whose surplus crops led to trade and the commercial life of cities.

The First Leaders

From these early societies the first leaders emerged, men who in moments of crisis and difficulty could contribute that extra stroke of originality and invention. Since the continued good fortune of ordinary people depended so much on natural forces, it is understandable that the man who could overcome them was looked up to as a god. All the early chieftains and leaders were given this god-like quality by the people. The folk tales of every nation are filled with references to the marvellous powers of its early kings.

15

The Sumerians

There is no general agreement about the origins of the Sumerians. Most likely they came from the hill country of central Asia and entered Mesopotamia possibly by sea through the Persian Gulf. By about 3500 B.C. they had established themselves in a number of places in the southern part of the Tigris/Euphrates valley and the land where they settled was known as Sumer.

The first Sumerian settlements were built on mounds of high ground which raised villages above the level of the surrounding land, which was often flooded. Houses were made of reed matting and wooden beams with a covering of mud plaster. They had wooden doors which turned in stone sockets, and floors were of beaten mud.

The people lived a simple life for hundreds of years, the villages gradually giving way to cities in the fourth millenium B.C. (a millenium is 1,000 years). At some time during this period it is believed that the whole area of Lower Mesopotamia was overwhelmed by a great flood. The probable truth of this event is echoed in several Flood stories in ancient literature, notably the Old Testament tale of Noah and the Ark.

Whatever unknown disasters befell the first Sumerians, they were strong enough to overcome them. We think of them today as city-dwellers because our knowledge rests on the discoveries made in the great cities. But nothing is known of the immense struggles there must have been to transform isolated mud-hut villages into such impressive places as Ur and Erech.

Irrigating the Land

One of the most important things which the early Sumerians had to do was to control the waters of the Euphrates River. Although little rain fell in the lower reaches of Mesopotamia, every year the river flooded and the surrounding land was nearly always swampy. To make more of this land available for crop-raising and animal-herding, wet areas had to be drained and the deserts watered.

By a long process of trial and error the Sumerians learned the science of irrigation. They built embankments to hold back the river and directed the water through a complex system of canals, dams and reservoirs. This sort of large-scale operation needed the combined effort of many people. Working together in this way made the building of cities possible.

The sequence of events can be seen clearly enough. By controlling the rivers more land was cleared and the production of crops increased. Although money did not exist as a means of exchange, there was a surplus of food. This could be used to barter with other people for things the Sumerians needed—timber, metals, minerals and precious stones —which they could not produce themselves.

The Art of Writing

The art of writing is one of the earliest signs of a civilised people. As the structure of city life built up in Mesopotamia, trade and barter increased and created new occupations, such as merchant and importer. Buildings became more complicated and the craft of the architect came into being. Priests were invested with the power which comes from being the official mouthpiece through which man speaks to the gods.

The home of an early Sumerian nobleman

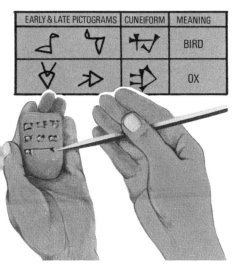

EARLY & LATE PICTOGRAMS		CUNEIFORM	MEANING
			BIRD
			OX

Cuneiform writing developed from early pictograms, or pictures used as symbols. Wedge-shaped signs were inscribed with a stylus on soft clay tablets which were baked.

More and more, people began to specialise in particular jobs. One obvious result of all this activity was that some system was needed to make a permanent record of transactions and events. Memory is faulty and out of necessity writing was invented. And from the time of its invention we can date the beginning of truly recorded history.

The oldest known writing is on two sides of a limestone tablet found in the city of Kish. It dates from about 3500 B.C. and confirms that writing at first consisted of crude pictures of objects, which we call pictograms. This Sumerian invention preceded the similar system called hieroglyphics which the Egyptians created.

These systems of picture writing eventually gave way to syllabic scripts, based on different signs for the sounds of different syllables, and so to an alphabetical script. But the process took hundreds of years to develop.

The most widespread form of writing in the ancient world was called cuneiform, a word which means wedge-shaped. Although it was the basic script for Hittite, Babylonian, Assyrian and Persian peoples it had been forgotten in the classical period of Greece and Rome. Rediscovered in modern times it was finally deciphered during the nineteenth century. A young German teacher named Georg Grotefend worked out the meaning of the first ten letters of a cuneiform script as a result of a bet! But the main work was done by an Englishman, Henry Rawlinson, whose translations of the Darius monument at Behistun were presented to the Royal Asiatic Society in 1846.

Headdress and jewellery of the Sumerian queen Shub-ad discovered in the royal tombs at Ur. The head was modelled from a female skull found in the same grave.

Cuneiform signs have been described 'like bird tracks on the wet sand'. They were made by a wedge-shaped stylus, which may have been metal or a length of reed cut off square at the end, impressed on to damp clay tablets. When the tablets were filled they were baked until they were hard.

The Gods

Writing began because of the need for bookkeeping and since the centre for commercial transactions was the temple, writing was associated with religion from the beginning, although it was not religious in origin.

When the Sumerians left the Elamite hills to settle in the Euphrates valley they brought their gods with them. The pantheon, or family of gods, was large, with special deities who were patrons of natural forces—a god of fire, a god of water, a god of the air.

Each of the Sumerian cities adopted a particular god who was the focus for every kind of activity. The whole territory became the property of the god and all work was done in his name. The king was the god's representative to the people and his priests controlled the city's fortunes.

In this way, trade, education, town planning and the law were all directed from the temple in the god's name. The people were entertained by

This statue of Gudea, a governor of Lagash, is over 4,000 years old. It shows the typical features and shaven head of the men of this period. It is a fine example of Sumerian sculpture and is made from diorite, a hard stone which is very difficult to work.

regular religious festivals and artists and craftsmen were encouraged to create beautiful things to dedicate to the gods. This association between the 'church', learning and the arts—which persists throughout history—was begun in the early civilisations.

The Law

From the earliest times, any collection of people who have set out to live together peaceably must have had a system of rules—however crude—which everyone tried to obey. These rules were perhaps imposed by the strong upon the weak, and may have been to the advantage of the strong rather than for the general good.

They may also have been arrived at by mutual agreement for the benefit of society as a whole. Whatever the system or its merits, someone had to see that the rules were obeyed. In the Sumerian city states it was the priests who had this task. The word of the law was the word of god. Although some effort was made to work towards a fair system of trial, the punishments for offences were savage and cruel.

The First Cities

In the ruins of one of the oldest cities in the world, at Kish near Babylon, can be seen the remains of a royal palace. On the evidence of the ruins it was an impressive building, yet it was made entirely from mud. In a land where there was no stone and little wood available, the early Sumerians used unbaked mud bricks held together by a pliable mixture of mud and water.

One important fact they learned right away was the necessity of raising these buildings above the level of flood water. The easiest way to do this was to build on an earth mound, in just the same way that the reed-hut villages had been constructed in earlier times.

It was a natural step to smooth down the sides of these earth mounds as they were built and in this way the beginnings of a walled city are seen. The habit of building on earth mounds was continued in the grander structures of Sumerian cities, notably the temples. The one at Eridu built about 3500 B.C. is recognised as the earliest example, on which all subsequent temples were modelled. Its imposing porticos and columns built high above a mud-brick base set a pattern which was repeated all over Mesopotamia.

The Ziggurat of Ur

The most famous Sumerian monument to have survived in part is the Ziggurat of Ur, built chiefly by Ur Nammu in about 2100 B.C. Although its central core is mud-brick, the exterior is contained by kiln-fired bricks, which accounts for its fine state of preservation. Burnt mud-bricks were used from an early period but usually only on important buildings or to strengthen foundations.

Every great Sumerian city had its ziggurat erected in honour of its local god. The most famous was the one at Babylon to the god Marduk, which is now totally destroyed. It is remembered today as the Tower of Babel, which is mentioned in the Old Testament Book of Genesis. The word Babel originally meant 'gateway to God', but for the Hebrews the Tower of Babel became a symbol of confusion because it was dedicated to a false god.

The Ziggurat of Ur was a three-storeyed step pyramid which supported the shrine of the god Nannar. The approach to the shrine was by three imposing flights of steps. The lower part of the Ziggurat still exists today in good condition, and the upper part can be reconstructed with reasonable accuracy from the remains.

The building contains the interesting feature that its rectangular walls have a deliberate slight outward curve, which pleases the eye and gives the whole structure the appearance of greater solidity. The architects used a principle which was revived by the Greeks when they built the Parthenon —that of a slight distortion which corrects the imperfections in observation of the human eye.

The Home of the Gods

The Ziggurat dominated the whole city of Ur. Wherever people worked they had only to look up and see the raised temple of their patron god shining in the sky. As a hill people they were used to looking up to the mountains as the home of the gods. On the flat plains of Mesopotamia the ziggurats they built became artificial mountains and holy places.

A reconstruction of the Ziggurat of Ur as it may have looked about 2000 B.C. The temple at the top was dedicated to the moon-god Nanna.

The standard of Ur consists of two panels mounted back to back on a wooden frame and decorated with scenes of war and peace. It may have been part of a musical instrument.

Although it had been subject to the ups and downs of fortune, Ur had been the most important city in Sumer since about 2600 B.C. Today its ruins show better than any other place in Mesopotamia what a great city of Sumeria looked like. It was a walled city built on a raised mound, the site of many previous settlements. Its buildings spread over an area of over ten square kilometres (nearly four square miles), although some were outside the city proper.

A detailed reconstruction of its streets has been made by archaeologists. The plan of Ur, unlike that of the orderly but even older city of Mohenjo-daro in the Indus Valley, exhibits all the signs of a place which has grown up piecemeal over a long period. It took perhaps 1,500 years for Ur to change gradually from a village into a city. The haphazard arrangement of its roads and buildings

has much in common with some modern European cities of great age.

There are narrow streets, blind alleys, open bazaars, large and small buildings jostling one another for space. The impression is of a busy, bustling place, crammed with people, for its population has been estimated at about 350,000.

The houses of Ur, whatever their size or importance, tended to be built to a similar pattern. Usually two-storeyed, rooms were grouped around a central courtyard, those on the upper floor opening on to a wooden balcony. The roofs sloped inwards, so that when it rained the water ran down gutters to discharge into a sunken drain in the middle of the courtyard.

These houses were occupied mostly by ordinary middle class people. They were the result of many years of experiment to find the type of house most suited to life in close-packed urban conditions. How successfully they suited the climate and conditions may be judged by the fact that to this day many Arab houses in such places as Baghdad still follow the same basic pattern.

Excavations at Ur

The city of Ur was first excavated during 1927/8 by the English archaeologist Sir Leonard Woolley. This great event in the history of archaeology followed earlier digs in the Tigris/Euphrates area which had been begun by a French consular official in 1877. Before that date nothing positive was known about the Sumerian civilisation, which was to prove even older than the Egyptian.

In the royal graves at Ur valuable finds were made which showed that the Sumerians were master craftsmen in the art of making jewellery and precious objects from gold and silver. One of the most celebrated of these is the mosaic Standard of Ur, which is covered with picture-book drawings showing life in Sumer. One side of the

standard depicts civilian life and the other is filled with military scenes. The drawings give a clear picture of the social life of the people and their appearance and dress.

The Standard also shows the uniforms and weapons of the professional army. In Mesopotamia where the city-states were constantly warring with one another, more or less permanent armies had become necessary. The foot soldiers were equipped with bronze helmets, shields and long spears. Others had heavy studded leather cloaks and battle-axes. The chariots, which were drawn by four asses, carried two men, one to drive and one to fight.

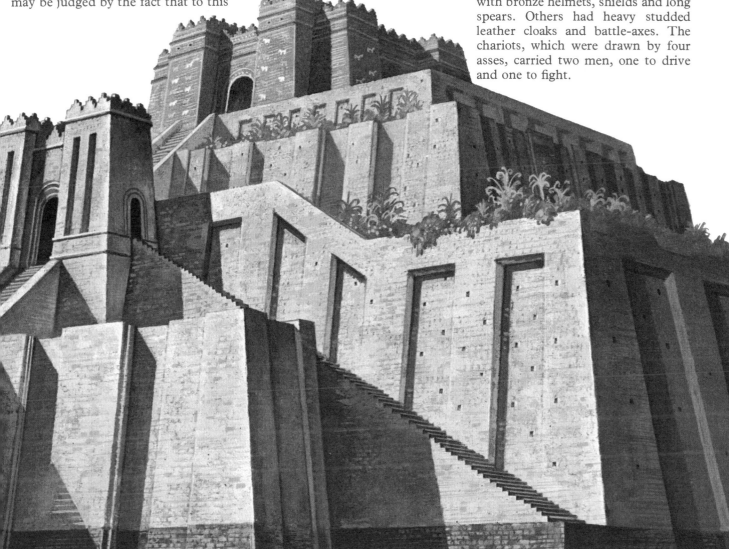

Ancient Egypt

The country of Egypt in early times was a narrow strip of green land, 16 to 32 kilometres (10 to 20 miles) wide, winding through the deserts of north-east Africa. It ran from modern Aswan in the south to the Mediterranean Sea, a distance of about 1200 kilometres (745 miles). Along its centre flowed the River Nile, which gave life to the fertile land on either side. At its mouth the Nile forms a wide delta and flows into the sea.

Very little rain falls in Egypt itself and the green valley of the Nile exists only because of the heavy summer rains which fall on high mountains farther south. The rain cascades off the mountain-sides, fills the African lakes and sends torrents of water along the Nile to overflow its banks and flood the land. Every year large areas of the valley are under water for about two months. When the water subsides it leaves behind a layer of rich black mud. It was in this narrow area of the Nile valley, with its dark soil, that people from the surrounding desert areas first settled to farm the land and grow crops.

A United Nation

These first farming communities date back to about 5000 B.C. The people settled in different areas and formed themselves into clans, each with its own leader or chieftain. Sometimes peaceably, and sometimes by fighting, the small clans came together and

Before the union of Egypt under one pharaoh it was the custom of the kings of Upper and Lower Egypt to wear different crowns. When the nation was united the two crowns were combined into one, although the king continued to wear the separate crowns on some occasions. From the left are shown the white crown of Upper Egypt, the red crown of Lower Egypt, the double crown of the united kingdom, and the pharaoh's ceremonial battle crown.

formed larger ones. This process eventually led to the existence of two main groups, one in the north around the Nile delta and the other in the south in the narrow valley of the river. The people of the northern group invaded the south and the two parts of Egypt, Lower and Upper, were united under one leader in about 3200 B.C. He was the legendary first pharaoh, or king, whose name may have been Menes or Narmer.

The first pharaohs ruled without serious challenge to their authority for about 300 years. This period covered the First and Second Dynasties of pharaohs. The different stages of Egyptian history are marked by the successive dynasties of kings, each of which consisted of a number of rulers from the same family who followed one after another.

The governments of ancient Egypt were highly organised and efficient and the pharaoh took an active part in his country's affairs. Egypt was split into a number of districts and each

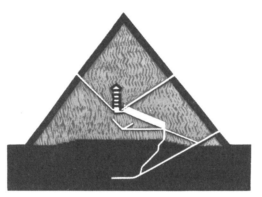

The great pyramid of Cheops, or Khufu, the second king of the Fourth Dynasty, was built about 2580 B.C. It contains a number of corridors and galleries which lead to the various tomb chambers, and ventilation shafts to allow air to circulate. It is the largest of all the pyramids in Egypt. It measures 230·4 metres (756 feet) on each side, was originally 146·6 metres (481 feet) high and covers 5·3 hectares (13 acres). It is built of over two million stone blocks weighing about 2½ tons each. It has been estimated that it took 100,000 men 20 years to complete. The smooth outer casing has now worn away.

was controlled by a governor responsible to the king. There were many other officials with special tasks, one of the most important being to guard the irrigation works. Since successful farming depended on irrigation, that is the spreading of the flood water across as many fields as possible by means of channels and dams, it was vital that everything was properly guarded and maintained.

A civil service of officials kept the pharaoh informed of all that was done in his name. In this the scribes played an important part. They copied out instructions, made reports, recorded work performed and kept a tally of the taxes collected. This web of business life was made possible by the use of such things as reed pens for writing and papyrus for making paper, as well as the development of a written script and the invention of a form of calendar.

Because they could read and write, scribes held important positions at the centre of government in Egypt, where most of the people were uneducated peasants.

Funeral boats carry the body of a dead pharaoh to his burial in the pyramids. Causeways led directly from the water's edge to the interior of the monuments.

The Pyramid Age
Memphis became the new capital of Egypt at the start of the Third Dynasty (c.2800 B.C.), which is about the time when the Old Kingdom begins. Little is known of the early pharaohs, except that they were all-powerful beings, worshipped as gods even while they lived. The people's reverence for the pharaoh is shown at its highest during the great age of pyramid building which followed in the Fourth Dynasty. The massive and monumental pyramids were built to house not only the soul of the king but his body as well. The pharaoh was so great a being that he must never be allowed to die and only by preserving his body could he live for ever. This is why for thousands of years the bodies of the Egyptian kings were mummified.

Pyramids have their origin in the simple sand mounds which were

Books of the Dead were papyrus manuscripts placed in tombs. They were full of magic spells and drawings which were supposed to help a dead person on his journey to the other world after death. This page is from the Book of the Dead of Ani, a scribe.

piled above the earliest Egyptian pit-graves. The first pyramid-shaped tomb was built for Zoser, one of the kings of the Third Dynasty. This is the famous Step Pyramid at Saqqara, one of the building marvels of the ancient world. Its rectangular stone terraces rise to a height of 61 metres (200 feet). It was designed by the architect Imhotep, who was also the king's chief minister. Imhotep was a man of many talents, skilled in mathematics, astronomy and medicine.

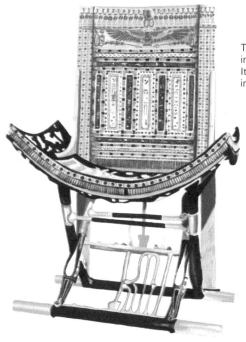

This seat was found in Tutankhamun's tomb. It was probably used in religious ceremonies.

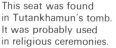

The design of this neck ornament, or gorget, is based on one found in Tutankhamun's tomb.

The Middle Kingdom

The long story of Egypt's history has three main chapters. Each chapter represents a period of national greatness when power was centred on the pharaoh and his control of an organised government. These periods are known as the Old Kingdom, the Middle Kingdom and the New Kingdom, or Empire. Separating them are two intervals of confused history in which civil wars and foreign invasions disturbed the established pattern of society. There are few historical records to tell us accurately

what happened during these dark ages of anarchy.

The first of them came towards the end of the Sixth Dynasty. The Egyptian nobility—the princes and dukes of the time—defied the king and fought among themselves. Egypt ceased to be a united nation and became a collection of warring states. Asiatic peoples from Syria invaded the country, and although little is known about them they brought an end to the Old Kingdom.

About 2100 B.C. a Theban family rose to power in the south. They opposed the new rulers, who had abandoned Memphis and settled in central Egypt. After fierce struggles the southerners triumphed and the Eleventh Dynasty of kings was begun, which in the reign of Mentuhotep III again united Egypt. Thebes, until then an unknown town, became the capital city and remained supreme for a thousand years.

The Classical Age

Ancient Egypt lasted for many hundreds of years and had a sense of permanence and continuity. As a nation she had grown in isolation, cut off by deserts from the rest of Africa and Asia. Even the foreign invaders, who from time to time ruled the country in her later history, were absorbed into the Egyptian way of life and did little to change it. Not until Egypt became involved in the fortunes of the Mediterranean countries was she permanently influenced by other races of men.

The standards of art and architecture, and the forms of religious belief and ceremony, were established in the Old Kingdom. The succeeding centuries developed them within the conventions already laid down. This can be seen in the style of figure painting, which for generation after generation obeyed certain rules about the positioning of the body. For example, it was the custom to paint the human face in profile but with the eye seen as if from the front. Although the Middle Kingdom is considered the finest period of artistic achievement, the great works continued to be produced within the traditional framework.

The period of the Twelfth Dynasty (c.2000–1788 B.C.) was one of the most settled in the whole history of Egypt. There was undisturbed peace and prosperity for over 200 years. The new pharaohs had learned, during the troubled times from which they had just emerged, the wisdom of choosing a successor to the throne and sharing it with him while both were still alive. By this association of the crown prince and the pharaoh as joint rulers the usual squabbles over succession were avoided.

This 'Classical Age' reached its peak during the reigns of Sesostris III and his son Ammenemes III. These two warrior kings not only extended Egypt's frontiers but carried out great public works at home and developed the country's prosperity.

The Feudal Age

The Middle Kingdom is sometimes called the 'Feudal Age', as the structure of society was in some ways similar to the feudal system in medieval Europe. There is perhaps a parallel in the struggles between the king and his nobles in both periods. The peace of the Twelfth Dynasty was only made possible because Sesostris was able to subdue and control the local chiefs and priests.

But what of the peasants? What sort of life did the poor and uneducated people in Egypt lead? The truth is that it varied very little from any previous or succeeding age, right up to modern times. The serf's life was hard. He could neither read nor write, and toiled on the land from dawn to dusk, resting only in the

middle of the day for the traditional break when the sun was at its height. In the flood season when the Nile overflowed across the land there was little he could do in the fields, and he laboured in the quarries or dug canals.

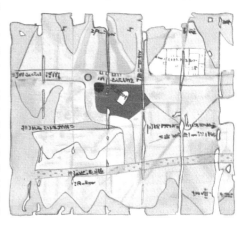

This papyrus map of gold mines and quarries, now in Turin Museum, dates from the fourteenth century B.C.

The Hypostyle Hall in the temple at Karnak, dedicated to the Theban god Amun, contained 134 painted columns.

But despite this harsh life there are many tomb paintings showing the ordinary people going about their work, seemingly content and at ease. Even the supreme example of oppression—the massed slave labour which built the pyramids—is probably misleading. Men were certainly forced to work but their religious belief was so strong and their awe of the pharaoh so great, that they carried out this terrible task almost as a spiritual act, something to be remembered in their favour when souls were judged by the gods.

Despite the wide gap between the wealthy and the poor there is some evidence from tomb inscriptions that nobles genuinely cared for their slaves and tried to look after their welfare and health.

Another feature of the 'Feudal Age' was the growth of a middle class of citizens. This was because trade with other countries created such people as merchants, agents and carriers—

Painted limestone bust of Nefertiti, the wife of the pharaoh Akhnaten.

occupations which had not existed before. Another change was the appearance of the foreign slave. War and conquest in other lands brought captives back to Egypt who stayed to serve their new masters.

Women were very much tied to the household and passed their time in such domestic activities as cooking, spinning and weaving. Perhaps it indicates the relative importance of men and women that the latter are often drawn in pictures on a smaller scale than men. It was also the custom in paintings to show the pharaoh a great deal bigger than ordinary mortals and this emphasis on the size of an image did have meaning. Another thing that painters did was to portray men with dark reddish-coloured skins, presumably because they spent most of their days out of doors, whereas women are given light yellow-coloured flesh tones.

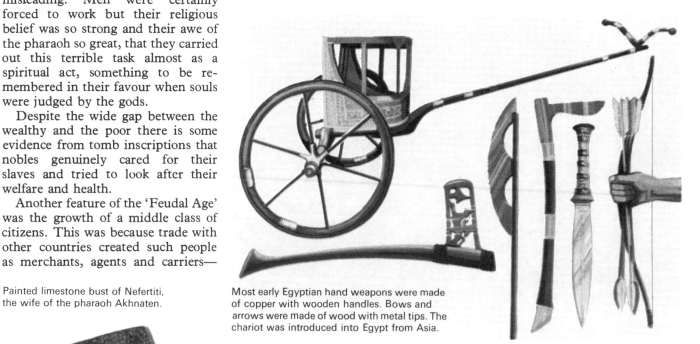

Most early Egyptian hand weapons were made of copper with wooden handles. Bows and arrows were made of wood with metal tips. The chariot was introduced into Egypt from Asia.

The Egyptian Soldier

From earliest times the people of Egypt accepted war as an inevitable part of their existence. By nature the Egyptian was not a ferocious fighter. In modern times he was once likened to a bicycle, which although it cannot stand up on its own is very useful under the control of a skilful master. Historians believe that throughout her history Egypt's military power was dependent upon mercenaries—foreign troops hired for service.

The appearance of soldiers of the Egyptian armies is well illustrated by sets of models found in the pharaohs' tombs. They depict heavily armed infantry carrying metal-tipped spears and wooden shields covered in leather. There is also a contingent of Nubian troops with bows and arrows. Archers played an important part in fighting in the ancient world. It was not until the fall of the Middle Kingdom dynasties that the horse and chariot were employed in warfare by the Egyptians.

The Hyksos Invaders

The second dark age, which came between the Middle and New Kingdoms, was dominated by a race of invaders from Asia called the Hyksos. As the scholar-priest Manetho (c. third century B.C.) wrote in his *History of Egypt*, 'For what cause I know not, a blast of God smote us'.

Compared with the highly civilised Egyptians the Hyksos were a crude and barbaric people. But they were expert fighters, with horses and chariots, and completely outclassed the Egyptian soldiers. The Hyksos crushed the delta princes and overran the rest of the country, bringing fire and destruction, looting and tearing down the temples. They set up a great fortress at Avaris, east of the delta, and from there they ruled both their Syrian empire and the land of Egypt. A succession of their leaders adopted the title of pharaoh and for a time they subdued even the southern tribes around Thebes.

After about 200 years the long-awaited war of liberation began. It was the Theban prince Amosis who

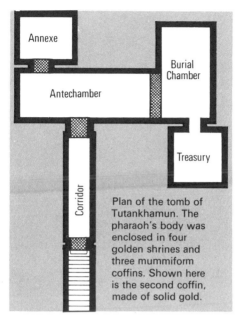

Plan of the tomb of Tutankhamun. The pharaoh's body was enclosed in four golden shrines and three mummiform coffins. Shown here is the second coffin, made of solid gold.

finally drove the Hyksos from Egypt in about 1580 B.C. Adopting the arms and tactics of the foreigners the Egyptian army became a formidable fighting force and their spirit matched their new weapons.

Amosis founded the Eighteenth Dynasty of pharaohs and, not content with victory in his own land, pursued a vigorous war of revenge in western Asia. His successors continued this aggressive policy and under the most successful of all Egypt's generals, Thutmosis III, the Empire began its most glorious phase. The whole civilised world was to acknowledge Egypt as the greatest power.

Thutmosis's great-grandson, Amenhotep III, was the most splendid of the pharaohs. He had no political worries, the military campaigns were over, and he devoted himself to gracious living and the glories of art. Beautiful houses and magnificent temples were built, great public works undertaken, and music, painting and crafts of all kinds flourished. Pageants and processions entertained the people, who shared in this feeling of an age of wealth and beauty. A devoted follower of the god Amun, Amenhotep III allowed the priests great wealth and power.

The Worship of Aten

It was perhaps a natural reaction that the character of the next outstanding figure in the history of the Empire, Amenhotep IV, who became pharaoh in about 1372 B.C., was completely different from that of his father. Amenhotep IV changed the course of Egypt's history in an entirely different way from the great generals and conquerors of his dynasty. He was possessed by an overwhelming religious belief in the existence of one god, the sun-god Aten. He also hated the rich priests of Amun, whom he considered evil.

Amenhotep IV changed his name to Akhnaten, which means 'Aten is satisfied', and ordered all the people of the great empire to worship only the sun-god. He tried to destroy the old gods, and abandoned Thebes with its many temples to set up a new capital city farther down the river, called Amarna.

It was difficult for the people of Egypt to accept the new faith. The power of the old gods which had existed for hundreds of years could not be cast off lightly. The priests opposed the new religion since it threatened their very existence. Once more Egypt was plunged into a disordered and discontented state. Akhnaten may have been a genuine idealist and seeker after truth but he was a failure as a ruler of a great empire. Practical government broke down and by the middle of the twelfth century B.C. the power of the Egyptian Empire was fading.

Two great pharaohs stand out from the troubled history of Egypt in the remaining twelve dynasties before Ptolemy I inherited from Alexander the Great what was left of a once mighty empire. They were Seti I (c. 1320–1300 B.C.) and Rameses II (c. 1300–1225 B.C.). During their reigns the country showed some of its old imperial glory. Rameses in particular was guided by vast ambitions for himself and his country, and he proved a worthy successor to Thutmosis III in wars with the Hittites.

After his death Egypt declined and for centuries was fought over and occupied by a succession of conquerors—among them Libyans, Nubians, Persians and Assyrians.

Thutmosis III (c. 1504–1450 B.C.)
He was one of the greatest of all pharaohs and reigned jointly with Queen Hatshepsut until her death. As sole ruler he soon became the national hero of the Eighteenth Dynasty, restoring Egypt's power and prosperity. A brilliant general (he has been called the 'Napoleon of Egypt') he defeated Syria at the battle of Megiddo (c. 1479 B.C.) and freed his country from foreign invaders. He campaigned in Asia and extended the Empire, building warships to control the Phoenicians. He was also a great builder of temples, particularly the great temple of Amun at Karnak. He erected several famous obelisks, one of which was brought to London in the nineteenth century and put up beside the River Thames, where it is known as 'Cleopatra's Needle'. Thutmosis was buried in the Valley of the Kings near Thebes.

Bronze head of the cat-goddess Bastet.

Wine was made in Egypt from grapevines introduced from Asia about 3000 B.C.

Sandals made from papyrus and reed.

Bed with a head-rest, used instead of a pillow.

The Egyptians used geometry and arithmetic for practical purposes. Below is seen part of a mathematical papyrus with calculations for working out the area of a triangular-shaped field.

The papyrus plant had many uses in ancient Egypt. Most important was the making of fine white paper. The plant stem was cut into pieces which were beaten until thin enough to be shaped into layers of paper.

Egyptian Civilisation

Much of our knowledge of the Egyptian way of life in ancient times comes from wall paintings and the models of everyday things which were buried with people in their tombs. Shown here are reconstructions of a small number of the many images of ancient Egyptian civilisation.

Life for members of the pharaoh's court and other wealthy people must have been very pleasant. They lived in bright, airy houses, cleverly designed to keep the occupants cool under the hot, cloudless skies. Buildings were made from wood and sun-dried bricks. Craftsmanship and artistry, in the making of objects and in the decoration of the interiors of buildings, were of a very high standard. The Egyptian who could afford such pleasures liked good food and drink, was fond of entertaining and provided music and dancing for his guests, and all kinds of games were popular.

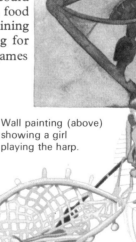

Wall painting (above) showing a girl playing the harp.

Wooden models of ships found in a tomb.

The Indus Valley

The Indus Valley is a great plain about 950 miles long in the north-west of the Indian sub-continent. Through it flows the River Indus and its tributaries. Today most of the valley is barren land but the soil was once rich and fertile.

Far less is known about the development of civilisation in India and China than in Mesopotamia and Egypt, although a similar pattern of life based on a fertile river valley is common to all. Before the archaeologists began their investigations of the sites in 1921 the only evidence for the existence of the great cities of Mohenjo-daro and Harappa was in the legendary tales of Indian gods.

Even today a great deal of mystery surrounds these extraordinary places and the people who built and lived in them. There are many blank spaces in the history of the early Indian cultures which historians are only just beginning to fill, helped by the relics of human existence which archaeologists dig out of the ground.

So far some forty other towns and villages have been unearthed up and down the river basin but none of these rivals the two 'capital' cities in size or interest. Whether or not they were the chief cities of two different kingdoms is not known. It seems likely however that the government of so large an area—by ancient standards—made it necessary to have two controlling centres. So the Indus Valley civilisation may have been split into north and south in the same way that Egypt was divided into Upper and Lower.

Town Planning

The earliest dates usually given for the building of Mohenjo-daro and Harappa are about 3000 B.C. It is believed they fell into decay about 1750 B.C., before finally being overthrown by Indo-European invasions from the north. The most striking thing about the two cities, which were almost identical although they were nearly 400 miles apart, is the careful and precise way in which they were planned.

Each was about a mile square and consisted of rectangular blocks of buildings divided by a regular grid of wide streets and minor lanes. As examples of efficient town-planning and civic organisation they have no equals in the ancient world.

Most places where men live and work grow up gradually, with simple

One of the best known pieces of Indus Valley sculpture is this bearded figure.

buildings giving way successively to bigger and better ones. In this way groups of primitive huts evolve into villages and so into towns and cities. But Mohenjo-daro and Harappa were laid out as if fully planned from the beginning. The houses were solidly built of brick with bathrooms and lavatories. All had proper drainage systems to take away rain water and cesspools for sewage disposal.

Successful Traders

The people who built the cities came from places outside the areas where they settled. No one is sure of their origins, but certain similarities in their way of life link them with the people of Sumer. They farmed the land, growing wheat and barley and many fruits such as melons and dates.

They were also the earliest people to cultivate cotton. They domesticated animals and selective breeding of cattle, camels and horses was common. But above all they were successful traders. The prosperous merchant class and the priests were the most important people in the land.

Yet despite their contacts with the outside world this civilisation lasted for over a thousand years with hardly any apparent change at all in the way of life or the style of art and architecture. It is probable that within such a self-contained community the ruling classes had nothing to gain from change of any sort —and very much to lose.

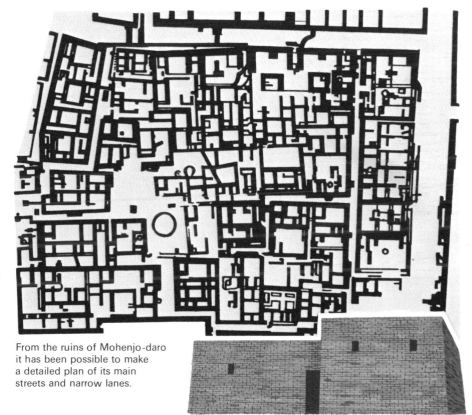

From the ruins of Mohenjo-daro it has been possible to make a detailed plan of its main streets and narrow lanes.

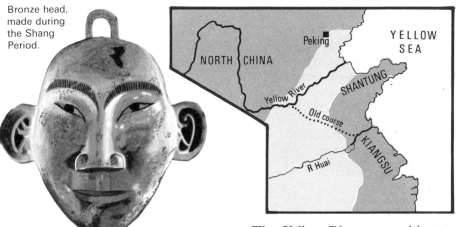

Bronze head, made during the Shang Period.

The Yellow River

The history of China is even more self-contained than that of other civilisations. From earliest times the Chinese have been a single people not greatly affected by foreign invaders. Many things in their culture, such as their system of writing and some of their artistic skills, have undergone little change for 3,000 years or more. It is only in recent years that real scientific knowledge of the prehistory of ancient China has been possible. Proper excavation of archaeological sites was not begun in earnest before the late 1920s.

The earliest Chinese people settled in the basin of the Yellow River (known now by its Chinese name as the Hwang-Ho River). They were cut off from the rest of the world in a way which is still partly true today. Of course, the area of land occupied then was only a fraction of the vast country we now know as China.

Early China

It is probable that most prehistoric groups of pastoral peoples, who learned to live from the land by growing crops, were isolated from each other in different parts of the world by natural barriers, such as mountains and deserts. But the Chinese civilisation remained unaffected by world developments for a long time.

Yet for thousands of years before the first dynasties of kings appeared, nomadic people had wandered across the hills and plains of China and beyond. It is likely that some of the crafts and skills of civilised life were learned from societies in the Middle East and brought back to China by these travellers. In this sense China cannot really be isolated from developments in the rest of Asia.

The Yellow River was subject to the same kind of flooding as the Nile and, as in Egypt, deposits of fertile mud made it possible for the early settlers to farm the land. The central plain of China, over which the Yellow River spread, is one of the best agricultural areas in the world. But the flooding of the river did not bring only good; sometimes it was on so vast a scale that it caused great disasters.

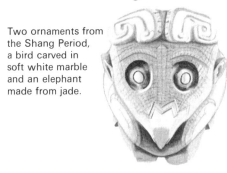

Two ornaments from the Shang Period, a bird carved in soft white marble and an elephant made from jade.

Legendary Emperors

Most of the early history of China is legendary, with marvellous tales of great emperors who lived for hundreds of years and whose deeds were extraordinary. One of them, known as the Yellow Emperor, is said to have been able to speak fluently from birth, and is supposed to have come into this world as a result of a flash of lightning which struck his mother.

Like all traditional founders of a great race the old Chinese leaders were shown in these stories to possess deep wisdom and the power of gods. They were credited with divine inspiration, which enabled them to teach people the basic principles of hunting, fishing, herding and the raising of crops; and how to manufacture utensils of wood, pottery and stone. They also invented an alphabet of written characters and a system of laws and taught the practice of medicine using herbs.

The first dynasty of emperors to emerge from the mists of fable into the half light of presumed historical fact, are the Hsia, whose eighteen sovereigns reigned from 2205 to 1766 B.C. They were followed by members of the Shang or Yin dynasty (1766–1122 B.C.).

These dates are traditional and if Chinese historians of the old world are to be believed the characters of the men who occupied the throne varied between angelic goodness and ferocious cruelty. But even in the middle of the second millennium B.C., when there were reliable and detailed records of civilisation in the Middle East, it is difficult to separate fact from fiction in the dramatic tale of Chinese history.

Great Empires

The fertile lands of Mesopotamia were a centre to which all the nomadic peoples of south-west Asia were attracted. The great empires of Babylon, Assyria and Persia were formed around them and they were the cause of the first great territorial wars.

The early civilisations had grown up more or less independently, with larger and larger units of people coming together by agreement or conquest. But war was now to be waged on a grand scale and great leaders were to emerge with positive aims of personal gain and glory. One of the first was Sargon of Akkad, the ruler of a Semitic people who had settled in an area north of Sumer.

The struggle between the Sumerians of the south and the Akkadians of the north caused a clash between two cultures which raised civilisation in the ancient world to a higher level. Throughout history, when the dust of battle has settled and the opponents have learned to live in peace together, such conflicts have often resulted in a richer life for all.

Sargon of Akkad

Sargon of Akkad founded his dynasty about 2400 B.C., with its capital in the town of Kish. His conquest over the city states of Sumer appears to have been swift and complete. He then extended his domain—the first great empire of the ancient world—beyond the boundaries of the Euphrates River by subduing the lands of Elam in the east and Assur in the north. To the west Sargon ruled over the distant lands which bordered the Mediterranean Sea.

But it was not easy in those early days to keep control of an empire which spread so widely, and after Sargon's death none of his successors was able to rule with the same force and authority. Akkadian power began to wane and new cities rose to prominence to take control of their own affairs. The most important of these was Babylon, which gave its name to the new empire of Babylonia.

Assurbanipal, king of Assyria, surveys his army. The figures of the king and his horse are based on sculptures which decorated the walls of his palace at Nineveh.

Babylonia and Assyria

The city of Babylon grew up on the banks of the River Euphrates. It had already gained some importance during the reigns of Sargon and the Akkadian kings, but the days of its true greatness were yet to come.

In Sumer and Akkad, the struggle for leadership between the city-states resulted in first one and then the other taking the lead. Lagash, Ur, Larsa and Uruk were the chief contenders for power. None succeeded in gaining any lasting authority and for several hundred years the whole area of Mesopotamia was split between rival and warring factions.

It is difficult to separate the historical stories of Babylonia and Assyria. From earliest times they are woven together into a mixed pattern of strength and weakness in which the two great empires alternately merge and part. The power of a kingdom depended almost entirely upon the personality and energy of the man who sat on the throne. Different peoples at different times were raised to the heights of power, taken there by the forcefulness of one man: when that man died, authority died with

him and there was a period of confusion and rebellion before a new king appeared. Again and again this pattern was repeated in the 2,000 years of Babylonian and Assyrian greatness.

In this new period of history, the Elamites were the first people to emerge with any unified power and their control was centred on the area of Sumer. In the north, a new force took command: this was the Amorite people who had migrated into Akkad from the north-west and established themselves in the city of Babylon.

Hammurabi the Great

So Sumerians and Akkadians were replaced by Elamites and Amorites, each a war-like people. It soon became clear that there was not room for both. One or the other had to yield and the skirmishing between them reached a point of decision during the reign of the Amorite king, Hammurabi (eighteenth century B.C.).

As one of the first dominant figures to emerge clearly from the incomplete records of the ancient world, Hammurabi fully merits the title of

'Great'. His aggressive policy brought the southern cities under his control. The Elamites were defeated and the whole of Sumer acknowledged Hammurabi as ruler.

After bringing north and south together and establishing Babylon as the new capital, Hammurabi spent the remaining years of his life building up his cities and improving life for the people. Many of his letters have been found. They were dictated by him to a scribe who 'wrote' with a reed stylus on clay tablets which were then baked. These letters record Hammurabi's orders to his overseers and his thoughts on government.

His builders repaired the great temples and erected new palaces and public buildings. His engineers provided new methods of water supply and extended irrigation in the fields. He set up schools and encouraged the education of children. The ruins of some of these schoolhouses have been dug up and in one of them a clay tablet was found with a copybook exercise written on it—'He who shall excel in tablet writing shall shine like the sun'.

The Ishtar Gate stood at the main approach to Babylon and was built in the sixth century B.C. during the reign of Nebuchadnezzar II. Richly glazed brickwork is shown on the right.

He worked for the genuine unity of the people throughout the country, trying to end the racial bitterness and strife between north and south. The different religions were respected and both languages, Akkadian and Sumerian, were officially recognised and used in state documents.

The Code of Laws

The crowning act of Hammurabi's career was his formation of a set of laws which controlled the acts of individuals and formed the basis for all legal decisions. Hammurabi's Code of Laws was always intended by him to be the one deed by which he should be remembered. All his life, even in the midst of battle, he thought about these principles of law and worked on

Creation stories in Babylonian mythology tell of the god Marduk (right) who slew the dragon-goddess Tiamat (left) and from the two halves of her body created both the heavens and the earth.

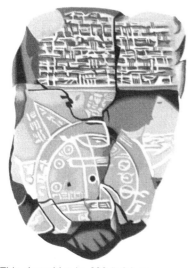

This clay tablet (c. 600 B.C.) shows an early Babylonian map of the world and records the campaigns of Sargon I.

them. Only in the final peaceful years of his reign was he able to give form and purpose to them. They are his monument, more than his victories in battle.

It was during Hammurabi's reign that all the different elements of the Mesopotamian lands came together to form a united Babylonian Empire. Another thing which helped to increase Babylon's stature was the merging into one god, called Marduk, of the powers of the chief gods of all the rival cities. As Marduk had been Babylon's god and protector since the founding of the city he served not only to unify religious beliefs, but turned everyone's eyes to Babylon as the focal point of worship.

After Hammurabi's death the first period of Babylon's glory ended abruptly with an invasion by the Hittites, who came from Cappadocia

in Asia Minor. They were attracted to Babylon by stories of its greatness and wealth. Finding the empire in some disarray, with rival kingdoms challenging the central authority, the Hittites attacked the city: with such success apparently that for a time a Hittite chieftain sat on the throne in Babylon.

The Kassites

The Hittites do not appear to have stayed for long or made any lasting impression. Such records as there are of this period tell us very little of what happened. A new name does appear in the story of Babylonian history, that of the Kassites, a people from the highlands of Elam, northwest of Babylon. Their dominion over Babylon lasted for over 500 years and

they were one of the first people to use the horse in military campaigns.

Babylonian chroniclers name Gandash as the first Kassite ruler and refer to him as 'King of the Four Regions, King of Sumer and Akkad, King of Babylon'. Some information about the events of the period can be gathered from the so-called boundary stones, or steles (a number of which have survived), which were set up in different parts of the land to record the deeds of gods and warriors.

In general it can be stated that the power struggle between the various peoples of the area continued as fiercely as ever. One thing is certain:

The Laws of Hammurabi

The Code of Laws is engraved in cuneiform writing on a stone pillar nearly eight feet high. There are over 3,600 lines which extend right round the shaft of the pillar. The relief carving at the top of the pillar depicts Hammurabi, on the left, receiving the symbols of justice from the Babylonian sun-god. Hammurabi's laws are the earliest complete code of laws to have survived from the ancient world. Although a great part of the laws are based on the simple principle of revenge— an eye for an eye, a tooth for a tooth— they did represent a genuine attempt to set up a proper system of justice which all could recognise and understand. The stone pillar, which dates from the eighteenth century B.C., was discovered in 1901 at Susa, in Persia, where it had been taken by the Elamites as a trophy of war in the twelfth century B.C. The pillar now rests in the Louvre, Paris.

The magnificent palace at Nineveh on the River Tigris is reconstructed in this drawing. The remains of the city were first excavated by the English archaeologist Sir Henry Layard in 1845. On the left is shown one of the human-headed lion figures flanking the palace portals.

from the time of Sargon I the ambition of all rulers was that of world conquest. Some came nearer to it than others, bearing in mind that the 'world' in those days consisted of near-eastern, African and some Mediterranean lands, but no one achieved it. Kassite rule had its good moments but it was no more successful in keeping the land unified than those which came before.

The most significant events of this time were taking place in the country of Assur, a strip of high ground to the north of Babylon in the upper reaches of the Tigris. The rulers of this land were quite independent of the south and it was they who were to assume in fuller measure than any others in the ancient world the role of world conquerors.

The Assyrians

The history of Assur, or Assyria as it was to become, goes back as far as that of Babylon. Settlements in Assur developed separately from those of the Sumer/Akkad area. But not until about the twelfth century B.C. did Assyria grow sufficiently in strength to be a serious challenge to the south. The Kassite rulers had long ago given up any thoughts of making the Assyrians a subject race. Already prudence had forced them to agree to a treaty respecting boundaries which established Assyria's sovereign territory.

Assyria's first entry into the arena of southern affairs was gained through the marriage of an Assyrian princess to the Kassite ruler of Babylon. The child of the marriage was murdered during civil wars which broke out in Babylon. Assyria, now more confident, set out to quash internal fighting and take a strong hand in government.

The history of this period is relatively well documented because of finds at Tell el-Amarna in Egypt of letters between the pharaohs of Egypt and the governors of Palestine and Syria. It is clear from them that Assyria was the dominant power and had finally captured and subdued Babylon. Once again, however, when the aggressive ruler of the day died, this Assyrian dominance was lost and the same pattern of confusion and petty squabbles was repeated.

The City of Nineveh

For the moment, however, the Assyrian Empire entered its greatest, and final, period of glory in the eighth century B.C. Tiglathpileser III founded a new dynasty of kings in c.750 B.C., with a new capital city at Nineveh on the banks of the Tigris, and their authority was firmly based on the strength of a highly trained and professional army.

By this time Babylonia was regarded as no more than a southern province, ruled by one of the relatives of the Assyrian king. In his efforts to stop the perpetual rebellions Tiglathpileser relied not only on the strength

of the army but also on his policy of settling loyal Assyrian people as colonists in various parts of the empire. The lands of Palestine, Syria and Judea all became subject to the Assyrian king whose strenuous efforts to govern all these varied lands efficiently brought an air of permanence to Mesopotamia.

Tiglathpileser's successor, Sargon II (c.721–705 B.C.), despite his efforts to allow Babylonia greater freedom in the government of her affairs, had to deal with renewed uprisings. This he did with the great cruelty and ruthlessness which characterised all the Assyrian rulers. In 689 B.C., during the reign of Sennacherib, Babylon was at last entirely destroyed by the Assyrians, who diverted the course of the Euphrates to flood the ruins of the city.

Sennacherib was assassinated in 681 B.C. and was succeeded by his youngest son Esarhaddon, who devoted his life to the conquest of Egypt. In c.670 B.C. Esarhaddon planted his victory standard on the Nile when the old capital of Memphis fell. The government of Egypt was reorganised and controlled by Assyria whose empire now embraced a wider area

than ever before. It included the island of Cyprus, which Assyria's newly formed navy had razed and subdued.

The full magnificence of Assyria's rule was shown during the reign of Assurbanipal (c.669–626 B.C.), who is also known by the Greek version of his name, Sardanapalus. His long reign sums up all the splendours of an ancient empire.

Nineveh, the capital of Assyria, was a city of great kings. More splendid even than Babylon and a rival to the once great Egyptian city of Thebes, it was full of treasures looted from conquered lands. Within the twelve-kilometre (eight-mile) circuit of its walls were two mounds, now called Kouyunjik and Nebi Yunus, on which were built the royal palaces and temples. Nearby were the quarries of marble which gave an almost inexhaustible supply of stone to the skilled architects and craftsmen. Reconstructions of the palaces suggest that they were supported and decorated by airy columns and soaring terraces that show the same combination of lightness and strength which were the hallmarks of Greek buildings.

In the 1850s more than 30,000

clay tablets, the remains of Assurbanipal's celebrated library, were discovered. They have become one of the main sources of Babylonian history. Other witnesses to the splendour of his life are the stone reliefs depicting scenes from his campaigns.

New Babylon
When Assurbanipal died in 626 B.C., Babylon again revolted. In 604 B.C. Nebuchadnezzar II succeeded in creating a new Babylonian Empire. The dynasty founded by Nebuchadnezzar lasted until the final overthrow of Babylon. He proved himself to be a great warrior and devoted himself to the restoration of the city, where he built the famous Hanging Gardens. His success was astonishing. By 562 B.C. he had defeated the Egyptians at Carchemish, crushed Syria and Palestine, subdued the Mediterranean coastal towns and was about to invade Egypt. His realm was almost equal in size and influence to that of Assyria in her greatest days. While Nebuchadnezzar lived Babylon prospered, but after his death the kingdom was again subjected to the conflicting ambitions of nobles and priests.

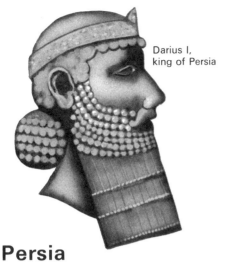

Darius I,
king of Persia

Persia

The Persians were one of the Aryan-speaking tribes which emigrated from central Asia into southern lands about 1200 B.C. They settled in the area between the Caspian Sea and the Persian Gulf and made their capital at Susa. For many years they acknowledged the kings of neighbouring Media as their masters. Then about 550 B.C. Cyrus the Persian, a prince of the house of Achaemenes, rebelled against the Median king Astyages and united the kindred peoples of the Medes and Persians under his rule.

Cyrus was the greatest of the Persian kings, and as was usual in ancient times was regarded by his people as a god-like figure. Yet the thing which distinguishes Cyrus from other early 'divine' monarchs is his humanity. In an age when brutality and ruthless extermination of an enemy was the rule, Cyrus spared the life of his conquered foe Astyages and won great popular support by his concern for ordinary people.

The kingdom of Lydia in Asia Minor had treaties of alliance with Media and the two powers were held together by ties of marriage. One of the earliest peoples to use coinage, the Lydians were great traders and bankers with a reputation for wealth echoed in the names of their famous kings, Midas and Croesus. Lydia determined that the upstart Cyrus should be put down.

She looked around for allies and was busy trying to persuade Egypt and Sparta to join her when Cyrus swooped on Sardis, the Lydian capital, and took Croesus prisoner, almost before the campaign had begun. Lydia and her subject cities on the Ionian coast became part of the new Persian empire.

Babylon Overthrown

Cyrus was well aware that the quickest road to peace lay in subduing other potential enemies before they attacked him. He extended his rule eastwards into Bactria and then marched south against Babylon. Here the cruel and worthless Belshazzar was king of an empire which had rotted away after the death of Nebuchadnezzar. Babylon was ripe for change and almost welcomed Cyrus's challenge. His reputation as an honourable and fair man had preceded him and the people looked upon him as a liberator.

Cyrus was now master of all the country which stretched from the Caspian Sea to the shores of the Aegean. In only twelve years the Persian empire had become one of the largest ever known in the ancient world.

In his conquests Cyrus had received an unusual degree of help from the people of the regimes he fought. As emperor and king of Babylon no strong voice was raised against him during the remaining ten years of his life. For the times in which he lived Cyrus's rule was mild. He allowed religious freedom to all and many of the old gods and rites returned. He ignored Egypt, and such fighting as there was took place on his eastern borders against wild nomadic tribes for whom war remained an inevitable sport. During one of these campaigns in 529 B.C. Cyrus met his death.

His son and successor, Cambyses, was filled with wider ambitions. He decided to bring Egypt within Persian rule. Aided by the treachery of one of the captains of the Egyptian army of mercenary troops who deserted to serve the Persian king, Cambyses annexed Egypt with some ease in 525 B.C.

Proclaiming himself pharaoh, Cambyses adopted the worship of Egyptian gods, but quickly offended the priests by his light-hearted attitude to his new religion. When his

This reconstruction of Persepolis is based on a model of the city made in the nineteenth century. The building of Persepolis was begun by Darius I in 518 B.C. and completed by his successors Xerxes and Artaxerxes I. The city was raised 9 metres (30 feet) above ground on a platform erected on a natural mound of earth.

Golden bracelet with winged animals, an ornament of Persian design, part of the fifth-century Oxus treasure, discovered in 1877 near the borders of Afghanistan.

military expeditions to Nubia and Carthage were wiped out Cambyses is said to have lost his reason and insulted the Egyptian gods. Things went from bad to worse and there occurred a revolt against him inside Persia itself. On his way to battle Cambyses died suddenly and the empire was dangerously near to breaking up.

That it not only regained its balance but also extended its power was due entirely to its new ruler, Darius I, a distant cousin of Cambyses's. Darius crushed rebellion wherever it tried to raise its head, using some of the old methods of terror and ruthlessness

which Cyrus had forsworn. He then set about the task of reorganising the government of his vast empire so that it might remain secure—something at which he succeeded so well that there was peace and stability for over twenty years.

The Satraps

He divided the empire into a number of provinces and over each appointed a ruler, called a satrap, to be directly responsible to him for good government. The most important provinces, or satrapies, were Lydia, Media, Assyria, Babylonia, Egypt and India. The satrap was governor, judge and commander-in-chief of the army in his district. He was always a high-born noble known personally to Darius and appointed by him.

Within his province the satrap had absolute power but only to the extent that every major decision was referred back to Darius by a complicated system of reports and recommendations. Darius's inspectors made frequent and lightning visits to the satrapies to make sure that everything was proceeding as it should. Communications throughout the empire were maintained by an efficient postal service and by a great building programme of roads, bridges and canals. Wealth in the form of tribute money flowed into Darius's treasury, and he became lord of almost the entire civilised world.

Zoroaster

Most religions and particularly those of the Indo-European races are based on worship of the forces of nature. This is a natural reflection of primitive man's life, which depended on nature's good moments for its continued existence. As man developed from being a hunting to a farming

animal and so to the earliest civilisations, he continued to seek fortune and favour from the powerful gods of nature. The great teacher of the Persians, Zoroaster, taught them to worship Ahuramazda, the god of light and fire, and Mithras, who represented the undying sun. Against them were set the forces of evil and darkness led by the devil, Ahrimanes.

East meets West

At the very height of its strength the great Persian empire was made to face and eventually fall before the challenge of the relatively tiny power of the Greek city-states. This armed collision between Persia and Greece was a momentous moment in the history of man—the first direct conflict between East and West.

The Persians often used images of animals in their metalwork and sculpture, as seen in this fifth-century gold cup (above) and the double-bull capital (below)..The cup is known as the Rhyton cup and is a fine example of the craftsmanship practised under the rule of Achaemenian princes. It was unearthed in 1955 in almost perfect condition. The bull capital once decorated the top of a column in the palace of Darius at Susa, supporting the painted roof of the magnificent throne room.

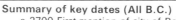

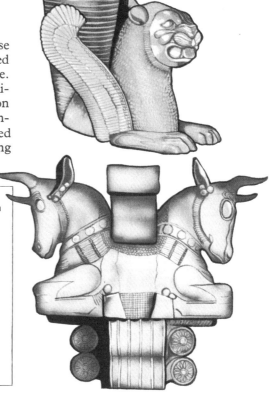

Summary of key dates (All B.C.)
- c.2700 First mention of city of Babylon
- c.2400 Dynasty of Sargon of Akkad founded
- c.2300 First Hittite invasions of Asia Minor
- c.1800 Hammurabi's Code of Laws. Kassites in Babylon
- c.750 Dynasty of Tiglathpileser III founded
- c.721–705 Reign of Sargon II
- c.689 Babylon destroyed by Sennacherib the Assyrian
- c.669–626 Lifespan of Assurbanipal
- 548–486 Lifespan of Darius I
- 529 Death of Cyrus I

Hittite soldier

Invaders and Nomads

Throughout the early periods of civilisation in Europe and Asia groups of people were always on the move from one area to another. Sometimes the groups were small and made little impact on the settled communities through which they passed. They were nomads, who moved from place to place as a way of life. When they did stay somewhere which suited them, they merged easily into the existing social life of the people.

Other groups were much larger and formed the mass migrations which often changed the course of history. The most important of these were by Aryan-speaking peoples, known as Indo-Europeans. About the middle of the third millennium B.C. they began to move from the steppes and plains of central Eurasia into the richer lands of Asia Minor, Mesopotamia, Persia and India.

The Hittites

One group of Indo-Europeans were the Hittites and they are believed to have entered Asia Minor from the Caucasus in southern Russia. Asia Minor, that part of Asiatic Turkey now called by its medieval name,

Anatolia, is a centre of great importance in the ancient history of man. This land forms a bridge between Europe and Asia and for centuries it was the home of great and powerful nations. The most important of these was the Hittite tribe, the warlike people who clashed with Rameses II and his Egyptian army at the Battle of Kadesh in 1296 B.C.

It is only in recent years that anything positive has been known about the Hittites. In 1931 excavations at the capital Hattusas (known today as Boghaskoy) revealed thousands of clay tablets inscribed in cuneiform writing. They record the names of kings and the dates of battles and treaties and give many details of the social life of the people. Other finds have borne out the claim that the Hittites were fine craftsmen in metal.

For more than a thousand years (c.2300–1170 B.C.) the Hittites held sway in central Anatolia and resisted the efforts of their enemies to overthrow them. Much of their success was due to the mountainous nature of the country which cut them off from their neighbours. Only on the western plateau, where Troy commanded the approaches to the Dardanelles, were

Wall sculpture showing scenes from the battle of Kadesh between the Egyptians and Hittites.

they exposed to attack. And it was across this natural land bridge with the Balkan peninsula that invading forces, among them the Achaeans, eventually drove the Hittites into the eastern mountains. It was at this time in the twelfth century B.C. that Troy itself fell, thus giving an historical background to the legends of Homer.

The Aryans in India
There were two main movements of Aryan peoples from central Asia: one to the south-west and one to the south-east. They were not planned as mass migrations, although this is what they became. Conquest was not the principal aim but settlement in new areas was. Since the newcomers wanted to be masters of the land they chose, clashes with the indigenous population (indigenous meaning people already living in an area) could not be avoided.

The word Aryan comes from a word in the Indian language Sanskrit meaning 'free-born'. It was used in India to apply to the higher castes—the priests, warriors and traders. Historically it is doubtful whether there is such a thing as an Aryan race.

It is more accurate to group 'Aryan' people together because they have a common family of languages: the classical Aryan languages are Sanskrit, Latin and Greek.

Part of the group of Indo-Europeans or Aryans, which moved south-eastwards, crossed the Himalayas into India about 1500 B.C. With them went their women and children and their herds of animals. They came to the area now known as Baluchistan and looked around for somewhere to settle. It was about this time that the cities of the Indus Valley finally succumbed to an invader, and the coincidence of timing has led to the belief that it was the Indo-Europeans who finally overthrew Mohenjo-daro and Harappa.

The most important religious book of the early Aryan people, the *Rigveda*, talks of Indra the war-god—the 'fort destroyer'—whose legendary exploits certainly fit the theory that the Aryans destroyed the Indus valley people.

Mohenjo-daro Destroyed
The record as far as Mohenjo-daro is concerned is clear. Excavations have revealed the fact that the city perished suddenly and violently by fire. People were slaughtered where they stood and their bones have been discovered in the agonised positions in which they died. The evidence from Harappa is less certain, as the remains of the city were plundered by railway builders in the nineteenth century, but it seems likely that its fate was the same. After the destruction of the cities there is nothing, no trace or record that anyone occupied the ruined sites.

The new masters of India moved across to the Ganges valley and easily conquered the people there. The subject tribes were made to perform the hard and unpleasant tasks and the Indo-Europeans set up a caste system which spread across the whole of India. They kept themselves apart from the local people whom they regarded as an inferior race.

At this point in time the record fails completely. Although Indian culture is one of the oldest in the world the country has no historical records which compare with those of other ancient civilisations. There followed some thousand years of complete darkness before a clear picture emerges of a revived and fully developed Indian civilisation during the fourth century B.C.

Asoka and Buddhism
Asoka was king of the Mauryan dynasty in India during the third century B.C. He was an important figure in the history of the East. He was converted to Buddhism and made it a state religion. The lion capital, above, stood on a column which Asoka erected near the spot where Buddha delivered his first sermon. Many of these pillars were put up by Asoka, commemorating sacred events in the Buddha's life. The lion capital itself became a familiar symbol in Indian architecture. The *chakra*, or wheel, at the lion's feet was adopted by Asoka as a symbol of peaceful change. Today it appears on the national flag of India. Buddhism was a religion founded by Gautama, the son of an Indian prince, in the sixth century B.C. When he gave up his rich life to devote himself to teaching and meditation, he came to be known as the Buddha, or 'the enlightened one'. Later the number of Buddhas multiplied and they were worshipped as gods.

The Hebrews

The Hebrew people, better known as the Jews, are the most remarkable race in world history, for they have survived from the days of the early civilisations until our own day despite merciless persecution and endless disruption. They have kept their identity, where all other races have lost it, by faithfully following their religion as set out in the biblical writings known to Christians as the Old Testament. They are the people of this wonderful book and their history has come full circle. Today the state of Israel has been founded again proudly and dangerously in the ancient land.

The Old Testament

Most people come to know about the old civilisations through the pages of the Old Testament. Because of this it seems that the Jewish nation was at the centre of ancient history and that everything turned upon their experiences. In fact, the Jews were not important in western Asia and of only minor concern to the great empires around them. However the coastal strip of Palestine was the favourite cockpit of war when Egypt, in the south, fought with the other empires coming from the north. Although small, the Jews were involved in almost all the important happenings of the time.

Migration of tribes westwards from the Tigris and Euphrates to the Mediterranean area was a constant feature of early times. With one of those waves of migration Abraham moved westwards into the land of Israel, as it was later called. From him, as their revered ancestor, the Jews trace their descent and their claim to rightful possession of the Holy Land. The story of Joseph explains how the Jews were drawn into the land of Egypt although there is no record of their stay. But many Semites, some of whom are seen making bricks in Egyptian pictures, were slaves there at this period.

The great Exodus from bondage in Egypt is a landmark in Jewish history. The Jews entered Egypt as a nomadic shepherd tribe and came out a united and organised people.

The Promised Land

When Egypt began to decline the desert peoples were in a ferment. The Jews wandered in these areas for forty years growing in strength and preparing themselves for the assault on the Promised Land. During this time Moses, the great leader and lawgiver, drew up excellent and far-reaching laws for the guidance of the growing nation but he died before the great invasion. This new Jewish nation was no longer entirely agricultural, for the people built in many places in Egypt and the story of the golden calf shows that they knew how to use the Egyptian mineworkings in Sinai.

The conquest was accomplished by Joshua, Moses's second-in-command, and the land was divided between the Jews into areas which they were to hold for ever. But there was no central government and every man tried to do what was right in his own eyes. The times were dangerous and leaders were necessary. The Book of Judges records the outstanding men who suppressed rebellion and strove for peace and true religion. But this was not enough and the Jews forced the leader of the priests to give them a king. So the long story of the kings begins with Saul, Jonathan and David. In David the Jews found a

leader whose courage, culture and personal zest for living made him the perfect king. He was a devout man and the Psalms echo the happy union of spiritual and temporal life in his reign.

Michelangelo's statue of Moses

Moses, the Hebrew prophet and lawgiver, lived in the fifteenth century B.C. He is said to have led the people of Israel out of Egypt towards the Holy Land. The course of their wanderings in the desert is shown on the map.

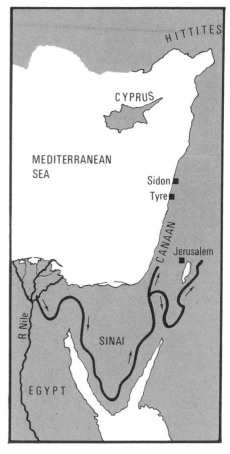

The Bible tells us that because God was angry with the wickedness of mankind He decided to destroy all life on earth by creating a great flood. From the disaster He proposed to save Noah and his family, and a breeding pair of every type of living creature. Noah was told to build an ark in which to shelter during the deluge. When the waters receded, Noah's family and the animals were able to emerge and start life again. This story appears in varying forms in early literature. Historians did not believe them but modern research has shown that they usually contain elements of truth. Evidence of a flood has been discovered in Mesopotamia. A deep bed of clay was dug up with pottery beneath it. Above it was pottery of a new settlement, suggesting there had been a great flood at an earlier period.

Israel and Judah

Solomon was the most ambitious and politically successful of the kings. His reputation with the priests was bad as his foreign wives caused him to dabble in other religions. But for the first and only time, Israel was a power of note in the Near East. Solomon made foreign alliances with the Phoenicians and the Pharaoh of Egypt whose daughter he married. A fine temple was built and trade was good, but the people were heavily taxed.

The dazzling success lasted only as long as Solomon's life. After a few years the little kingdom split itself into two parts. The northern ten tribes chose the name of Israel and took Samaria for their capital. The remaining two tribes in the south chose the name of Judah and were governed from Jerusalem. This split was never to be healed.

The northern kingdom was less faithful to the strict religious traditions. Constantly in doubt about whether to ally itself to Assyria or to Egypt, it often made the wrong and disastrous choice. Eventually the ruthless Sargon of Assyria carried off thousands of Jews to his own land and replaced them with Assyrian colonists. The mixed race which resulted became known as Samaritans. Their religion lost its high moral standards and in the time of Christ the Jews had no dealings with the Samaritans.

In the south, Judah managed to survive longer. This was partly because they paid more attention to the prophets who, with no thought for their own safety, preached against wicked practices and called for a righteous society. There was tremendous jubilation when the mighty Assyrian empire fell, in which the Jews joined enthusiastically. Their joy was short-lived for Nebuchadnezzar included Judah in his conquest of Egypt and destroyed Jerusalem, carrying the Jews off to captivity in Babylon. In Babylon the Jews sang those songs of exile which have so powerfully moved them ever since.

Wanderings of the Jews

The Seventy Years' Captivity in Babylon was good for the Jews. They searched their hearts and decided to place their future in their religion. Their sacred writings were brought together and preserved and the synagogue was founded as the centre of Jewish life. Henceforward the Book and the Synagogue as a place of assembly accompanied the Jews in all their world-wide wanderings. Eventually the more enlightened Persians allowed the Jews to return to their land and set up their state again.

When the Greeks replaced the Persians as overlords of the Near East, Judah suffered cruelly in the wars between Syria and Egypt. At times the Jews were overrun and suffered religious persecution. Thousands were sent to populate the new city of Alexandria and the surrounding territory. But the flame of Jewish patriotism burned fiercely at this time and a succession of great leaders with fanatical and often unwise courage fought bitterly against their persecutors. The most famous family were the Maccabees. Judas Maccabeus re-dedicated and fortified the temple in Jerusalem after a great disaster. After his death his brother brought peace but he, like Judas, was assassinated. Hatred against the Samaritans rose to fever pitch during this time.

Some sixty years before Christ, the Romans took over Judaea and the end of the story was near. Although the Romans deposed the infamous Herod, finding him too cruel even by their standards of repression, they intended to rule in their own empire. Unwisely the Jews revolted again. The last terrible act in the tragedy was the destruction of Jerusalem in A.D. 70 by Titus, carried out with an efficient ferocity which was final. The surviving Jews were sold as slaves until they caused a glut on the market of the empire. The terrible dispersion of the Jews as a homeless and wandering people had begun.

The Story of Joseph

Joseph, the favourite son of Jacob's old age, aroused the murderous envy of his brothers. They sold him to passing slave traders and told his father he was dead. In Egypt, where he was taken, Joseph did well and became steward to Potiphar, who was captain of the pharaoh's bodyguard. Potiphar's wife falsely accused Joseph of attacking her and he was disgraced and put in prison. Even there, Joseph prospered. He was put in charge of other prisoners and began to explain their dreams. When the pharaoh was troubled by dreams Joseph was brought to him. Because he could see into the future Joseph was able to save Egypt from famine. He was given a place of honour as the pharaoh's servant. During the famine the Hebrews went to Egypt to seek corn and Joseph was reunited with his father and brothers, and forgave them.

The Phoenicians

The Phoenicians had their beginnings on the narrow coastal strip of the eastern Mediterranean running northwards from Mount Carmel. They were Semites, like their near neighbours the Jews, and the links between the two peoples were often very close. In early times there was constant activity in this area and the Phoenicians do not emerge as a distinct people until about 1500 B.C. Caught between mighty Egypt to the south and the successive great powers who ruled Syria to the north, the Phoenicians were always hard pressed to maintain independence for very long. Early in their history, the struggle for existence made them take to the sea where they realised their true destiny.

The Phoenicians were the outstanding seamen of the ancient world. Full of restless curiosity, they became the first true explorers to whom the horizon always beckoned. They traded successfully throughout the Mediterranean from an early date and were renowned for their love of profit and skill in striking a hard bargain.

The Rise of Carthage
At first the great port of Tyre in the homeland dominated Phoenician affairs. Then successive disasters at the hands of warring empires caused power to shift to her great daughter colony Carthage in North Africa. Carthage rose to even greater heights of power and wealth in the western Mediterranean but eventually Rome challenged and deliberately destroyed her.

The Bible supplies a good deal of information about the Phoenicians, for Hiram, king of Tyre, was an active ally of David and Solomon in the prosperous days of the Jewish kingdom. Building materials and technical help were supplied for the construction of Solomon's Temple and there were marriage ties between the kings. Later the prophet Ezekiel describes the merchandise and riches of Tyre in great detail. In fact, Phoenicia and Israel underwent much the same experiences at the hands of the great powers.

Westwards, however, the early story was one of continued success. Always seeking trade rather than colonies, the Phoenicians avoided clashes with local people wherever they went, particularly the Etruscans and Greeks. They even made non-aggression treaties with the early

Romans. The Phoenicians had an expert eye for deep-water harbours and Cadiz and Valletta in Malta were two of their typical outposts. Their ships were seaworthy to a degree which made it possible for them to pass the Pillars of Hercules (Strait of Gibraltar) and sail oceanic waters.

At a busy Phoenician port trading ships are loaded with cargo bound for the Mediterranean colonies.

The Punic Wars
The Romans however were growing in strength and intended to be the first power in the western Mediterranean. As a stop-gap they signed treaties until their strength was great enough to challenge the Phoenicians directly. The Punic Wars, as they were called, were decisive; Rome not only defeated Carthage but destroyed the Phoenicians as a nation.

The Romans were a race of soldiers who knew nothing of the sea whereas the Phoenicians had magnificent navies long skilled in the Persian and Greek wars. It was a contest between a sea-power and a land-power. Rome, ignorant of seamanship and ship building and less wealthy and poorer in resources compared with the Phoenicians, decided to wipe them out of her path. With fanatical determination and icy courage Rome embarked on a period of supreme self-sacrifice. Navies and armies were lost but again and again her discipline replaced the losses and renewed the conflict.

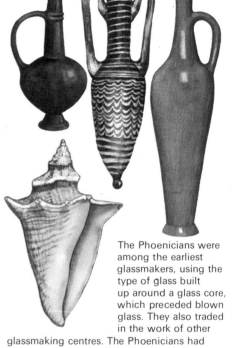

The Phoenicians were among the earliest glassmakers, using the type of glass built up around a glass core, which preceded blown glass. They also traded in the work of other glassmaking centres. The Phoenicians had almost a monopoly of dyeing, producing the famous Tyrian purple from the shellfish murex (left) which provided a strong staining liquid.

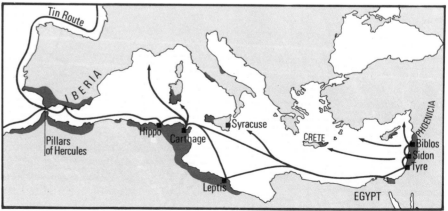

Phoenician colonies in the Mediterranean.

Ships were built on Phoenician models and rowers were even trained on dry land to provide oarsmen for these war galleys. The practical Roman genius invented the corvus. This was a broad gangplank hoisted to the mast which had a gigantic spike mounted at one end. When it was released, it crashed and fixed itself into enemy decks and the invincible Roman infantry boarded the vessels with ease.

PHOENICIAN	ANCIENT GREEK	ENGLISH
⋈ ⋇	∧ ∧ ⋉ A	A
𝑞	⅃ 𝐵 B	B
𐤊 𐤊	𐤊 𐤊 K K	K
○	⊙ ◇ □ ○	0
𐤌	⋎ ⋎ ⋀ M	M
𐤔 V	M ∫ Σ C	S

The Phoenicians devised at least two systems for writing down their spoken language. The diagram above illustrates how Phoenician lettering developed through Greek to Latin.

There were three phases to the Punic Wars spread through the period from 264–146 B.C. Rome now controlled Italy but felt insecure because Sicily was in foreign hands. She began to interfere in the island's affairs and war became inevitable. After incredible hardships the Romans triumphed and Sicily became the first Roman province. A peace dictated by the exhaustion of both sides followed, but it was used to prepare for further fighting.

The Young Hannibal

The scene then changed to Spain where Carthage's leading general, Hamilcar Barca, was organising the Carthaginian empire as a land-base for operations against Italy. One of his most important acts was to take his nine-year-old son, Hannibal, to the altar and solemnly cause him to swear eternal hatred to the Romans. Thus one of the world's very greatest generals acquired his destiny almost in infancy. For a time there was a stalemate and Rome and Carthage divided Spain between them along the line of the Ebro. But Hannibal was growing up.

As soon as he was ready, Hannibal picked a quarrel with Rome and the second Punic War began. Hannibal with his famous elephants followed the difficult coastal route to Italy and crossed the Alps, where most of the elephants died, and descended into Italy. The Roman armies at Lake Trasimene and Cannae were cut to pieces. For years, with virtually no support from home, Hannibal campaigned in Italy winning every pitched battle.

Finally Fabius realised that the best plan was to contain Hannibal and wear him down, denying him supplies and thus weakening his armies from within. Meanwhile Scipio Africanus was triumphant in Spain and passed into Africa driving all before him.

Hannibal was recalled to defend Carthage and was defeated by Scipio at Zama in 202 B.C. Once again Roman discipline and stamina had triumphed over genius in the enemy command.

Rome was not satisfied with crippling Carthage. Fifty years later an opportunity occurred to force the matter further. This time Carthage was attacked and, after a long and bitter siege, was completely wiped out. A plough was drawn over the site of the city by the victorious Romans and the Phoenicians of Carthage disappeared from history.

Thus ended the story of the finest seamen of the ancient world. Their ships had covered the whole of the Mediterranean and penetrated the Atlantic Ocean. All the merchandise of the earth had passed through their hands until the day the Romans destroyed them.

```
Summary of key dates (All B.C.)
c. 2000–1200 Indo-European invasions
       c. 2000 Phoenicia emerges as sea-
               power
       c. 1600 Phoenicia conquered by
               Egypt
       c. 1500 Mohenjo-daro destroyed
       c. 1300 Exodus of Jews from Egypt
       c. 1296 Battle of Kadesh
       c. 1095 Saul becomes first king of
               the Jews
       c. 1012 Temple in Jerusalem built by
               Solomon
        c. 950 Hebrew kingdom divided
               into Israel and Judah
        c. 700 Carthage founded
       264–146 Punic wars
       247–182 Lifespan of Hannibal
           202 Hannibal defeated by Scipio
      A.D. 70 Jerusalem destroyed by
               Romans
```

The Oriental World

The last emperors of the Shang dynasty had a terrible reputation for cruelty and idleness. According to the traditional history of China they were overthrown in 1122 B.C. by people from the western province of Chou. The Chou's leader, Won-wang, had been cast into prison by the Shang because he spoke out against the regime, and there he died. During his imprisonment he wrote a revolutionary book, listing all the faults of the emperor's rule and laying down guide-lines for good government. This book is believed to be the oldest work of Chinese literature. It was Won-wang's son, Wu-wang, who avenged his father by winning a great battle against the Shang, afterwards becoming the first emperor of the new Chou dynasty.

The Great Wall of China

code was strictly obeyed, because to exceed the minimum degree of violence was dishonourable and would certainly invoke the wrath of the gods.

By about the eleventh century B.C. new settlements of people were springing up all over China, many of them hundreds of miles from the original centre of Chinese civilisation. The Chou people themselves lived on the western edges of the country and were the nation's chief defence against the barbarian tribes who constantly threatened invasion.

The Chou People
The natural rise of new communities was encouraged by the first Chou emperor, who rewarded his chief followers with gifts of land. These local 'barons' grew powerful, and from small beginnings a number of semi-independent states arose, some of them quite remote from each other. In this way the authority and control of the emperor over a land which

Confucius lived from 551 to 479 B.C. He gave up his life as a magistrate to work as a wandering teacher. His sayings, published after his death, were concerned more with man's conduct in this life than with religion.

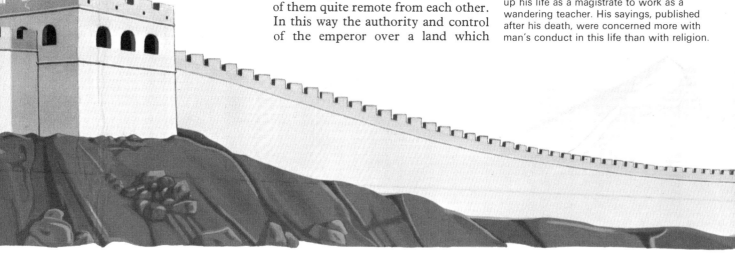

It was during the period of the Chou dynasty that many of the methods of Chinese government which have lasted until recent times, were first practised. The Chinese preoccupation with ceremony also dates from these early times. Great importance was placed on correct behaviour between different grades of society. There was a proper form of dress, speech and movement. Control and deliberation were prized above all things in both private and public life. All people paid respect to tradition and worshipped their ancestors.

The logical, and perhaps highly sensible, end of this love of ceremony can be seen in the form of courtly warfare which the Chinese practised in the seventh century B.C. A battle was transformed into a tournament and only a moderate amount of force was allowed in pursuit of victory. The

was fast expanding was gradually weakened.

By the third century B.C. the Chou emperor possessed only a mere shadow of power. The five principal outlying states which then made up provincial China were equally strong and aggressive, and it was only a matter of time before one of them took over. The move was made by the king of Ts'in, who annexed all Chou territory in 249 B.C. The first Ts'in emperor came to the throne soon after, in 246 B.C. This remarkable young man, he was only thirteen years old at the time, was named Cheng—his adopted name Shih Hwang-ti means 'first universal emperor'.

Shih Hwang-ti saw himself as the saviour of his people, welding together all the unruly peoples of his vast country into a unified nation. He was a dedicated reformer and a tireless

builder of roads, bridges, canals, palaces and public buildings. He abolished the feudal system in all the provinces and revived the authority of the emperor by appointing new overlords who were directly responsible to him.

He wanted his reign to be the beginning of a new era for China. Not only was the past to be forgotten, it was to be erased from people's memories. The emperor's determination to break with old beliefs and traditions led to the edict of 214 B.C. by which the destruction of all existing books was ordered. At public ceremonies throughout the land people were compelled to bring their precious writings to be burned. History and philosophy were to perish in the flames. In this way Shih Hwang-ti hoped to banish from men's minds the teachings of the past.

Of course, the scheme failed in its

objective. Some books were saved and many Chinese scholars, with the remarkable memories for which their race is renowned, simply committed whole books to heart and then set them down again on paper to await better times.

The Great Wall of China

Shih Hwang-ti is remembered not only as the man who tried to wipe out his country's past but as the builder of the Great Wall of China. In fact, defensive walls along the northern frontiers of China were first built during the fifth century B.C. 'Fear not the tiger of the south, but beware the rooster of the north'—so runs an old Chinese saying, and the people had cause to be fearful of the wild barbarians of the northern steppes. Shih Hwang-ti's wall was created by joining existing walls and extending them to form a continuous line of defence over 3,000 kilometres (2,000 miles) long. The famous remains of

The Chinese buried funerary models in tombs. This Han period pottery model represented a home for the spirit.

like when done to yourself do not do to others'. Confucius did not write down the principles of his system for a moral society. He said he was not a maker of ideas but a transmitter of thoughts. Nor did he claim any divine knowledge or inspiration from any god. He was of the world, and for him the acid test was how a man behaved towards his fellow men in this life, without thought for any reward in the next.

The other great school of Chinese philosophy, Taoism (from the word *tao*, meaning 'the way'), said to have been founded by Lao-Tzu in the sixth century B.C., teaches man to withdraw from the world and come close to nature. The ideal Taoist accepts himself and his environment for what they are. He is passive and receptive, and does not seek to change his situation. Here the key words are harmony, acceptance, simplicity. The great virtue is expressed in the Chinese word *wu-wei*, which means 'do nothing'.

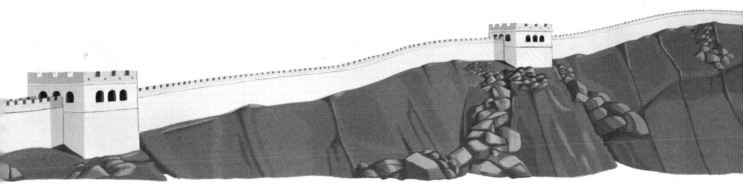

the Great Wall of China which can still be seen today are largely those of walls built in the fifteenth century A.D. and are much farther south than the old walls.

Confucius

Naturally enough Shih Hwang-ti's policies aroused great opposition and he was hated by the aristocracy who admired the old heroes of feudal times, and the scholars who revered the memory of the great teacher Confucius. The philosophy of Confucianism was directly critical of the emperor but it survived the 'burning of the books'.

Confucius had been born into a noble family and was raised within the traditions of a strict moral code of behaviour. But sixth-century Chinese life saddened him. Its glorification of war and heroic military

deeds encouraged violence and cruelty. The government was weak, life was cheap and a great gulf existed between the aristocracy and the poor. 'The world,' said one of his followers, 'had fallen into decay, and right principles had disappeared. Confucius was frightened by what he saw, and he undertook the work of reformation.' At the height of his fame, Confucius had over 3,000 disciples who followed his wanderings across China.

Confucius did not teach a religion; he was concerned with individual conduct. He believed that man should not only live virtuously but that he should do so within a framework of formal behaviour. His key words were kindness, respect, obedience, loyalty. His golden rule, which was capable of being expressed by one character in Chinese that has no direct translation into English, was 'what you do not

Both Confucianism and Taoism have had immense influence on the Chinese and were the basis for a way of life which lasted into the twentieth century.

Three-legged bronze cauldron, Shang period.

Writing and Printing

The literature of China is very old and has a continuing line of development right up to modern times from the very earliest verse written probably about the eleventh century B.C. It is also a vast and varied literature. The earliest writing was done on pieces of bamboo and wooden tablets, with a pen made from bamboo frayed at one end and dipped in coloured liquid. Later a brush made from hair was used and the writing done on silk or, more frequently, on paper, which was a Chinese invention of the second century A.D. So from this time Chinese artists were using the same materials as their descendants sometimes do today.

The earliest attempts at printing may have been inspired by the taking of rubbings on inscriptions carved on stone, some time in the ninth century A.D. This led to the idea of taking impressions on paper from wooden blocks, and by the tenth century this method was widely used in the production of books.

Priests of the Shinto faith, state religion of Japan since the eighteenth century.

Movable types of baked clay are said to have been invented by Pi Sheng about 1043 but it was not until possibly some time in the fourteenth century that these were made of wooden blocks. Due to the nature of the Chinese language, with its thousands of pictograms, movable type did not become popular in China as it did in the West after its introduction by Gutenberg in the fifteenth century. The Chinese printers found it easier and quicker to cut a complete block of the characters needed rather than search among six or seven thousand different characters for each individual piece. Nevertheless, the invention of movable type belongs properly to the Chinese, although they found it to be unsuitable for their needs.

The Origins of Japan

The earliest inhabitants of the islands of Japan were a race of people called the Ainu, of whom there are traces dating from the New Stone Age. About 1000 B.C. migrants from Korea are believed to have crossed the sea to the westerly island of Kyushu. Others, it is thought, came from south-east China. These people were the ancestors of the modern Japanese. It is not until some time in the first century A.D. that any written historical records appear.

Shinto Grand Shrine of Ise in Japan

Between the third and sixth centuries A.D. in Japan, *haniwa* figures, such as this simple head of a woman, were made from fired clay and placed around burial grounds.

The Ainu were quite distinct from the Japanese in every way. The Ainu had a larger physique and a great deal more thick wavy hair than the Japanese. Their women, in fact, even went to the length of tattooing moustaches on their upper lips. At one time the Ainu occupied all the islands of Japan but the new migrants pushed them gradually northwards until today there are only a few of them left on the northern island of Hokkaido.

During its early history Japan seems to have been solidly under the influence of China. There was regular contact between the countries through envoys and traders, but there is no evidence of a Chinese conquest of Japan. It is natural that the much older civilisation of the Chinese should be copied by the Japanese, and that Chinese wisdom and learning should have had great impact. But true to the tradition which they have followed into modern times, the Japanese learned quickly and efficiently. There was also a lot of traffic between Japan and Korea in those early days but usually for the purpose of making war.

44

Northern Europe

The early civilisations of man grew up in southern Asia and in places around the Mediterranean Sea because conditions there favoured a settled agricultural life. In northern Europe it took much longer for the land to recover from the effects of the Ice Ages. For centuries it offered only the barest livelihood to primitive man. Yet the Aryan-speaking tribes who moved across the Caucasus and through Asia Minor into middle-eastern lands, also pushed across the great rivers and mountains of central Europe to colonise France, Spain, Germany, Britain and Scandinavia.

These very early Europeans speak to us only through the objects of stone and metal which later people left behind. There is no written history, and usually such communities as existed are grouped and studied together because of some common factor in their way of life. For this reason, archaeologists talk of beaker folk, megalith builders and lake dwellers.

These groups of people did not exist in one place in Europe but were scattered over a wide area. In general they were cut off from the more advanced civilisations of the Mediterranean area by such natural mountain barriers as the Alps and the Pyrenees. But for the purposes of trade there was contact between people in northern Europe and the Mediterranean from an early date. There are many instances where the influence of the cultured southerners on the northern 'barbarians' can be detected. For example, some archaeologists point to similarities between the construction of Stonehenge in England and shaft-graves at Mycenae and suggest the employment of a master architect from Greece. Others maintain there is a strong link between Maltese temples and the temple-like monument at Stonehenge, although there is no direct evidence of any contact between Malta and Britain.

Megalith-builders

One of the recurring arguments among ethnologists (scientists who study the cultural history of man) is the extent to which a new method or step forward in man's cultural history is likely to have been discovered by various people in different places and at different times, independently of one another. The earliest megalith building is of a simple enough kind to allow the thought that men far apart from each other could have arrived at the same constructional methods.

The word megalith comes from two Greek words meaning big and stone, and it is used to describe a method of building prehistoric monuments with huge stones. It was widespread throughout western Europe and its probable origin was in tomb building in certain Mediterranean islands. As so many of the sites in western Europe where traces

Bronze Age trumpets from Denmark and a Beaker pot from Wiltshire in England.

of megalith building have been found are on or near the coast, it is thought that the idea was spread from place to place by seafaring people. There is little to suggest what early ships of this period may have looked like, apart from hazy representations of sailing vessels on pottery and stone carvings, but it seems certain that there was much movement by sea between coastal 'towns'.

The building of such monuments has much to do with early religion and the disposal and protection of the bodies of the dead. This religion was based on ancestor worship and a 'mother-goddess' cult, and spread from the western Mediterranean to other parts of Europe. Although cremation (the burning of bodies) was practised in the later Stone Age, the earliest method of dealing with the dead was to bury the body in a cave or in the earth. Sometimes very elaborate structures were created for

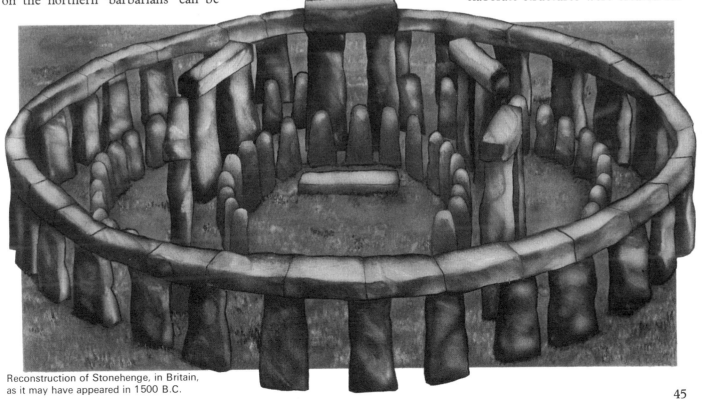

Reconstruction of Stonehenge, in Britain, as it may have appeared in 1500 B.C.

Many Bronze Age people were sun-worshippers. This model of a chariot drawing a disk representing the sun was found in Trundholm, Denmark.

vistas down which worshippers could watch the rise of a sun-god. A later development of the line of standing stones is the stone cricle, and it is this combination of lines and circles that has led to all kinds of theories about their purpose. One of the best examples, although sadly reduced by the understandable activities of a bygone farmer who spent much time and energy removing stones from the path of his cultivation, is at Avebury in England. Another is Stonehenge, the greatest prehistoric monument in Europe.

the housing of the dead and they indicate a strong religious conviction about the necessity of treating people's remains with respect. But the tremendous impulses which drove men to build such monuments as Stonehenge can only be guessed at.

Standing Stones

The simplest form of tomb is called a dolmen. Two or more stones are fixed upright in the earth, and a third stone is laid across them in the shape of a roof. Bodies were placed inside, under the roof, and the structure

was then covered with earth to form a mound. An even simpler and more widespread type of monument was the menhir, or standing stone. People in every part of the world have set stones on end for a variety of reasons —it is the commonest form of expression using natural materials. Among its many uses, the standing stone has served as a memorial, boundary stone, date marker, and as an aid to astronomical calculations.

The most extensive collection of standing stones is in France, where at Carnac and other places in Brittany there are great rows of them set up in what are called alignments. No one knows the real purpose of these stones, except to suggest that they are ceremonial avenues or perhaps

Lakes and Beakers

Some of the first people to settle in Europe did so in the mountainous areas of Switzerland where they built villages upon shallow lakes. These artificial islands were created on the same principle that inspired medieval castle builders to erect fortress islands with moats around them. An alternative to putting a ring of water around a piece of land was to take the 'land' and place it in the middle of an expanse of water. Large trees were felled and their trunks driven into the lake bed to form supports for platforms above the water, on which huts were built. Farming was carried out on the shore, on land cleared by the lavish cutting of timber. Livestock were kept on the platforms, although in summer the cattle were driven on to the Alpine pastures, much as they

A Celtic village scene in northern Europe about 2,000 years ago.

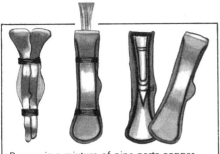

Bronze is a mixture of nine parts copper and one part tin. Some of the first people to use this alloy made the heads of their battle-axes, called palstaves, from it. While the metal was in liquid form it was poured into moulds. Here the two parts of the mould are shown bound together, then the liquid being poured in and finally the separated halves containing the axe-head.

are today. But the people lived in comparative safety from wild beasts or their human enemies on these isolated platform villages, which were approached by narrow causeways. The remains of lake villages have been found in many parts of Europe.

The beaker folk were a race of people who came from Spain, skilled in the making of a type of pottery which gave them their name. Many of these beautiful pots, which are the symbol of a new European culture, have been found in burial grounds. The bell-shaped beakers were wide-mouthed vessels ornamented with geometric designs, used for storing food. Their makers spread from the Iberian peninsula into France, Britain and the Netherlands and mixed with Nordic people from the steppes of Russia to produce the ancestors typical of the modern races of northern Europe.

Skara Brae

One of the most interesting of all archaeological finds in Europe is the village at Skara Brae in the Orkney Islands. Although it dates from the beginning of the Bronze Age in Britain the people who lived there belonged to a Stone Age culture. Their village was a compact community of stone-built houses which, centuries ago, the stormy winds buried beneath sand blown from the nearby sea-washed dunes. A similar storm in the winter of 1850 partially uncovered the site and some exploration of it began.

But it was not until 1930 that a complete examination of the village was made. This revealed the remarkable fact that Skara Brae was a kind of Pompeii of northern Europe. For the houses had been left by their occupants at short notice, as if they had been forced to escape before their homes were buried beneath the sand. Excavation showed that the stone walls and roofs of the village had been buried beneath kitchen waste, as generation after generation of inhabitants piled their rubbish around the outer walls to keep out the bitterly cold winds. Apart from holes left in roofs to allow smoke to escape, the whole community was buried under its own refuse long before the sand swept across the exposed site, obliterating it and filling every corner.

Within their snug little houses, these Stone-Age people had beds enclosed by stone slabs, stone dressers with household implements upon them, stone cupboards and shelves, and a central square hearth. In an area where there was virtually no wood everything was of stone. But it is possible to imagine the warmth and comfort of the place, with mattresses of heather and skins upon the beds. It is a picture of simple

Summary of key dates (All B.C.)
 c. 4000–3000 First settlements along the
  Danube river
 c. 2500 Lake dwellings in Europe
 c. 2000 Tin mines in Cornwall
 c. 2000–1000 Bell beaker folk in Europe
 c. 2000–900 Pile villages in Europe
 c. 1500 Erection of Stonehenge
 c. 1500–1300 High Bronze Age in Europe
 c. 1200 Wheeled vehicles in use in
  Europe
 c. 750 Migrations of Celtic peoples
  into Britain
 c. 600 Hallstatt culture in Europe
 c. 250 Invasions of Britain by
  La Tène Iron Age people

peasant life which altered very little for thousands of years—the family grouped around the hearth, warming themselves before the peat fire, surrounded by their simple utensils and belongings. In the barren, wind-swept Orkneys, Skara Brae was one of the last outposts of the early civilisations which had their origin in the warmer and kinder climate of near-eastern lands.

This Celtic warrior carries a typical Bronze Age shield.

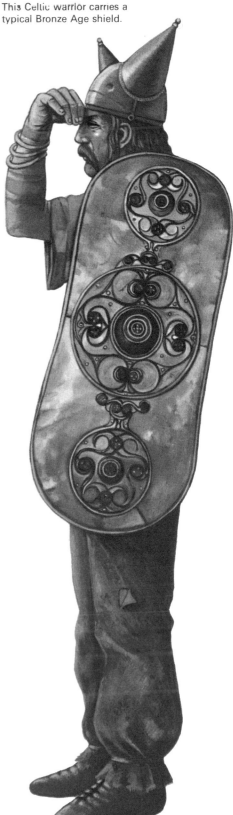

The Greek World

With the appearance of the exciting Greeks, world history becomes vividly alive. Suddenly, individual men are important, unlike the faceless subjects crushed by the all-powerful monarchs of the East. The Greeks were men in their own right who took independence to a fanatical extreme and thereby established new standards of human dignity. They were neither rich nor numerous, and even in the face of terrible danger the separate city-states were unwilling to combine. Yet no people have had a greater zest for living or for accepting every physical and intellectual challenge.

The Early Greeks

Originally the Greeks, like the Romans, were part of that great Indo-European movement of peoples which flowed into Europe. However, the Greeks did not find the land unoccupied when they moved in from the north. In southern Greece and in Crete there was a considerable civilisation which went back to the Bronze Age and beyond.

The islands of the Aegean Sea formed stepping stones to Asia, and Crete was a halfway house to Egypt, so that much of what earlier civilisations of the East had to offer had already been absorbed before the Greeks arrived. For many centuries these early settlements were unfortified and therefore were living in peace. With these peoples the earliest Greeks mingled. The resulting Mycenaean civilisation spread its influence over the sea routes. The massive beehive tombs of its most successful period, which have been excavated, are very impressive. About 1400 B.C. Knossos and the other chief Cretan cities were destroyed by unknown raiders and soon afterwards the Mycenaeans in southern Greece began to fortify their cities very heavily.

The Minoans of Crete

The ruler of Knossos, the most important city of Crete, became the chief power in the island about 2000 B.C. when the Minoan civilisation was at a peak. He was considered to be almost divine. His great palace at Knossos was a magnificent building surrounded by terraces of houses and paved streets. Fine frescoes, with delicate designs and lively scenes, are painted on the walls of the palace.

The Minoans, judging by their pictures, had a great love of sport. Not only are they shown dancing but also boxing and indulging in curious gymnastic displays which involved boys and girls jumping over the backs of bulls. Such a scene recalls the legend of the Minotaur, the fabulous man with a bull's head. The story says that seven youths and seven maidens supplied by Athens, should be sent periodically to be devoured by the monster. However, the valiant Theseus with the help of Ariadne, a Cretan princess, penetrated the baffling labyrinth, killed the Minotaur,

Cretan two-handled flask decorated with an octopus.

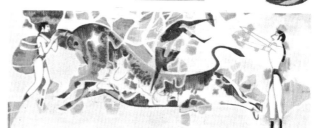

Cretan bull-leaping fresco

Heinrich Schliemann, German archaeologist, found this beaten gold death mask at Mycenae and called it the 'mask of Agamemnon'. Above is a reconstruction of Mycenae about 1600 B.C.

and escaped safely again to Greece.

The Mycenaean civilisation fell on evil days soon after the fall of Crete in a series of troubles which involved warfare with the city of Troy. This struggle between the Greeks and the Trojans was almost certainly a trade war for control of the sea routes but in Homer's *Iliad* it has been given a more romantic story involving Helen, the most beautiful woman in Greece.

The Trojan War
The *Iliad* tells the story of the cause and conduct of the war. Paris, son of the king of Troy, when asked to decide the most beautiful of three goddesses, had been bribed by one of them, Aphrodite, to give her the prize—a golden apple. In return she promised him that he should have the most beautiful mortal woman in the world. Whereupon he persuaded Helen, the wife of the Spartan king Menelaus, to elope with him to Troy.

To recover Helen, the Greeks collected a great force from the whole of southern Greece under Agamemnon, the brother of the weak Menelaus.

Upon arrival at Troy the Greeks challenged the Trojans to surrender Helen but they firmly refused to do so. For ten years the siege continued with varying success while the gods and goddesses meddled in the fortunes of both sides on behalf of their favourites. There was an epic quarrel between Agamemnon and the mighty Achilles which caused a serious split in the Greek ranks for a long time. At last by the stratagem of the wooden horse, the city was taken and destroyed.

Homer's other great work, the *Odyssey*, tells the story of Odysseus (or Ulysses as he is better known) and his companions on their return journey from Troy to their homes in Greece. These thrilling adventures occupied a further ten years and have become part of the world's great literature. But to the Greeks of those days the works of Homer were far more than good stories, they had the religious force of a holy book. This was the way men and women behaved in the heroic age: the courage of the heroes, the faithfulness of Odysseus's wife, the deserted Penelope. This was the way in which all Greeks must learn to live their lives. Throughout Greece, professional performers gave public recitals of Homer to enthralled audiences.

The City-states
The Greeks were the first Europeans to rule a world empire, although their homeland was not large and they were not numerous. They had, however, a lovely and pleasant land, more fertile than it is today, with a happy balance between town and country and between land and sea. In Greece, the

The stratagem which brought victory to the Greeks and defeat to the Trojans in Homer's *Iliad* was the making of the wooden horse. Until this point in the story Homer had been at pains to keep the two sides equal in success, but the stalemate of the war was broken by a trick. The Greeks built a huge wooden horse which was large enough to conceal a number of hand-picked warriors. The horse was then hauled right up to the walls of Troy and left there. The Trojans watched it for a long time with suspicion. There was a furious debate among them about the action to be taken. Finally the Trojans sallied out and dragged the horse

Homer

within the city. After careful examination they went away and left it unguarded. When night fell the Greek raiding party emerged from the horse and opened the gates to the Greek army while the Trojans slept.

mountains and the sea are never far away and the quickest way to travel is often by water. Not all Greeks lived on the mainland. In fact, the earliest Greek brilliance was seen in the cities of Asia Minor. The expansion of Greece was rapid, many of the prominent cities founding colonies from one end of the Mediterranean Sea to the other, and even on the southern shores of the Black Sea.

Greek Government

The progress of Greece was never smooth because of the intense independence of each individual Greek. Yet all were proud to be Greek and considered themselves with some right to be the finest race on earth.

The Greeks had many slaves and, except for a short period of wild experiment, slaves and women were not allowed to vote. Every freeman had the vote and, more importantly, the right to attend government assemblies in person—a right which he exercised. In order that every freeman represented himself in government, he heard the speeches first-hand, voted on the outcome, and was personally responsible for carrying out the laws.

Only freemen were allowed to fight for their city. Thus everyone was a politician, critic and soldier.

Many Greek coins bore the city badge of Athens—an owl—with the head of the goddess Athene on the reverse.

There were bloody quarrels but no one could shelve the responsibility. This form of political organisation kept the city state small, for the assembly had to be within a reasonable walking distance. Athens itself was never larger than a good-sized country town, ruling an area the size of a small county or province. Military service was compulsory and Socrates and Aeschylus both fought for their city.

Gradually two city-states emerged as the leaders, Athens and Sparta. In every way they were a contrast. Athens was a sea-power and thereby open to foreign influences and enterprising in outlook. Sparta was a land-power, locked in tradition. She was also a military state, run like a barracks with frightening discipline of its men from early boyhood. They were subjected to harsh and prolonged endurance tests which weeded out the weaklings and kept the supremely fit, who became an élite. Today we admire Athens but old Greece venerated Sparta and her invincible infantry. It was inevitable that the two should clash as they did later in a terrible civil war (called the Peloponnesian War) which permanently weakened both of them.

In the sixth century B.C. Sparta was the most powerful state in Greece. All male citizens were soldiers and spent their days in some form of military training.

The Importance of Vases

Our knowledge of the ancient world is mainly obtained from archaeologists, who dig carefully into the sites of old cities and retrieve fragments of the past which they piece together into a logical story. 'Pots', as all clay vessels are called, are most helpful to the archaeologist. The potter has always been most necessary to man and has existed in all kinds of civilisations. Although broken, the pots decay very little and therefore supply frequent evidence which reveals their makers and their dates. Some are of immense beauty while

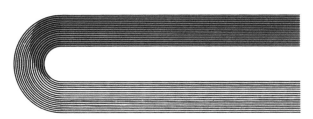

Athletes were immortalised in stone by the sculptors of ancient Greece. On the right are shown copies of two famous works, *Wrestlers* and *The discus thrower*.

The Olympic Games

In ancient Greece there were four great festivals, the Olympian, Pythean, Isthmian and Nemean, to which people came from all parts of the world. The Olympian festival in honour of the god Zeus was held at midsummer every fourth year. The periods of four years between the games were known as Olympiads and they were used in dating historical events. The Olympic Games were the chief part of the festival. There is a record of the victors since 776 B.C. The number of events in the games was added to over the years and included foot races, boxing, chariot races and the pentathlon (a contest of five events comprising running, wrestling, the long jump and throwing the javelin and the discus). The stadium at Olympia was shaped like a long horseshoe (see above) and could seat 40,000 people. A truce was proclaimed between the Greek states during the games and all fighting between them stopped so that competitors from all over the Peloponnese might be given safe conduct to attend.

others are humble, but there are endless shapes and varieties of decoration and texture, which make them a ready-made time scale for the historian.

The Unity of Greece

The Greek nation appears at first sight to consist of dozens of separate units all fighting against each other—it is not easy to see the central core which holds it together. Yet the people knew very definitely they were Greek. Their unity was due to language and religion. They all used a language which many consider the finest the world has known and in it they had heroic stories which they respected with religious conviction.

Their religion was unusual. Not only was it strong but it was very wide in scope. Great festivals were held which were for the Greeks alone. There was enormous rivalry between cities to win the prizes for excellence in competitions which included drama and athletics. There was nothing strange to the Greeks in this, for they believed in a balance between a healthy mind and a healthy body. The plays centred round some burning question of moral importance to Greeks. It was an exciting sort of religious experience. From these great festivals the Olympic Games were born.

Perhaps the most important of the festivals were the games held at Olympia in southernmost Greece. Only freeborn Greeks were allowed to enter and women were not allowed to watch. The festival lasted five days, beginning with opening ceremonies and ending with feasts to celebrate the occasion. Runners, horsemen, boxers and wrestlers all competed and there were group events like the Pentathlon. To win an important event made one a public hero and a foremost citizen of one's city for life, so the competition was intense. Philip of Macedon, the father of Alexander, once won the chariot race and this achievement was recorded on his own coinage.

The Persian Wars

The growing strength of the city-states and the widespread success of their colonies around the shores of the Mediterranean Sea now brought the Greeks into direct conflict with the Persian Empire, the greatest power of the day. The Greeks of Asia Minor lived on the extreme western boundary of the Persian Empire but the Greeks in mainland Greece were not in contact with the Persians at all.

The finest Greek vases were made in the fifth century B.C. They were used both for dry storage and liquids, such as wine, water and oil.

However in 546 B.C. Cyrus, the famous conqueror of Nebuchadnezzar as recorded in the Book of Daniel, moved against the wealthy kingdom of Lydia, which had been increasing its power under Croesus, the king whose riches had become a legend. Lydia had acted as a buffer to the Greek cities of Asia Minor and when that kingdom fell decisively to Cyrus, all these cities came under direct Persian rule and were required to pay tribute and to serve in the Persian armies.

Fifty years later they revolted with naval help from across the Aegean Sea given by Athens and Eretria. Sardis, the old capital of Croesus, was captured and the Athenian ships went home. Darius, the new Persian king, quelled this revolt and was indeed reasonable in victory for he wanted Greek ships from the cities of Asia Minor to help him attack those western Greeks who had made his empire insecure.

The Plain of Marathon
The struggle which followed was a fight between a giant and a pygmy. The Persian Empire was immense and all its subject peoples were required to supply troops. Greece was not only small but hopelessly divided by proud independence. But these Greeks believed that each man was important and had rights, whereas the king of Persia was an eastern despot with absolute power over all his subjects.

Under Mardonius, the huge Persian army rolled ponderously into Europe and eventually reached the borders of Macedonia. The Greek cities were invited to submit but declined. By 491 B.C. Athens and Eretria knew that a direct attack across the Aegean would be the next move. In the face of this fearful danger, Athens and Sparta drew nearer together and they had the advantage of advice from Miltiades who was skilled in Persian ways.

Darius despatched his fleets and a landing was made on Euboea resulting in the capture of Eretria. The main Persian force of 25,000 men was then landed on the plain of Marathon unopposed. Immediately Athens sent her heavy-armed hoplites to occupy the foothills overlooking the Persian landing. There were barely 10,000 Athenians assisted by 1000 men from Plataea. Pheidippides, the famous runner was despatched to Sparta to warn them of the Persian invasion, whereupon the Spartans marched but did not arrive in time.

The Greeks, advised by Miltiades, attacked at dawn having thinned their line in the centre and packed the wings so that when the two armies clashed there was a pincer movement which encircled the Persian force. The more heavily armed Greeks took a terrible toll of the Persians with little loss to themselves. However the surviving Persians boarded their ships and set sail for Athens hoping to avenge themselves on the unprotected city. But the Athenians raced home and arrived before the Persian fleet, whereupon the thwarted Persians sailed away.

There was an uneasy pause of ten years while Darius prepared a full-scale invasion. In this period, a great find of silver was made at Larium which brought a large sum to the treasury, and Themistocles persuaded the Athenians to invest it in a larger navy. The Spartans meanwhile fortified the isthmus in order to hold the south of the country. Darius then died but soon his successor Xerxes advanced relentlessly by the land route towards Greece.

Sparta called a conference of all the cities and was given the command on land and sea. The narrow pass of Thermopylae was chosen for the first engagement and there the Greeks halted the Persians for two days but the stalemate was broken when the traitor Ephialtes led the Persian Immortals by a secret path to the Greek rear. Leonidas sent the main body of the army back but stayed with his Spartans to fight a glorious delaying action in which every one of his men fell fighting to gain precious time.

The Battle of Salamis
Despite the Spartan heroism, the Persians advanced steadily upon Athens by land and sea. On land there was no hope of stopping them and a desperate decision was taken by Athens after bitter discussion: this was to abandon the city to the enemy and to trust solely in their ships. All the aged, the women and the children were evacuated to nearby islands whence they were agonised witnesses of the burning of their beloved Athens. The men filled the ships and engaged the Persian fleets. By wily tactics and superior seamanship, the Greeks destroyed Persian naval power

In one of the great sea fights of all time the Greeks gave battle to the Persian fleet in the narrow waters around the island of Salamis. The Persians were out-manoeuvred and the Greeks rammed and boarded many of the enemy ships to win an important victory.

in the battle of Salamis and the Persian army, weakened by disease and famine, was compelled to retreat.

The following year, the Persians made their last attack but were heavily defeated by Sparta at Plataea. By these superb victories, Europe was saved and the way paved for Alexander the Great.

The Golden Age

After the astonishing defeat of Persia, the Greeks were filled with that boundless confidence which only comes to a people once or twice at the greatest moments of their history. Athens had played a leading part in the Greek victory at Marathon and at Salamis. She was now the equal of Sparta and poised for further success. The political foundations of Athens were already the finest in Greece due to the work of the great statesmen Solon and Pisistratus. Now under the dazzling leadership of Pericles (490– 429 B.C.), Athens was to come to her supreme perfection.

The Building of Athens

Although Europe and mainland Greece were safe, the huge Persian Empire still existed. The Ionian

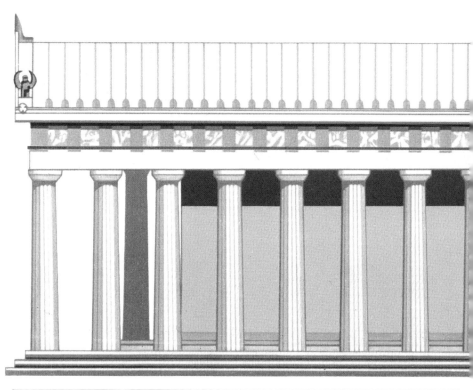

Greeks of Asia Minor were still in danger and they looked to the new sea-power of Athens for protection. So Athens organised all the interested maritime states into a defensive league based on the sacred island of Delos. While danger was high, the league was very popular and the assessment of ships to be contributed by the member cities, made by Aristides the Just, was never questioned.

Athens was very active at sea but as danger receded some members shirked their dues. Athens decided to take matters into her own hands. She moved the treasury from Delos to the safety of her own city and compelled payment from the unwilling. All disputes were also handled in the Athenian courts so that the league was being transformed into an empire. These necessary actions helped to create the bitterness which later led to the civil war with Sparta and closed Athens's finest hour with disaster.

Sea-power brought great wealth to Athens and Pericles did not hesitate to use it to adorn the city with the artistic power at his command. The

The Athenian Pericles (c.490–429 B.C.) was one of the most brilliant statesmen in the history of Greece. Born of distinguished parents, whose forebears had long been leading citizens of Athens, he made full use of his opportunities. Pericles did not look for public popularity and remained a dignified, cultured man, quietly detached in his bearing. His all-round ability, his honesty and his genuine superiority over others made him a natural leader, in the cool judgement of Thucydides, the great historian. Pericles's first successes were all political. He increased the people's share in government and accepted the danger of rivalry with Sparta. Peace with Persia gave him funds and opportunity in the general prosperity to rebuild Athens to his own sure taste. Soon after the Peloponnesian war began a plague ravaged Athens and Pericles died of a fever.

The Doric column was the one used most by the Greeks and has the simplest form of capital with no base at the bottom. It was used by Phidias on the Parthenon, the most perfect example of Doric architecture in Greece.

The second order of Greek architecture is based on the Ionic column. This is taller than the Doric, with fluting which is deeper and narrower. At the top of the column there are balancing scroll ends and the whole column stands on a base.

The Corinthian column was more ornate than the earlier forms. The shaft was thinner and the fluting even narrower. The capital was decorated with an intricate design of acanthus leaves. This type of column was very popular with the Romans.

bitterest Athenian memory had been watching while the Persians burned their city, so now they crowned the Acropolis with the cool beauty of the Parthenon, which has floated above Athens ever since.

The arts were nearing perfection at this time. Statues idealised human bodily perfection, the proportions of the buildings were a harmony of design, and the decoration was carried out by the finest artists, like Phidias. Inside the houses were articles of rare beauty. The rebuilding of the city was as extensive as it was brilliant.

On every hand there was a flowering of the Greek genius. Great writers and artists produced the finest drama the world has seen. Art and entertainment of this magnificent quality were enthusiastically received by the whole citizen body of Athens, and testify to their superb taste.

Greek Drama

In the kindly Mediterranean climate, it was possible to organise large-scale festivals with some ease and there was a long history of dramatic development from early times. But in 534 B.C., Pisistratus, who did so much for Athens, reorganised the festival of Dionysus, who is best known as the god of wine. This festival thereafter brought performances of plays before the public and provided a theatre for the tragedies of Sophocles, Euripides and Aeschylus, and the comedies of Aristophanes, many of which are still regularly performed today.

The plays written then remain as eternal masterpieces in the repertoire of the world's classical theatre. In the festival the tragedies were performed first, followed by the comedies, which were usually witty imitations of the serious plays already acted. This

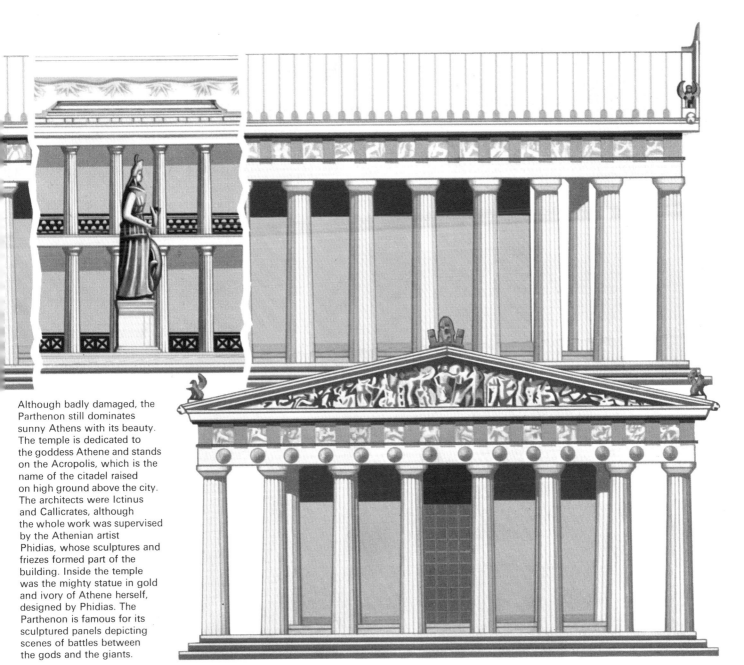

Although badly damaged, the Parthenon still dominates sunny Athens with its beauty. The temple is dedicated to the goddess Athene and stands on the Acropolis, which is the name of the citadel raised on high ground above the city. The architects were Ictinus and Callicrates, although the whole work was supervised by the Athenian artist Phidias, whose sculptures and friezes formed part of the building. Inside the temple was the mighty statue in gold and ivory of Athene herself, designed by Phidias. The Parthenon is famous for its sculptured panels depicting scenes of battles between the gods and the giants.

holding up of serious ideas to searching ridicule in the same festival was an acid test of their value and a creator of sound judgement.

The Greek plays which have come down to us are impressive and powerful. The audience was at a religious festival to consider some great moral question about which everyone had very strong feelings. Never has there been such communication between audience, actors and writers; they were all completely involved. The play attempted to explore the basic truths of life with as much stark simplicity as possible. Consequently the playwrights selected their material very carefully, kept to a strong central theme, and expressed themselves in a stark and forceful style. The chorus, however, which both sang and danced, acted as a foil to the main line of the dialogue.

The Peloponnesian War

It was always easy to offend Greek independence and there were many who envied the Athenian success. Those who felt like this drew away to Sparta and the tension grew between the two leading cities. Athens, who probably felt a reckoning between them was inevitable, pushed her rival Corinth into the arms of Sparta. The war began half-heartedly in 431 B.C. and has been brilliantly described for us by the great historian Thucydides.

Misfortune now dogged the Athenians, for plague grievously attacked the crowded city. Pericles, the wise leader, died shortly after the long war began. In unusual contrast, Sparta produced a great leader in Brasidas, who won over many Athenian allies. Wisdom prevailed for a time and there was an interval of six years' peace.

Then the dangerous Alcibiades gained the ear of Athens and persuaded her to send a great expedition to attack Syracuse. The expedition was not only ill-advised but was also betrayed by the treacherous Alcibiades. Athens surrendered at Syracuse and dug in behind fortifications on her chief port Piraeus. The land fighting now switched to the Black Sea corn route on which Athens's survival depended. Sparta eventually took Athens but with rare mercy spared the beautiful city of Pericles. Both cities, however, were permanently exhausted by war and power passed into new hands.

Greek Intellect

Although the Greeks inherited much from earlier civilisations, the heights to which they soared left all previous human thought behind both for quality and range. There seems to have been no mental challenge which they dared not face; whether it came in pure philosophy or applied science.

Nevertheless different parts of the Greek world were particularly successful in different fields. Scientific thought and discoveries first prospered in Ionia, that is in the Greek cities of Asia Minor. The work was then taken up by the colonies in the west, such as Syracuse, and the final chapters of brilliant science were written at Alexandria when Greek power was declining. Philosophy, which explored the whole realm of the intellect's possibilities and the basis of all our moral ideas, came to full flower in the marvellous Athens created by Pericles.

True Science

The Greek believed that the universe and all it contained could be understood if only man would apply his reason logically to the world around him. Thus modern science was born and exact knowledge began to be recorded. Thales of Miletus was a typical representative of the alert, well-informed Greek. He was a man of affairs who had travelled widely and learned enough about astronomy to understand the nature of eclipses. Thus he was able to foretell the eclipse of 585 B.C. not by priestly soothsaying but because he knew scientifically it would happen. This was the first absolutely certain date in world history.

Thales also thought the basic matter of the universe was water, which had a liquid, gaseous and solid form. Greeks were looking for simple universal explanations of matter. Thales's follower Anaximander made the first map and thought the earth was suspended in space by a balance of forces. He also thought life came from water and that a fish was the ancestor of man.

Democritus thought the world was made up of an uncountable number of atoms which were continually being brought together and separating again. Other Greeks guessed the world was round and that the sun was the larger planet. It is easy to appreciate that this free imagination of the Greek mind, coupled with careful observation of life around them, formed the basis of modern experimental science and twentieth-century physics.

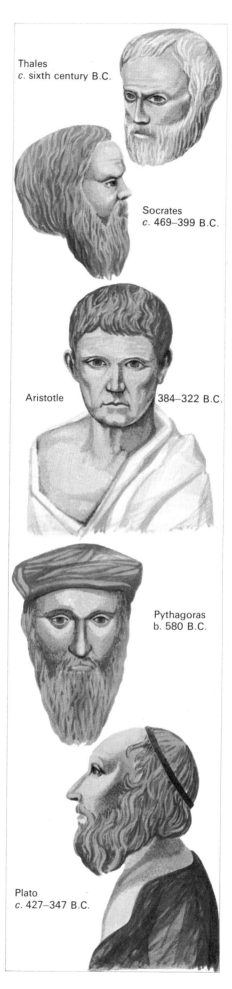

Thales
c. sixth century B.C.

Socrates
c. 469–399 B.C.

Aristotle   384–322 B.C.

Pythagoras
b. 580 B.C.

Plato
c. 427–347 B.C.

Sometimes imagination outran reality. The Greeks were fascinated by the beautiful laws and harmonies which they discovered in mathematics. Pythagoras discovered the mathematical nature of music. He tried to apply mathematical laws to the moral questions which belong to religion. Of course, they could not work in so abstract a field but there is a clear link between Greek thought and Einstein's famous equations explaining relativity. In our own day such discoveries have unified the physical universe and made atomic physics a new avenue for human progress.

Socrates and Plato

Living in the Athens of Pericles was Socrates, considered by the Delphic Oracle the wisest man in Greece. This remarkable man, together with Plato and Aristotle, permanently affected the course of human thought. Socrates wrote nothing, but we have his teaching in the beautiful words of Plato who wrote *The Republic*, one of the best plans for an ideal society that man has produced. Socrates was a man of great physical and moral courage. He fought for his city, saving the life of Alcibiades, and defied the whole political order of his day in his persistent quest for truth. Wearing the same coat summer and winter, Socrates was poor and ugly but 'all glorious within'. He cared for his soul, not for wordly goods and always saw the comical contradictions in human nature. He has remained famous for the type of logical enquiry which if followed to its conclusion will lead to the discovery of truth.

Aristotle

Aristotle spent the first part of his life in Athens with Plato and then went on his travels. During this time he became tutor to the young Alexander for three years. Returning to Athens, he became responsible for the famous school in the Lyceum which occupied him almost to his death. Aristotle had an encyclopedic brain. For his own use he placed on record the best of the knowledge of his day. This covered an amazing range of subjects which are still studied in universities today. The schoolmen of the Middle Ages held him in almost religious awe and brought many of his and Plato's ideas into Christian thought.

Alexander the Great

The Macedonian phalanx consisted of infantry armed with very long spears.

The exhaustion of Athens and Sparta after the great civil war caused them to lose the leadership of Greece. For a short time Thebes became the chief city, its supremacy being based on a new type of military formation, the phalanx. As a young man Philip of Macedon served with the armies of Thebes and learned their new tactics. Philip returned to his own country and organised a tough professional army which forced unity on the unwilling Greeks by superior military power. In this hothouse of war Philip trained the boy Alexander.

Training of Alexander
From thirteen to sixteen years of age Alexander was tutored by Aristotle but then he assumed the control of Macedonia while his father was absent on campaign. At eighteen he commanded the left wing of the cavalry at the crucial battle of Chaeronia (338 B.C.) which subdued Greece. When Philip was assassinated two years later, probably with the active help of Olympias, Alexander's mother, the young man stood on the threshold of manhood, ruler of his country and head of a fine professional army.

Campaigns of Alexander
In the next three years Alexander was to conquer the whole civilised world and to show himself a superb master of war. The revenge campaign against Persia had been planned by Philip and carefully prepared. Alexander readily accepted the task. His heavy cavalry, siege engines and deep formations of infantry swept all before them.

At the first meeting on the Granicus, he defeated the Persians and freed permanently the Greek cities of Asia Minor. The Persians then assembled a huge army to defend Syria. Alexander tore it to shreds and moved on to Tyre, the great Phoenician city which controlled the eastern Mediterranean. The position of Tyre on an island required the construction of a great causeway. It took many months but Tyre fell.

Alexander swept on into Egypt and founded a city in his own honour—Alexandria—to replace Tyre. Nothing could stop him. Persepolis was burned and he entered Babylon. But now the luxury of the East and Alexander's weakness for divine honours began to conquer the young genius. He reached the Caspian Sea in the north and India in the east but his men rebelled.

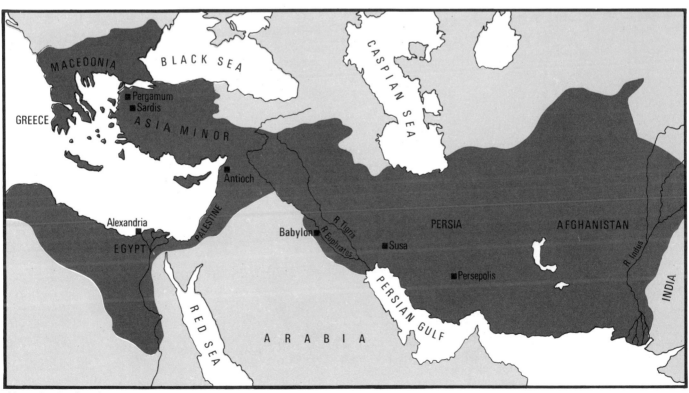

Alexander the Great's empire extended from the Mediterranean to the borders of India.

Summary of key dates (All B.C.)
359 Accession of Philip II of Macedon
338 Battle of Chaeronia
336 Accession of Alexander the Great
333 Battle of Issus, Alexander defeats
    Darius of Persia
326 Alexander conquers Punjab
323 Death of Alexander. Ptolemy I founds
    Egyptian dynasty
307 Alexandrian Library begun by
    Ptolemy I

Suddenly at thirty-three, he died of fever in Babylon.

Alexander left no son to continue his work and his empire became the prey of warring generals who finally resolved themselves into the rival powers of Syria and Egypt. But his death was not the end of Greek influence on the lands so rapidly conquered. The pupil of Aristotle fully intended that the benefits of Greek civilisation should follow his conquests. It was his custom to found Greek communities everywhere he went.

Greek speedily became the international language of the Near East so that three hundred years later the New Testament was written in Greek to reach the widest possible audience. Egypt proved to be the richest seed-bed for Greek ideas and Alexandria fulfilled all its founder's hopes when the city swiftly rose to dominate the intellectual and commercial life of the eastern Mediterranean and to continue as capital of Egypt for a thousand years.

Greek Science in Egypt

In Egypt, Greek science once again flowered brilliantly. The Egyptians had traditional skill in construction and land measurement, which came to its zenith in the mathematical school founded by Euclid, one of whose pupils was the resourceful Archimedes. Galen, the physician whose knowledge influenced doctors for centuries, was another Alexandrian. It was a world of applied science and Eratosthenes measured the circumference of the earth almost exactly by using the reflections of the noonday sun in well shafts some distance apart.

Alexandria had been carefully sited on the Nile Delta at a point where the current kept the harbour free of silt.

Underground cisterns could conserve a year's water supply. The Pharos, or lighthouse, was one of the Seven Wonders of the Ancient World. The intellectual side of the city was catered for by its museum and library.

Alexander's Successors

But although Greek culture survived so splendidly in the eastern Mediterranean, Greece as a political nation was now broken and began to decay. After a long trial of strength, Alexander's successors split into the two powerful kingdoms of the Seleucids in Syria and the Ptolemies in Egypt, who were always fighting with each other. In the West, the power of Rome was growing daily but the Punic Wars shielded the Greek lands for a time from their attention.

At first, the Romans were lenient towards the Greeks because of the respect they had for Greek culture which they were striving to imitate. But this special relationship did not prevent the Romans moving in with their customary ruthless efficiency when the time was ripe. By the middle of the second century before Christ, both Macedonia and Greece had been annexed as Roman provinces. The Greeks in Egypt experienced a longer liberty but first Pompey and then Caesar moved against them and when Cleopatra died in 30 B.C., Alexandria, the world's greatest port, fell to the Roman Empire.

The Pharos at Alexandria

The Romans

Etruscan bronze figure of a legendary Greek monster called the chimaera.

This typical costume of an Etruscan woman is reconstructed from many figured monuments that have survived from ancient times.

After the flashing brilliance of the Greeks, the Romans do not immediately win our admiration. They achieved their amazing growth to world power by steady, well-planned effort which could draw on deep reserves of stamina and determination in the Roman character. Society was based on a man's loyalty to his family, then to his city, and finally to his country.

The Romans were loyal to their traditions and believed in a dignified seriousness of conduct and bearing. Although they did not hesitate to use severity to establish their rule if they were opposed, the Romans were basically reasonable and their empire advanced as much by treaty and mutual self-interest as it did by conquest.

The Etruscans

Although little is known for certain about the beginnings of the Romans, they were Indo-Europeans and entered Italy from the north. Italy was much more thickly populated than Greece at that time and already the Romans found themselves surrounded by four powerful nations. The Etruscans were established in what is now Tuscany, the Gauls held the great northern plain, and Sicily was in dispute between the Greeks and the Carthaginians. The city of Rome arose from a small group of farming villages in the plain of Latium. They

combined and chose the seven hills of Rome as their main centre.

When Rome is first heard of, it is a tiny city-state ruled over by Etruscan kings. Little is known about this mysterious people, and their language has not been deciphered by scholars. There is no doubt however about the high standards of their culture and early Rome benefited from its influence. The overlordship of the Etruscans was cruel and oppressive and eventually the Romans rebelled. The foreign kings were expelled and a republic was set up.

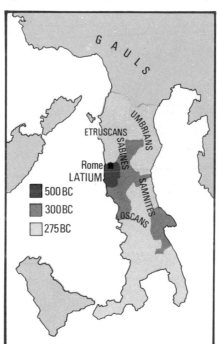

The growth of Rome

This bitter experience left the Romans with an enduring hatred of kingship which was still strong in the days of Julius Caesar.

Soon the Etruscans disappeared as a separate people and the Greeks were a spent force. It was left to the Carthaginians to defend their great commercial empire against the threat from Rome. At this time Rome was strictly a land power while the Phoenicians of Carthage were the finest sailors of the ancient world. With fanatical determination and dreadful loss of citizen armies, the Romans built ships and fought until they had utterly destroyed the Carthaginians.

Patricians and Plebeians

While the Romans were defeating their rivals in war, the domestic scene was not one of peace and harmony. The aristocrats ruled Rome through the all-powerful Senate and the laws fell with severity on the

Gaius Julius Caesar was a patrician by birth but saw his political future in supporting the popular party. Away from Rome on army service, his own gay life and the lavish public spectacles which he sponsored involved him in enormous debts on his return to the city. However, he made a success of his first important command in Spain. Wisely, he threw in his lot with Pompey and formed the famous triumvirate with him and Crassus. While Pompey rested on his laurels as victor of the east and remained in Rome to secure political power there, Caesar conducted his extensive campaigns in Spain and Gaul, including his two brief visits to Britain. Death removed Crassus and the rivalry between Caesar and Pompey came to a head. Pompey, backed by the Senate, expected submission but Caesar crossed the Rubicon and drove out Pompey to defeat and assassination. In 44 B.C. Ceasar received the unusual honour of dictatorship for life, and outraged republicans assassinated him.

heroic farmers who fought so courageously for their country. Thus began the long and bitter struggle between the Patricians, who represented the aristocratic families, and the Plebeians who represented the common people.

At first the Plebeians had no say in affairs whatsoever. The situation was so tense that there were two desperate moments of crisis when they almost abandoned the city. But gradually the Romans hammered out an agreement. Tribunes were appointed to represent the interests of the Plebeians and they play an increasingly important part in the history of the later republic. The common people gained better treatment through the new laws of state, which were respected by all Romans, rich and poor.

Burning patriotism and a genuine respect for law saved the early republic. When war threatened, the Romans suspended their normal life and for the duration of the war appointed a dictator whom all should obey without any question. After the fighting was done, he was required to lay down his great powers and to become a private citizen again. This ability to put the interest of the state above personal desires served Rome well in times of crisis.

After the crushing of Carthage, Rome was able to consolidate and extend her provinces east and west. The republic swiftly began to expand into an empire. The rich world of the older civilisations to the east was in hopeless chaos. To them Rome offered either peaceful alliance or conquest. The strength and organisation of Rome could not be resisted and the countries which had made up Alexander's empire became provinces of Rome. The Romans were magnificent civil engineers and brought prosperity to the lands they ruled.

The Power of the Army

Wealth and slaves flowed from the conquered lands and weakened the disciplined character of the Roman people. Political power passed to profiteers who used corrupt methods to gain their own ends. The free,

The triumphant return to Rome of the Imperial Army after a successful campaign.

small farmers of Italy, who had been the backbone of early achievements, lost their land in favour of large plantations worked by slaves. These landless men crowded into Rome itself and became a dangerous mob which the politicians had to quieten. Free issues of Egyptian corn and massive entertainments in the Colosseum were arranged for their benefit. Ambitious politicians exploited this unrest and power passed to the army and its commanders.

The last hundred years of the republic (first century B.C.) was violent and bloody. The ruthless army commanders now held the republic in their hands and battled with each other for the prize. Anarchy broke out and a grim civil war was fought between forces led by Marius and Sulla. The struggle for complete power spread from Italy throughout the Roman world. Finally two great commanders brought matters to a decision. Pompey became the master of the east and was favoured by the politicians in Rome. He was opposed by Caesar who had built up his power in the west. The task of subduing Spain and Gaul had been much more difficult than Pompey's easy conquests in the east. Caesar's battle-hardened legions defeated Pompey and Caesar stood alone as master of the Roman world.

Still the republican flame had not quite been destroyed. There was a move to make Julius Caesar a king and a body of conspirators banded

Roman parade helmet

The Roman army was the foundation of its power throughout the history of Rome. The main core was infantry originally supplied by the free citizens of the state. Then Marius, the Roman general, reorganised the army on a more permanent and professional basis. It was made up of legions of six thousand men arranged in ten cohorts and sixty centuries. The officers consisted of a legate, usually of noble birth, who was in overall command, and the cohorts were led by military tribunes. The centuries were numbered and led by centurions, men chosen on merit from the ranks. Promotion started in the higher numbers so that the centurion in charge of the first century was an outstanding man. The equipment and training of the army was of the highest standard.

The legionary was armed with a shield, a sword and a long spear.

The testudo, formed by soldiers joining shields together for protection.

together to prevent this betrayal of the republic. At the moment of his triumph, he was assassinated.

So, with Augustus, under whom Christ was born, began the long rule of the emperors. Italy now begins to fade in importance while the provinces of the empire begin to have more influence on the destiny of Rome.

The Roman Empire

When Julius Caesar was assassinated, the duty of revenge fell to Mark Antony, his second in command, and to Octavius, his nineteen-year-old adopted kinsman. The result of all the civil strife which then broke out

The Circus Maximus was a vast stadium in Rome, which could seat about 200,000 spectators.

throughout the Roman Empire was that the quiet young Octavius became the sole master of the Roman world.

At first the two leaders of Caesar's faction were jointly victorious but then Antony was foolishly persuaded by Cleopatra to rebel. He was decisively defeated at the battle of Actium in 31 B.C. and the dominance of the west over east was permanently established. With immense care and cold wisdom the young general, who now became known as Caesar Augustus, consolidated his power. First and foremost he retained the command of all the armed forces for life and held all the key state offices in person. Having the reality of power, he concealed it.

Caesar Augustus

With the mild title of Princeps, or first citizen, Augustus was effectively the first of the true emperors but he was most careful to show suitable respect to the Senate and all outward forms of republican and religious procedure. Nevertheless the Senate

was really powerless, for only Augustus could introduce business and he had complete power of veto on what was done. Even the persecution of opponents was put through the law courts for form's sake. His wisdom and self-control were to give the empire fifty years of invaluable peace. He reduced the size of the army and placed the remaining legions, every one of which he had commanded at some time, on frontier duty.

Throughout the peaceful empire ran the Roman law together with the Roman language and customs. Since wars were only with barbarians, taxes were light. Rome was poor, but liberal gifts of free corn and frequent entertainments kept the populace docile. Meanwhile Augustus administered the provinces wisely, an

The toga was a woollen outer garment, semicircular in shape, worn by men in ancient Rome. One end hung in front of the body and the other was thrown over the left shoulder, taken round the back and under the right arm and then thrown over the left shoulder again.

example his imperial followers were to copy, and wealth poured into Rome.

The Senate was incompetent and too aristocratic to consider any form of work. So their power was quietly whittled away in favour of a civil service recruited from the rising middle class, many of whom were Augustus's own freed slaves. For the first time there were no pirates in the Mediterranean and there were no frontiers or customs barriers throughout the empire. Somewhat boastfully but with much truth, Augustus said that he 'found Rome brick and left it marble'.

There was one ominous warning from the German frontier, however. The army attempted to push the northern frontier to the Elbe in order to shorten their defensive line but Varus and three legions were cut to pieces and the eagles were lost. The attempt was never repeated and northern Germany remained barbarian.

The Julian House

By the time of his death, Augustus had reached the position he had aimed at as a young man and he rounded off his magnificent service to the empire by choosing and adopting a worthy and efficient successor in Tiberius. This superb general ensured that the triumphant Germans stayed safely behind the Rhine and that the provinces were well ruled. But his nature was grim and suspicious, so that he persecuted the Roman nobles who might be plotting against him and kept a strict control over all his officials. It was fear of Tiberius which made Pontius Pilate such a wretched figure in the trial and crucifixion of Jesus.

The next three emperors were also of the Julian house and had the support of the army and the popular party; but they were to bring disgrace upon their kinsmen. Caligula was dangerously and viciously mad and finally had to be murdered to arrest his insane crimes. He was followed by an eccentric but better man in the physically feeble Claudius.

He is very important to the history of the British Isles for he followed up the two reconnaissances made by Julius Caesar with a full-scale invasion. With the help of an efficient staff (on which most of Rome's famous generals appeared) and extensive preparations, Claudius successfully invaded Britain. The country became part of the Roman Empire for nearly four hundred years.

The infamous Nero was the next emperor. He had artistic leanings and insisted on giving public performances of song and poetry. These disgusted the nobles to whom such a display was nauseous, particularly as the emperor should have been leading his legions against the barbarians. But the vain and foolish side of Nero's mind was accompanied by a dark and vicious cruelty. He persecuted the Christians with enthusiasm and counted the murder of his wife and mother among his crimes. Finally the unhappy man committed suicide.

This was the end of the Julian house, which had given Rome its first emperors. The depths to which absolute power can corrupt human nature had been horribly and thoroughly demonstrated.

The Army Rules

Now the all-powerful army began to choose its favourite commanders to be emperors and to threaten civil war if their choice was questioned. There was a gulf of sympathy and communication between the frontiers and the capital. The marching legions learned what easy plunder the soft, peaceful lands offered on their way to Rome. Often the legions chose well and

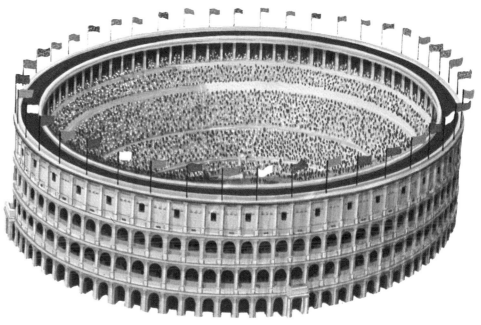

Vespasian and his son, Titus, who brutally destroyed Jerusalem, strengthened the army and chose senators on a broader basis than the old aristocracy. After so much civil war, their saner rule was a welcome interlude.

Between A.D. 96 and 180 there was a brief golden age when five good emperors, carefully chosen and linked by adoption, gave Rome a period of peace. Trajan conquered Dacia and brought the empire to its greatest extent. He loved to glorify his dominions with splendid public buildings, many of which remain today.

The most famous amphitheatre of the ancient world was the Colosseum in Rome, built in the first century A.D. by the emperor Vespasian.

He was followed by the energetic Hadrian, who twice toured the whole of his empire and built the famous defensive wall across Britain. The Stoic, Marcus Aurelius, closed this fine period—but the shadows were falling. This philosopher-emperor, renowned for his *Meditations*, was obliged to spend almost his whole reign on active service against the barbarians. Then he foolishly set aside the wise policy of adoption in favour of a worthless son.

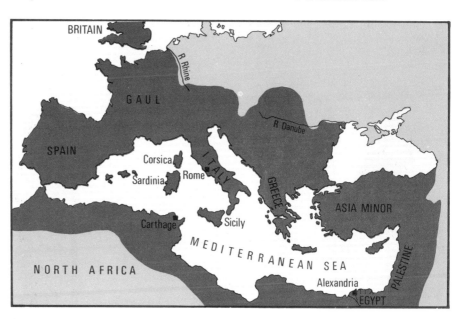

The Pont du Gard, a Roman aqueduct at Nimes in France.

The extent of the Roman Empire at the height of its power.

The troubles were now mounting for the empire. The all-important army was no longer composed of Romans. In Gaul they were nearly all Gauls and in Syria nearly all Syrians. Since Augustus the army had been greatly increased in numbers and the first necessity for the emperor was to see that they were paid.

The flow of treasure which came from the east and the plentiful supply of slaves were now drying up. So manpower was short and everywhere people were complaining about the rising prices and the heavy taxes. The eastern and western parts of the empire, which had never been welded together very firmly, now began to drift apart. When Caracalla gave Roman citizenship to all free men throughout the empire in A.D. 212, the true reason for his generosity was probably to increase the taxes which he could raise.

Frontier Troubles
A change in Persia at this time brought a new line of kings who made that country more warlike. Also the barbarians along the frontiers of the Rhine and Danube were discovering how helpless the lands were behind the fortifications. Often a new emperor was only supported by some of the provinces, so that civil war resulted. Under these conditions the

Roman legions were stretched to breaking point to deal with difficult situations on several fronts. Despite heroic feats of arms, the army could not carry out the impossible.

Money troubles grew worse and only Britain and North Africa, far removed from serious fighting, seem to have stayed prosperous. At this unhappy point Diocletian appeared and stopped the downhill slide firmly and efficiently for twenty years. He was a superb organiser who separated the work of the civil service from that of the army. Every worker was compelled in that time of crisis to stay in his job on pain of death. Whatever his conditions he had to put up with them. Diocletian accepted the fact that the east and west were more natural apart. So he ruled the east and chose a colleague to rule the west. Thereafter the separate halves of the Roman world went their own way. Such a man was bound to persecute the obstinate Christians but their day of release was near, under Constantine who was to become their patron and their ally.

The frontiers were now manned by reduced garrisons who could call on no reserves if their line gave way. In A.D. 406 the Rhine froze solid and a mighty host of barbarians flowed over into Gaul. The long-threatened collapse of the west occurred when Alaric the Goth sacked Rome in

The emperor Hadrian (A.D. 117–138) visited all the Roman provinces, including Britain, where he built a wall running from the Solway Firth to the river Tyne to mark the northern boundary of his empire.

A.D. 410. The eastern empire, however, Greek rather than Roman and more and more Christian in character, lingered on for a thousand years until the fall of Constantinople.

Roman Engineers
In the arts generally the Romans were content to follow others. First the Etruscans and then the Greeks gave them their models and they tended to copy them too slavishly. The Romans were not very imaginative and they showed little interest in exploring lands beyond their own frontiers. Their interests were practical and they were the finest civil engineers the world has seen until modern times.

The Romans liked space when they sited public buildings, unlike the Greeks who were inclined to crowd them together. Thus in nearly every Mediterranean town of any size there is a central square around which the principal buildings are arranged in Roman fashion.

The Romans developed two important new ideas, the arch and the vaulted ceiling. If the arch was often erected for military glory, it also supported bridges which are still used in Italy today. The use of bricks and cement made it possible for huge spans to be roofed over without the support of pillars. The dome of the Pantheon is immense, with a nine-metre (thirty-foot) wide opening for light and air in the middle as well. Baths usually had not only the bath area but also all the many adjoining rooms under one ceiling.

The Roman practical ideas worked. The roads ran straight as arrows over hill and dale and were usable in all weathers. The aqueduct as a means of transporting water seems rather clumsy but it was effective and one still supplies Rome with some of its water.

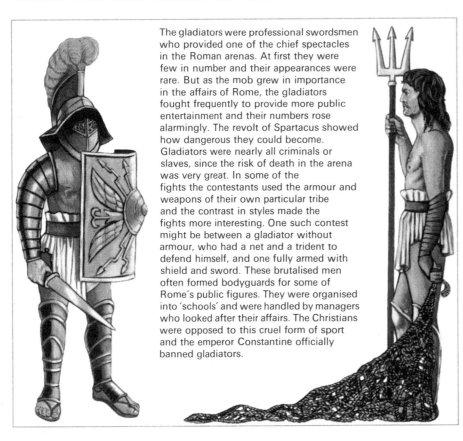

The gladiators were professional swordsmen who provided one of the chief spectacles in the Roman arenas. At first they were few in number and their appearances were rare. But as the mob grew in importance in the affairs of Rome, the gladiators fought frequently to provide more public entertainment and their numbers rose alarmingly. The revolt of Spartacus showed how dangerous they could become. Gladiators were nearly all criminals or slaves, since the risk of death in the arena was very great. In some of the fights the contestants used the armour and weapons of their own particular tribe and the contrast in styles made the fights more interesting. One such contest might be between a gladiator without armour, who had a net and a trident to defend himself, and one fully armed with shield and sword. These brutalised men often formed bodyguards for some of Rome's public figures. They were organised into 'schools' and were handled by managers who looked after their affairs. The Christians were opposed to this cruel form of sport and the emperor Constantine officially banned gladiators.

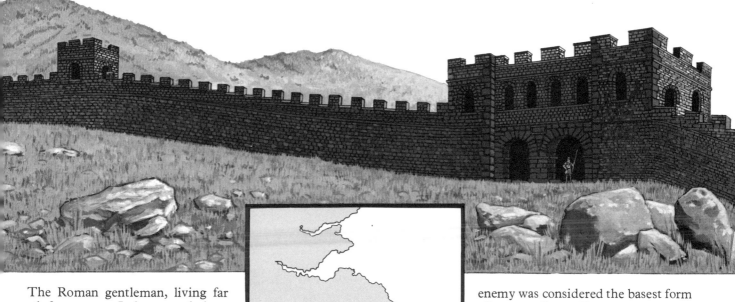

The Roman gentleman, living far north from sunny Italy, not only kept himself warm with imported wine but also had central heating. Air-bricks inside the walls and under the mosaic floors led back to a furnace which supplied the heat. The system was known as a hypocaust.

Roman buildings were built to last and are found, many in a fine state of preservation, throughout the old Roman lands. Rome naturally has the finest display of the emperors' love of building but Hadrian's wall, which marked the Roman frontier in Britain, shows how thorough was all their work.

Literature and Law
During the Augustan age three fine writers, Virgil, Horace and Livy, raised Latin to new peaks and produced a literature worthy of the empire. Today Latin has become the parent language of French, Italian, Portuguese and Spanish in the west. In the east also, one Latin language remains in Rumania due to Trajan's conquests beyond the Danube. All the people who speak these languages are aware of a common culture and a sense of belonging to each other.

The Romans had tremendous respect for law and through all their lands they introduced the rule of law once they had control. This law became the framework for the legal system in western Europe. The law courts themselves were held in a hall-like building called a basilica, which later became the model for the earliest Christian churches.

Roman discipline and devotion to duty created Rome from very slender resources and kept her strong through terrible trials. To surrender to the enemy was considered the basest form of cowardice. Every man was expected, as a matter of course, to fight to the death. When Pompeii was overwhelmed with molten lava from Mount Vesuvius, the sentry did not flinch from his post of duty. Today his skeleton is seen 'at attention', still on guard. No Roman would expect to find him otherwise.

Slave Labour
One great contrast to modern life was the complete lack of interest which the Romans had in any form of labour-saving. The use of slaves had taught them to employ muscle power for all forms of work. Ships of war were driven by banks of rowers under the whip of the overseer. Corn was ground by women hour after hour in little hand-mills. Where no carriages had springs, the wealthy found it more comfortable to be carried in a litter on the brawny shoulders of bearers. No thought was

The design of the letters which form the Latin alphabet has always been a highly skilful craft. In this respect the Romans were unexpectedly artistic. The lettering on their monuments is superb and, in particular, the lettering on the base of the Trajan Column in Rome has been the chief model for craftsmen throughout history. Experiment in the craft of lettering soon shows that each letter requires special treatment.

Both the size of the letters themselves and the spaces between them need to be carefully balanced to obtain the correct proportions. Gradually the simplicity and fineness of line were lost by the Romans and in the last century of the Empire there was an outburst of ornament and flourishes. In modern times there has been a new interest in lettering and the Trajan form has regained its place as a model for artists.

65

ever given to lightening the toil of the workers by their selfish masters.

Public amusements showed the bloodthirsty side of the Roman people but no political leader could stay in power without providing them. The shows put on to entertain the city mobs were disgusting and cruel. Gladiators hacked each other to death to amuse a crowd. The heroic Christians were thrown to wild beasts for their further delight.

The harsh and cruel side of Roman life cannot be excused. It passed away eventually, cleansed and changed by Christian teaching and the best of Christian behaviour. But the ordered framework of Roman organisation did not disappear despite the collapse of the empire. The Church replaced the missing organisation with one equally efficient. It offered scope for all men of talent and grew into a spiritual empire. The Gothic rulers were obliged to turn to the Church for help in running their kingdom. The conduct of affairs was bound to fall into the hands of those who could read and write and keep records. Thus in many ways the Church took over the work of the empire.

All these items of Roman household use have been recovered by archaeologists. Seen above are a corn measure, a balance, a strainer, a baking tin, a comb and a knife.

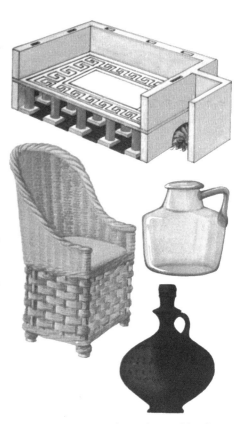

The hypocaust was a form of central heating by which a fire lit in a basement sent hot air beneath floors. Also seen are a wicker chair, a glass bottle and a wine flagon.

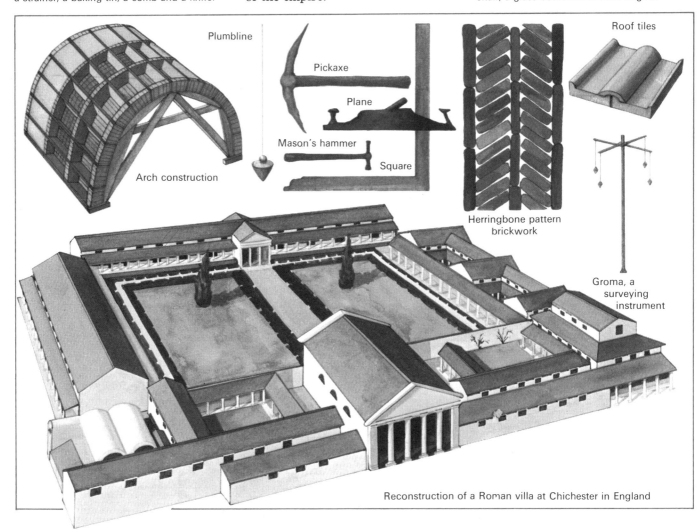

Plumbline

Pickaxe

Plane

Mason's hammer

Square

Arch construction

Herringbone pattern brickwork

Roof tiles

Groma, a surveying instrument

Reconstruction of a Roman villa at Chichester in England

The Christian World

Fear of death and concern about the future life have made religion important to all sorts and conditions of men throughout history. Of the higher religions, Christianity is the faith which has won the loyalty of the western world. Even if today many people do not believe, western civilisation assumes that everyone knows the moral teaching of Christ. Laws and customs are softened by mercy and ideas of justice are much concerned with forgiveness and people's welfare.

The Birth of Jesus

Jesus was born in Judaea in the reign of Caesar Augustus and brought up in the Jewish manner of his day. Thus, Christianity was born in Judaism and continued many of its ideas, building them into its own teaching. Jesus proclaimed himself to be the expected Messiah and also the son of God. The Jews could not understand how God could have a son in this way and they expected their Messiah to be a political leader when he appeared. The main part of the Jewish nation paid no attention to Jesus but his impact was so great that the leading Jews made the Romans destroy him. His crucifixion is the best known fact

in history to the western world. The death of Jesus on the cross was the beginning, not the end, of the Christian faith.

His disciples declared that they had seen the risen Christ whom death could not hold, and further that this death was a sacrifice which made men one with God again. They went everywhere preaching the great salvation and often meeting a martyr's death because of their faith.

At first the new members were all Jews but Christianity was designed to appeal to all mankind and it shook off the narrowness of Judaism. Alexander had ensured that a common language was understood throughout the Near East. The Old Testament had already

appeared in Greek and soon the New Testament followed. The missionary fervour and organising genius of St Paul gradually established a network of simple Christian communities which stretched from Jerusalem to Rome.

The Christian message brought hope to the unhappy slaves of the empire, promising them a glorious future beyond the present suffering of their bodies. In Christ all men were of equal importance once they had been baptised. Faith created Roman courage in these early humble Christians and they willingly defied the authorities rather than deny Christ. Believing that death could not prevail against them, the Christians triumphed over their persecutors until Christianity became the official religion of the empire.

In 1947 some old manuscripts were found hidden in caves in the desert of Judaea and were given the group name of the Dead Sea Scrolls. The manuscripts belonged to Jewish religious sects who had fled to the wilderness, bringing their libraries

with them. Some had survived unsuccessful revolts against the Romans. Others held religious views opposed to the traditional viewpoint. The documents are mostly copies of the Old Testament and other books. The best known sect were the Essenes.

The Middle Ages

The Middle Ages are well-named for they separate the world of the ancient empires from the modern way of life. In Europe for a thousand years from the fall of Rome to the voyages of Columbus, a special type of society flourished unlike anything which had been seen before. It was based on the power of Christianity to appeal to all men and women, regardless of race, language or economic advantage. A new type of conquest, called conversion, made men and women eager to join together to work for a cause superior to the narrow ambitions of one people or nationality.

Again and again ferocious tribes with only destruction in their minds were tamed and won over by the missionaries of the Christian Church. Once converted, they gave up their pagan ways and eagerly built magnificent churches and cathedrals to the glory of God. This Christian empire, however, was maintained by the sword and the pagan enemies of Christ were driven out. But the idea had been born of nations living together in harmony by common agreement.

The Church

During the Middle Ages the Christian Church rose to a pinnacle of wealth and power which raised the lofty cathedrals of the Age of Faith in the eleventh and twelfth centuries. From the most dangerous situations the Church triumphed over all its outward enemies but its power was finally shattered by division within its own ranks.

The old east and west divisions of the Roman Empire lived on in the Greek Orthodox and Catholic churches which divided Europe into two independent faiths. Christendom, the realm of Christ ruled by the Church, was the creation of the western Catholic Church. The Greek Orthodox Church accepted state control and did not compete with the eastern emperors. In the Catholic west, wealth brought serious abuse, but reformers, such as the monks of Cluny, rose up repeatedly to recall the Church to its duty. But as the growth of trade destroyed the feudal framework of society, the growing economic power of northern Europe made it independent. Reformers in the north began to proclaim that the true reformation of the Church was only possible by a fresh start. Consequently, the western Church became divided into Protestant and Catholic, whose bitter rivalry led to Christian civil war.

Pastoral Care

In its true work of pastoral care for the faithful, the success of the Church was far greater. The dark and savage pagan rites of the barbarian peoples were forgotten once they became Christians. Devoted men and women in religious houses cared for the sick, taught the principles of love and obedience, and showed with their own hands the true dignity of work. The world had acquired a conscience it was never again to lose completely. The fortunate were taught that they had a duty to the less fortunate and civilised nations today accept a measure of responsibility for the underprivileged.

Although the Church harnessed education to its own needs very severely, during the Dark Ages of pagan threat learning was kept alive solely by the servants of the Church. Perfection was part of the outlook of the Middle Ages. The books and buildings then produced were as perfect as artistic pride could make

Figure of a bishop from a set of bone chessmen made about the thirteenth century and found on the Isle of Lewis.

them. To men with their eyes on eternity, time did not matter. What one generation left unfinished the next generation continued with loving care.

The lot of the ordinary people in the Middle Ages was very much a mixture of good and bad. During the dangerous time of the barbarian raids, safety was the supreme need. A lord offered his skill in war and the use of his stronghold in return for loyalty and service from the people in his district. At first the offer was gladly accepted. But when the danger passed the men found that they had lost their freedom. The lord in his castle now ruled them and they had become peasants tied to the land on which they lived.

Increase in Trade

As trade increased and towns sprang up, the old world of Feudalism, based entirely on land ownership, began to weaken. Towns gave ordinary people strength by reason of their numbers, and the long fight for freedom had begun. Plague was a constant visitor to the narrow streets of medieval towns. But the Black Death, which ravaged Europe, was so severe that it caused a major shortage of labour. In England, the opportunity was seized to bring about the end of serfdom, centuries before other nations. The merchants grew up into a middle class, linking the people with the nobility. There was now a new career in trade for the bright young man and the Church was not the only road to promotion. At this point, the great ocean voyages altered the shape of the known world and a new age had begun.

This picture from a sixteenth-century Flemish Book of Hours is a fine example of medieval illustration

The Barbarian Invasions

'Barbarians' was the group name given to the German tribes and their allies who threatened the northern frontier of the Roman Empire in the west. The German tribes came from the Scandinavian area in two main waves. The Saxons and Franks moved towards the North Sea coast and the Rhine and eventually became the founders of England and France, while the Goths moved south to the Danube. The Goths were among the latest to arrive but they played a principal part in the defeat of the western empire. They were very successful at first but then their fortunes changed dramatically and they swiftly disappeared from history as a separate people.

The German tribes, who had been infiltrating into the Roman Empire for many years, had no general plan for attacking it. But they themselves

came under pressure from waves of fierce tribes coming out of central Asia. Thus they were driven against the Roman frontiers by the pressure of those behind them.

Goths and Huns

Many of the barbarian tribes, particularly the Goths, greatly admired the empire and they soon became valuable converts to Christianity. For years they had been recruited into the frontier legions and trained in the arts of war by the short-sighted Roman rulers.

Then the Germans felt the weight of a fresh attack from a new and terrible enemy. The Huns, a Mongolian people, rode with fire and sword into Europe, driving all ruthlessly before them. In return for acting as a buffer to protect the empire, the Goths were permitted to cross the Danube and settle inside the frontier fortifications. When quarrels led to fighting, the Goths soon showed that their cavalry were superior to the Roman forces. From that time the importance of infantry in warfare began to decline rapidly.

Since the Goths respected everything Roman, they were willing to adapt themselves to the Roman way of life. They had split by this time

into two main bodies, the Visigoths in the west and the Ostrogoths in the east. The Ostrogoths in the Balkans were the first barbarians to be converted to Christianity and the Bible was very soon translated into Gothic.

The Visigoths elected Alaric as their king and he led his forces into Italy and, somewhat reluctantly, sacked Rome in A.D. 410. He was followed by Odoacer who in 476 deposed the last feeble emperor and reigned as the official representative of the eastern empire.

The Ostrogoths now rose to power under the great king Theodoric, who killed Odoacer and drove the Visigoths westwards out of Italy. He ruled in Roman fashion from the more convenient city of Ravenna. His remarkable tomb is still there and some of the superb mosaics, which make Ravenna a treasure-house of early Christian art; date from his time. The Goths were the first

Summary of key dates

c. 400 Roman legions withdraw from Britain
410 Alaric the Goth sacks Rome
432 St Patrick's mission to Ireland
447 Attila rules kingdom of the Huns
460 Britain overrun by Angles, Saxons and Jutes
476 Romulus Augustulus, last western emperor, deposed by Odoacer
481 Clovis I becomes king of the Franks
597 St Augustine lands in Britain

Frankish warriors of the time of Clovis in the sixth century A.D.

barbarians to absorb a high degree of Roman civilisation from those who had converted them. Suddenly a curious accident destroyed them as a people.

Arianism

Christians in the early centuries were divided in their ideas about the nature of Christ. All the Goths had the misfortune to be converted by followers of Arius, the founder of Arianism, a Christian religion which the main Church condemned as a heresy. This simple fact separated the Goths from the other barbarian converts and kept them apart. The dispute was fierce and often backed by force of arms. The Goths totally lost the favour of the Church, who turned to the Franks. The Franks had learned their Christianity in the traditional way and became the champions of Christendom. In the next few years, the Goths suffered many defeats and were finally thrust out of the Catholic community and lost to history.

Meanwhile other German tribes had been crossing the Rhine in great numbers. The destructive Vandals laid waste Gaul and overflowed into Spain. Later they were themselves driven over into north Africa. There they captured Carthage and used the

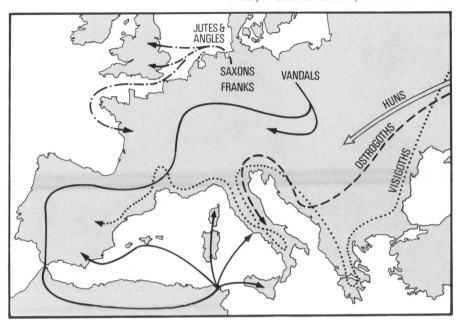

Principal routes followed by the barbarian tribes.

harbour as a base for piratical attacks which terrorised the whole Mediterranean. Not only were the Roman lines of communication cut but the food supply was endangered.

The Franks had now moved into northern Gaul while the Visigoths, driven out of Italy, ruled southern

Gaul and most of Spain. For a time disaster threatened when the merciless Atilla led his cruel horsemen to ravage the west. For a time Atilla was the supreme warlord from the Rhine to the Urals. But he had no talent for besieging fortified cities and the barbarian defenders of the Church

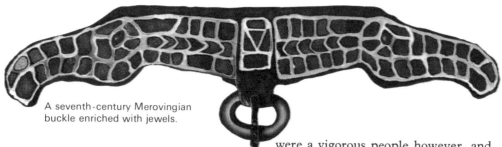

A seventh-century Merovingian buckle enriched with jewels.

rode out the storm. Finally he was defeated in Germany and he withdrew into Asia again, where his death prevented any further campaigns to the west.

Roman Britain

The Roman province of Britain did not escape the attacks of the barbarians. For many years Saxons had raided the eastern coast of England but had been kept at bay by a Roman fleet. As Rome recalled her legions and her ships to deal with troubles at home, the Romano-British were left

Sixth-century bronze Germanic medallion showing a horseman.

to defend themselves. From raiding, the Saxons passed to a definite invasion of Britain, with their allies the Jutes and the Angles. From their arrival in the middle of the fifth century to the coming of Augustine in A.D. 597, there is a virtual blank of one hundred and fifty years in the history of Britain.

In that period England was transformed. Almost every trace of Roman civilisation disappeared together with the Latin language. The advanced society of civilised and Christian life had been removed. Instead there were pagan Saxons, Jutes and Angles who despised cities and lived by farming. Their speech and their gods came from Germany and had no relationship with what had gone before. They

were a vigorous people however, and had a great respect for liberty and justice between free men.

At that time England was heavily wooded and had extensive marshes caused by undrained rivers. Natural independence and the difficulties of travel kept the tribes apart, and there was endless fighting before any unity even began to show itself. To this completely changed land came St Augustine and his band of monks to begin their work with the conversion of the Jutish kingdom of Kent.

The missionary expedition which was sent to convert the Saxons in England was typical of the rising power of the Church. Two remarkable men laid the foundations of this great advance: St Benedict and Gregory the Great. St Benedict, who died in the year that Gregory the Great was born (540). established the first order of monks in western Europe. Gregory was the first of those great statesmen of the Church who combined spiritual wisdom and high political ability.

The Celtic Church

Christianity had existed in England from a much earlier date. The earliest Christian martyr, St Alban, is said to have been beheaded about 303. But the fierce Saxons drove the previous inhabitants of England to the north and to the west. From their places of refuge they continued to practise their faith as the Celtic Church. But Augustine's work brought the newly converted Saxons gradually into the framework of the Roman Church. Thereby they became once again linked to Europe and the mainstream of civilisation.

In Gaul, Clovis the Frank rose to power. He was the founder of the Merovingian line of kings and thereby the founder of the French monarchy. Clovis was both a fierce warrior and also a staunch Catholic. Victorious over all his foes, he drove the heretic Goths out of France into Spain. Clovis abandoned Soissons and chose Paris for his capital and thus the framework of the future France was laid during his reign (481–511).

Clovis, who ruled from the Rhine to the Pyrenees, was only too anxious to fight for his Church and to extend its power. In that rough age, the Church was willing to accept the help of the fighting men in order to survive. So that not only was the French Catholic monarchy established from that day until 1830, but also the crusading spirit was born that was to unite priest and warrior against the heathen. From the time of Clovis the warriors of Christendom were to fight under the banners of the Cross.

Although there were severe trials ahead for both countries, England and France by their submission to the Church began to show remarkably rapid progress in civilisation. The foundations were then laid that were to bring the two countries to nationhood long before the rest of western Europe.

The Byzantine Empire

The reforms of Diocletian and Constantine were the deciding factors in separating the east and west in the Roman Empire. Constantine was now in supreme command in the east and his subjects were settling into those permanent classes of society which were to last for centuries. The peasant was tied to the land and the local dignitaries became the servants of the emperor.

Constantine

Constantine was elected to the throne by the troops. He certainly justified their choice for he never afterwards lost a battle. He was a man of the greatest vigour and his policy for the empire was unity before everything else. Although he himself never ceased to be a sun-worshipper and was baptised only at the last moment, Constantine chose to adopt Christianity as the official religion of the Roman Empire. Thereby he formed the union of Church and State which is a key to much of later history. Christendom was divided, as we have seen from the history of the Goths, by the heresy taught by Arius. At the Council of Nicaea in 325, Constantine summoned the factions to make up their differences and the great rift was healed. The still small but well organised Christian Church could now go forward with its civilising work.

With a soldier's eye for the best defensive position, Constantine chose the old city of Byzantium to be his new capital. The empire was looted for works of art and both public and private building went ahead feverishly. By 330, in six years, the new city rose as the symbol of Rome to the east. But although the city was to be a bulwark of Christianity against paganism, Greek was to triumph over Latin in this new world. The name Byzantine Empire is usually applied to the eastern empire after this time.

Justinian and Theodora

When the barbarian inroads destroyed the west, the Ostrogoths also troubled the east until the time of Justinian (527–625). This vigorous emperor married Theodora, a young actress of the poorest background. But she proved to be one of the great women of history and the equal of her husband. Justinian made peace with Persia and sent his great general Belisarius against the empire's enemies. The Vandals were destroyed in North Africa and, after a long struggle which reduced the country to ruin, the Goths were finally driven out of Italy and back into Germany.

Despite his conquests, Justinian is better remembered for three great gifts to the future. Among his many buildings, the superb church of St Sophia was constructed in Constantinople and most of the priceless mosaics in Ravenna. But it was in the

The mosque of St Sophia in Constantinople (now Istanbul) was originally a Christian Church built by the Roman emperor Justinian in the sixth century A.D. It became a mosque in 1453 and, beyond the addition of a number of minarets, was little altered and remains a perfect example of Byzantine architecture.

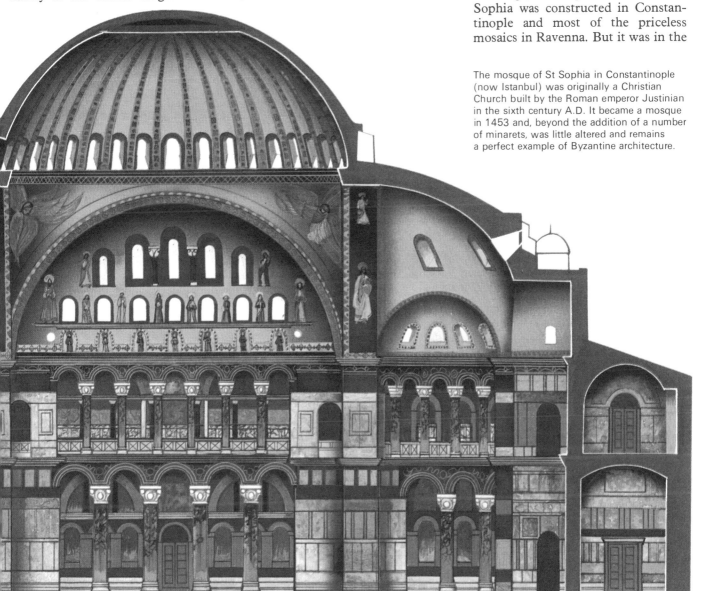

field of law that Justinian achieved his crowning success. He collected all the Roman laws together and made them into a system which he recorded for future study and imitation.

Justinian and Theodora both busied themselves in the religious disputes raging at the time which dangerously divided their subjects. Temporarily they achieved an outward appearance of unity but the root causes of division remained.

East and West

The work of Mohammed soon brought new waves of pagans against the Byzantine Empire. The Saracens lopped off the provinces of Egypt, Syria and Persia like ripe plums and moved in to attack Constantinople itself. Leo the Isaurian came to the throne at this point (711) and he used the strength of his capital, and the help of the Bulgars, to make Europe safe from the swords of Islam.

Once again religious matters proved dangerous. Leo listened to the complaints of those who condemned the number of idols in his dominions and

This mosaic portrait of Theodora, wife of the Roman Emperor Justinian, can be seen in the church of Saint Vitale at Ravenna in Italy.

Marble head of Constantine the Great, part of an enormous statue from the fourth-century Basilica Nova in Rome.

forbade the making of images. The western Church excommunicated the eastern Church and persuaded the Franks to become their champions against them. Thus the split between the Roman and Greek churches began to follow the political division of the old empire.

The Macedonian emperors (867–1016) took over from the Isaurians and produced several emperors who

injected new life into their dominions. South Italy and most of the Near East were regained and Crete rescued from the pirates. The emperors' skill in diplomacy enabled them to form friendships with the most unlikely allies.

The Byzantine Empire began to regain its rightful eminence. But the strong rulers were succeeded by feeble ones and two new foes attacked their lands. The Normans took Sicily and the reasonable Saracens were replaced by the ferocious and fanatical Seljuk Turks. The Seljuk leaders seized power from the weak, surviving rulers of Baghdad and Egypt and moved against the Byzantine Empire. Asia Minor was occupied after a great victory.

At this time of crisis, Alexius Comnenus came to the throne. This able young emperor first brought order to his own dominions and then faced the Turkish problem. Already the famous cities of Antioch and Jerusalem were in pagan hands. Alexius then decided to appeal to the West to save Christianity and wrote to Pope Urban II. The result was the First Crusade. Alexius simply wanted military help to recover his lost lands, but the Pope's interest was to recover the Holy Places of Jerusalem from pagan hands.

The Fall of Constantinople

The new allies had little in common. The Latins and Greeks had no respect for each other. The Byzantines, who had inherited both Greek and Roman civilisations, felt the strength of Rome was based on barbarians. Recently they had also converted the Russians and the Bulgars to Christianity as well as many lesser peoples. The Pope however could count on the warlike Normans who wanted to bring the East under the control of the West by force. Because of this basic disharmony, the Fourth Crusade turned aside to destroy Constantinople and to set up Latin rule there for fifty years. Thus the chance to destroy the Turks was lost and the break between eastern and western churches was widened beyond all hope of repair. Fresh waves of Turks entered Europe. They took Greece and advanced to the Danube, threatening Hungary. Constantinople was surrounded and cut off in every direction. At last, in 1453, the great city fell, to remain permanently in Turkish hands.

Mohammed and Islam

All the world's great faiths have come from Asia and the last to appear was Islam, in the deserts of Arabia. The name carries the idea of total submission to God. The stark power of Islam was excellently fitted to the harsh realities of the desert. The core of the Islamic faith has a majestic simplicity: Allah is the one true God and Mohammed is his prophet.

Before he gave himself entirely to the religious life, Mohammed had travelled widely along the busy caravan routes of the desert. There he met Jews and Christians and compared their ideas with his own. Finally Mohammed retired from the world of trade to devote himself entirely to religion. For long he meditated apart upon the true God.

Mohammed had genuine mystic power but also sound common sense. After a long preparation, he was ready to preach his ideas.

The Great Prophet
The vast sands of the desert under the unbroken glare of the sun made the distance between the one all-powerful God and man, his weak and helpless creature, easy to accept. Mohammed believed he was the last and greatest of the prophets. His task was to set the seal on the work of the prophets of the past. For Mohammed accepted Abraham, Moses and Jesus as true men of God.

Mohammed had no time for idols or for any representation by man of God's living creation. This limitation was to have a profound influence on Islamic art. Artists made their handwriting into an art form and worked out endless geometric designs.

Mohammed was a great moral teacher who attempted to raise the existing standards rather than to proclaim an impossible level of goodness which no one could reach. The Christian idea of sin is not found in Islam. The true believers are to enjoy a life of bliss in paradise whereas the wicked are to undergo torments.

The true believer prays five times a day, facing towards Mecca. The prayer is a short act of adoration and not a series of requests to God. If possible, each Moslem should make the pilgrimage to Mecca once in his lifetime. Intoxicating drink is strictly forbidden. The great feast of Ramadan lasts a month and fasting must be maintained between sunrise and sunset.

Today the Arabic-speaking world is remarkably faithful to Islam. If trouble threatens in one area, reactions are immediately felt throughout the whole world of Islam.

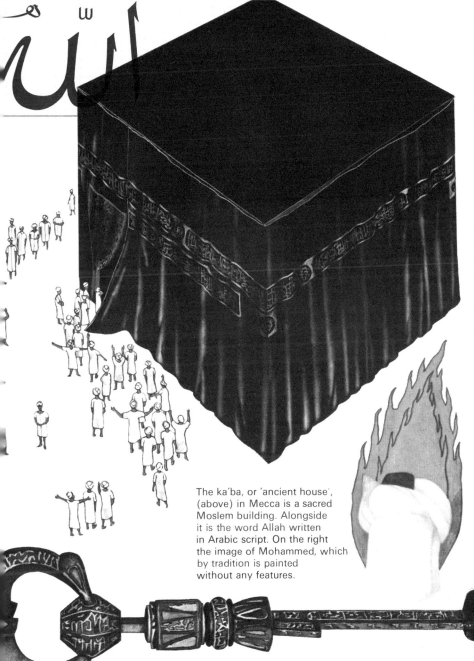

The ka'ba, or 'ancient house', (above) in Mecca is a sacred Moslem building. Alongside it is the word Allah written in Arabic script. On the right the image of Mohammed, which by tradition is painted without any features.

The key to the ka'ba

Summary of key dates

570	Birth of Mohammed
622	Mohammed's flight from Mecca to Medina
643–98	Moslem conquests in North Africa
711	Moslem invasion of Spain
720	Moslems cross Pyrenees into France
732	Franks under Charles Martel defeat Moslems at Tours
786	Haroun-al-Raschid caliph of Baghdad
827–40	Moslems invade Sicily and Italy
1492	Granada, last Moslem stronghold in Europe, taken by Spain

Mohammed

Mohammed was born in Mecca. He became an orphan when still very young and began his working life as a shepherd. Moving to the city, he received some training in business. At twenty-five, he married Khadija, a wealthy widow, fifteen years older than himself. The management of Khadija's affairs took Mohammed along the caravan routes and made him aware of the religious ideas of other men. He withdrew into the desert to meditate and received such a vision of divine light in the cave at the foot of Mount Hera that he felt compelled to preach. He aroused such murderous opposition that he fled secretly to Medina in 622. Fighting broke out over the new faith and Mecca was captured. In later life Mohammed became a lawgiver and politician. When he died in 632, he left no successor to carry on his work.

The Arab Conquests

Europe had no sooner begun to settle down after the vast changes caused by the barbarian invasions than a new and unexpected challenge threatened her. Arabia had never had importance or danger for the rulers of Europe until Mohammed appeared. For the first time Islam imposed a unity of purpose on the Arab tribes. Instead of quarrelling among themselves, they now turned their swords against the unbelievers. In the deserts were endless supplies of superb fighting men, mounted on swift horses. The speed of their advance completely disorganised the surrounding lands, and within a hundred years Islam had conquered from the Atlantic to the frontiers of India. This victory, as far as parts of Africa and Asia were concerned, has proved permanent. Christian Europe, however, sustained by its own faith, rode out the storm and survived.

Mohammed's Successors

Mohammed left no successor and there was a period of great confusion after his death. Temporarily the breathtaking victories of Omar the great caliph swept disputes aside. In ten years (634–643) he overran Egypt, Syria and Persia and assumed control of the whole Middle East. There was then a pause of fifty years. The new conquests had to be absorbed and trouble had broken out at home. Upon Omar's death a dispute arose over the succession. A party was formed which supported Ali, the son-in-law of Mohammed. Ali was eventually murdered and there was civil war until the Ummayad rulers of Damascus became supreme masters of the Arab world in 692. But the split between the two rival sects, called Shiites and Sunnites, has divided the Arab world ever since.

This temporary respite from attack proved of little help to the Byzantine Empire. The Arab armies resumed their lightning attacks once unity had been re-imposed. By 711 they had seized the whole coastline of North Africa and crossed over into Spain. Other armies invaded Asia Minor and the Greek islands, for the Arabs had now extended their activities to the waters of the Mediterranean. Constantinople itself was threatened by the Arab advance. Europe faced a giant pincer movement from the west in Spain and the east in Asia Minor.

Fortunately in both areas there was a saviour at hand. In France the Arabs were defeated and thrown back by Charles Martel after an epic battle near Poitiers. In the east, the vigorous Leo the Isaurian held out successfully against all the Arab attacks. Thus Europe became the fortress of Christendom and the pattern of the Middle Ages had been created.

The Caliphate

Meanwhile the caliphate had moved out of Arabia. For a short time it was at Damascus, where that ancient city of Greek culture considerably civilised the Arabs. A further dispute removed the caliphate to Baghdad where the magnificence and intellectual wealth of Persia also had its influence on Islam. One member of the ruling house of Damascus escaped to Spain where he became the founder of the Emirate of Cordova. There were now three great Arab centres—in Spain, Egypt and Persia —which remained separate until the Turks welded them together again.

Although the first caliphs were men of enormous power with irresistible armies, they were simple men living simple lives. No one could have foreseen that the world of Islam, once it absorbed the culture of the captured lands, was to lead the Middle Ages in science and philosophy. It also produced a fascinating world of art and architecture which was very decorative and highly individual.

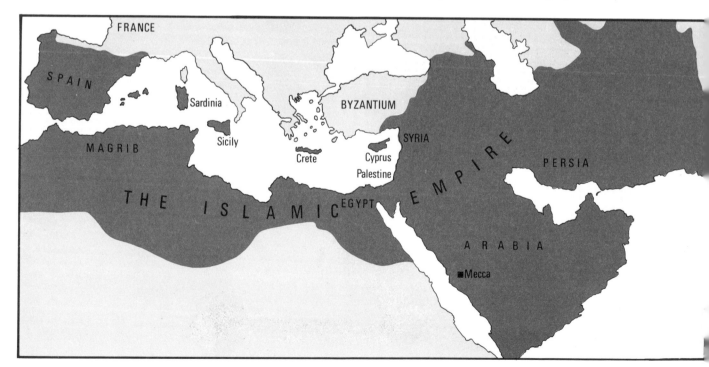

The people of the desert were united in their submission to the will of Allah. They converted their enemies by the power of the sword.

Mohammed had forbidden his followers to copy any living creatures in their artistic work because of his detestation of idolatry. Consequently the Arabs concentrated on line. Beautiful and elaborate designs were worked into their public buildings. The decorative nature of their handwriting was translated into stone and marble.

Arabic Learning

When the Abbasid family transferred the caliphate to Baghdad, the learning which the West had lost in the barbarian destructions became available to the Arabs in Persia. Poetry, practical science and medicine were equally important there. Haroun al-Raschid, who was written about in the *Thousand and One Nights*, is a symbol of that age.

Arabic had now become the language of the educated throughout the lands believing in Islam. Greek philosophy and science became translated into Arabic and was carried into Spain. The Jews were allies in this intellectual work. The wonderful navigation of the Portuguese and Spanish at a later date benefited from this source of knowledge. Maimonides, the greatest Jewish philosopher of the time, lived in Spain and wrote in Arabic.

In Spain the Arabs showed the superiority of their civilisation. As a desert people they knew the value of water. To them the coastal plains of Spain were a green paradise. They irrigated the dry land and turned it into a garden. In Granada they harnessed the melting snows of the Sierra Nevada to supply the endless fountains and pools of the Alhambra.

In Cordova, the capital of Moorish Spain, there was a university before such foundations were known in Christian Europe. Science and mathematics made spectacular progress because religion and science were studied apart from each other. Algebra is an Arabic word. An improved set of numbers derived from the East was brought from Egypt. Working under test conditions, the doctors discovered that contagious diseases required isolation if they were to be controlled. This knowledge was to defeat plague.

The fierce Berbers ended this refined civilisation soon after the year 1000. At the same time, from Persia the followers of Islam were conquering India which they ruled for five hundred years. This conquest resulted in the great Mogul Empire whose greatest artistic monument is the Taj Mahal in Agra.

The Alhambra Palace in Granada, Spain.

The Story of El Cid
Stories and legends have grown up around the name of El Cid as they have around the name of King Arthur. The historical character was Rodrigo Diaz de Bivar. His first name is often shortened to Ruy and he lived in the eleventh century. He was born near Burgos and died in Valencia in 1099. This warrior became Spain's great national hero and was known as El Cid Campeador, the Lord Champion. At first he fought for one of the local Spanish kings against his rival. Then he was exiled unjustly and he became a soldier of fortune, sometimes fighting for his own race and sometimes for the Moors. Feared by all, he became famous for his successes against the pagan Moors.

One of a series of stained glass windows in Notre Dame, Paris, which tells the story of the eleventh-century poem *The Song of Roland*.

who had invaded Italy in 568, and Charlemagne responded vigorously. He ended the Lombard kingdom and brought it under his own control. Rome fascinated him and he wanted its artistic and cultural life for the Frankish lands. The needs of the Pope and the enthusiasm of the great king were both happily satisfied when the Pope crowned Charlemagne as Emperor of the Romans on Christmas Day, 800. The idea of a political and spiritual Christendom under one government had been given practical shape.

The conquests of Charlemagne, who is claimed equally by the French and the Germans as a national hero, made the dream a temporary reality. After hard-fought campaigns, he battered the Saxons into submission and compelled them to accept Christianity. All central Europe was made safe for Christianity as far as the Elbe and the Middle Danube. Italy was incorporated into Charlemagne's lands and the Pope was under his control.

The Holy Roman Empire

The Holy Roman Empire was founded on the achievements of Charlemagne and continued, at least as a title, for a thousand years until the days of Napoleon. The idea of a united Europe, governed as one community and completely devoted to the Christian faith, still lives on as an ideal. The European Common Market owes something to this traditional dream.

The Merovingian kings, the successors of Clovis, had long been feeble. Their key men, the Mayors of the Palace, showed surprising loyalty to their useless masters but eventually started the Carolingian line of kings of whom Charlemagne was the greatest representative. He came to the throne in 768 with his brother Carloman. This subdivision of their kingdoms between all surviving sons was a Frankish custom which regularly caused civil war. Fortunately Carloman died quickly and Charlemagne was left the sole monarch for forty-three years.

Charlemagne the Great
Charlemagne was the perfect king and heroic leader. He was a big hearty man, brave and resourceful, who enjoyed life thoroughly. But he also had a high respect for the learning of the clergy and was always willing to listen to them.

The Pope appealed for help against the Lombards, a Germanic people

This richly decorated tenth-century book cover from the old province of Lorraine in France is ornamented with jewels.

The Song of Roland
Charlemagne's one major defeat was in northern Spain when part of his army, under Roland, was cut off by the Basques. But this reverse produced the greatest story of the Charlemagne legend, the eleventh-century *Song of Roland*. Although Charlemagne was a German, he ruled the old Gaul and it is French literature which created the principal stories about him.

The conquests of Charlemagne brought the Polish, Bohemian, Austrian and Hungarian lands into touch with civilisation. More ominously, his gift of old Lombard territory to the papacy created the Papal States which kept Italy divided until 1870. Charlemagne's domains now included most of the old western Roman Empire together with the German lands which the Romans had failed to conquer.

Charlemagne used his power to revive the intellectual life of his subjects. The Carolingian Renaissance had no Greek spirit of discovery or Italian passion for the arts. It was a solid work of sound education by good scholars. Alcuin of York was the greatest figure among many illustrious men. Monastic schools were founded and book production was increased. The School of the Palace had to follow the king on his constant journeys. Although the Holy Scriptures were the chief object of study, most of the Latin classics which have survived were also preserved by these scholars.

When Charlemagne died, his lands were divided among his three sons. The division grimly foreshadowed later history. One son took the German east, another the French west, and Lothair had a long strip of territory, running between his brothers' lands, from the coast of Holland down to Rome. The later rivalries of western Europe may be seen in this division of Charlemagne's empire.

Church and Emperor

From that time onwards the Holy Roman Empire became increasingly Germanic, dabbling in the affairs of Italy, sometimes as the ally and sometimes as the enemy of the Pope. France and England were busy resisting the Danes and Vikings who were raiding their coasts and river valleys. Meanwhile in the east the Magyars, a race of horse archers, had come in and occupied the Hungarian plain, thus dividing the north and south Slavs into separate groups. The king of the Saxons, Henry the Fowler, defeated the Magyars and later they became converted to Christianity. Conversion was the passport to

membership of the European family and Hungary became a bulwark of Christianity against the Turks.

In response to an appeal from the Pope, Otto I restored the position of Italy and the papacy in the tenth century. He was crowned Holy Roman Emperor by the grateful Pope but the title now carried little weight. Otto III, a little later, took it very seriously but the emperors who followed certainly did not do so. The German empire was too big to control properly and local landowners, petty princes and church authorities were setting up independently as feudal lords. The idea of nationhood had not yet been born.

The main challenge against the emperors' authority came, however, from the Church which they had so long favoured. The Church was now an important landowner. In the past there had been fighting bishops but now popes arose who had been strictly trained. The papacy was reformed and popes were now elected by the college of cardinals. Gregory VII made the rule that clergy must not marry, in order to make them wholly the servants of the Church. The new popes expected to rule Christendom as monarchs for Christ. The investiture struggle, as to who appoints bishops—emperor or pope— split Europe for centuries.

This image of Charlemagne is based on a fourteenth-century jewel-encrusted bust of the emperor from Aachen in Germany.

Charlemagne's talisman (above) was a jewel made of twin oval sapphires mounted back to back with a piece of wood, claimed to be from the cross of Jesus, set between them. It was buried with the emperor in 814 but was recovered from his tomb in the year 1000. Below is Charlemagne's cypher, used to sign documents.

The Holy Roman Empire extended over large areas of central Europe. It lasted from 800, the date of Charlemagne's crowning, until 1806.

The Church and Learning

Throughout the Dark Ages, when Christian Europe battled for survival, the Church continued its work of organisation and education whenever it could. Its members were almost the only people who could read or write and barbarian kings always had to turn to them for help. As soon as the exciting business of conquest was over, the work of administration demanded some scholarship.

The Church expected to last forever and it was the only channel by which a talented young man could advance from the lowest classes to a position of power and influence. Consequently, the Church was never short of brilliant servants. This natural process was encouraged by the strength of the monastic ideal.

The First Monasteries

Monks had been known in the East before the Christian age and the idea had been taken up in the eastern Roman Empire. But it was St Benedict who established the first monastery in the West. His life as a pious hermit attracted great attention and led him to found the monastery on Monte Cassino near Naples. His 'rule' was strict. His followers had to take the vows of obedience, chastity and poverty. His ideas had a very practical side, for manual work was added to study and prayer as a proper pursuit for the godly man. He taught that to work was to pray. The precise application of these strict principles was left to the local abbot so that they could be modified for special local needs. The rule which St Benedict taught remained the guiding pattern for later orders of monks.

The production of books by hand was a principal part of the labours of the monks. Time was no consideration for them. They were men who hoped for eternal life after death and were content to offer up their years in this world in patient service. The artistic quality of their best work is exquisite and almost unbelievable in its perfection. A monk would spend a lifetime writing and decorating a copy of the scriptures, which became thereafter a treasured possession in the library of a king or a bishop. The Book of Kells, the Lindisfarne Gospels, and the lovely Carolingian miniscule of the schools of Charlemagne testify to a widespread level of craftsmanship. Such work was an act of prayer.

The subject matter of the books was strictly controlled by the Church. The unfortunate disagreements between eastern and western churches caused the knowledge of Greek to

Eighth-century Irish stone cross.

This plan of a Benedictine monastery in St Gall in Switzerland, built at the beginning of the ninth century A.D., shows the extent of the buildings which were necessary to serve the physical needs of the monks, whose lives were centred around the core of the monastery, the church itself.

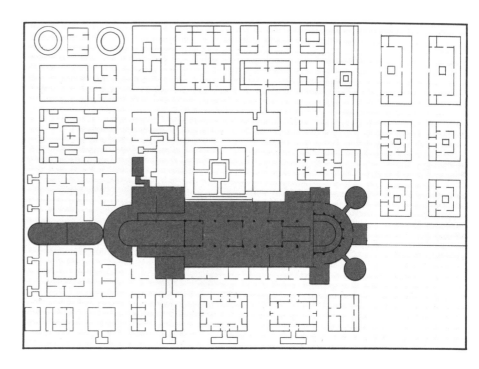

REGALIS VRBEMAII

Most modern types of lettering come from Roman capitals used on monumental inscriptions. Shown above are fifth-century capitals, square (top) and rustic.

palam

Roman uncial lettering was developed in the fourth century. It was a form more easily written by hand than the earlier capitals. Letters are round and flowing.

sic ergo

Half-uncials are letter forms which represent the vital change from capitals to small or lower case letters and were first used in the sixth century.

en angeli laudate &

Caroline or Carolingian miniscule developed on the continent of Europe. This medieval handwriting was part of the revival of learning in the ninth century.

disappear in the West, to be replaced by Latin in the church services and in the schools. The spirit of free enquiry and intellectual daring which is the breath of life in the Greek classics no longer found a place in the West. Law and order and respect for traditional practice carry on the Roman ideal rather than the Greek. By contrast with the learning of Islam, the learning of the Catholic West was no friend to science. But in a time of unrest and disorder a new spiritual empire based on the Roman pattern gave great strength to Christendom. The Latin classics were more fortunate and were often preserved.

The Power of the Church

Apart from the famous works of the theologians, such as St Augustine of Hippo's *City of God*, the whole world of everyday learning gave the Church enormous power with kings and rulers. The clerks of the Church kept the records on which every state of any size must rely for its continuing existence. The ability to collect taxes efficiently cannot be achieved without accurate clerks and the warrior never had much patience with paperwork.

The international character of the Church was of great advantage to the spread of learning. When one area was devastated, help could come from another more fortunate area. The monasteries of Northumbria had a spell of exceptional brilliance before the Danes destroyed them. The Venerable Bede, who had a vast store of learning, wrote the famous history of the English Church, and Alcuin of York went across the Channel to found the schools of Charlemagne. Boniface, who converted Germany, was an Englishman. The schools of Charlemagne continued the work. Later, France and Germany were able to send scholars to Alfred the Great to restore learning in ravaged Britain. The monastic movement was as international in character as it was widespread.

National Languages

In the Middle Ages, Latin became the international tongue of the educated. This common language helped the ready communication of ideas between all the learned men of Christendom but increasingly shut out the ignorant from understanding professional information. But gradually, as men began to think in terms of nationhood, the language of their homeland assumed greater importance. In response to this new feeling, some clerks began to write in the language of their race and to communicate directly with their people. Alfred the Great was very keen to promote this work in his day. These early excursions into national languages were the beginnings of all the western national literatures.

It must be remembered that the practical side to the Benedictines' work had produced remarkable results. It was their custom to choose unpromising sites in undeveloped country for their self-supporting monasteries. They cleared the forest, drained the land, and gave a lead in many ways to more intelligent agriculture. Their technical influence on good farming was a major feature of practical education in the Middle Ages. The care of the sick led the monks to the practice of medicine and nursing. Technical education became very much the business of everyday life in the great religious houses.

At various periods the powerful and wealthy Church grew slack in its duties. But always reformers arose to correct the balance by preaching a return to severer standards.

The *Book of Kells* was an early Irish illuminated manuscript of the four gospels from the New Testament of the Bible. The monogram page below contains the opening three words of the Gospel of St Matthew.

Danes, Vikings and Northmen

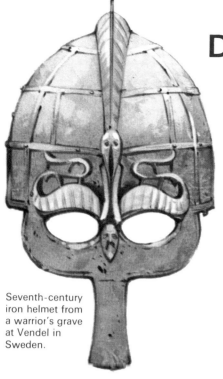

The last important attack made by the pagan north against Latin civilisation came from Scandinavia and it came by sea. The series of piratical raids, followed by invasion, lasted for about two hundred years. They were so ferocious in character that for a time the fate of civilisation in western Europe seemed to be in the balance. These Viking pirates came from Norway and Denmark. The Swedes, on the other hand, had gone inland and brought order and purpose to the disorganised Russians living along the great river highways of that country. Under their leader Rurik, they founded the principality of Kiev. The Swedes reached Constantinople and entered the service of the Byzantine rulers.

Viking Colonies

The courage and unshakable stamina of the Vikings enabled them to sail successfully in open boats over the cold waters of the North Atlantic. They colonised Iceland and Greenland. They then sailed on to a land they called Vinland which was probably the coast of Labrador. This means that the Vikings were the first people to reach America, centuries before Columbus. They settled also in island groups such as the Shetlands, the Orkneys and the Hebrides. The Isle of Man they used as a centre for raids in all directions.

Western Europe was very weak and disorganised after the death of Charlemagne. The speed of these ferocious pirates took everyone by surprise. They raided all the coasts and calm river valleys of the west. When they landed it was their custom to seize horses and raid farther inland. The Danes concentrated on the shorter sea routes of the North Sea while the Norwegians swept round the islands and coasts of northern Scotland and then to Ireland and the western coasts of Britain. The object of these early attacks was loot from the rich lands of the south. The raiders were particularly harsh on monasteries, where great wealth had been stored during the long happy years of peace. Now the monks were murdered and their buildings sent up in flames.

Danish Raids

Following the time of Augustine, England was divided into the kingdoms of Northumbria, Mercia and Wessex, who fought among themselves for supremacy. When the Danish raids first broke on England, Wessex was the most important. Their kings had been driving westward, taking over Somerset, Devon and Cornwall. For the first fifty years of the ninth century the Danes were content to make raids but in 851 they wintered in England and began a systematic conquest. The land from the Thames to the Clyde was soon overrun. Northumbria and Mercia went down and when Alfred came to the throne in 871 the Danes had Wessex by the throat. They took Reading in the same year and pushed on to Dorset and Wiltshire. The Celtic Cornish rose in rebellion and linked hands with the Danes. Alfred just escaped into the marshes of Somerset and held out in a winter camp at Athelney. One of Alfred's qualities was that he never despaired however black the situation appeared. From a desperate position he turned the tide of Scandinavian aggression and began the unification of England by leading the counter-attack against the Danes.

Despite the terrible harshness of the fighting, the Danes did not bring a new religion or a new language to Britain as the Saxons had done earlier. The two peoples were closely akin in race and speech and had no difficulty in understanding each other. Both had an equal love of law-making and justice and they began to merge into one people.

Saxon England

The next hundred years was a golden age for Saxon England and Alfred's grandsons ruled the whole country. But in 980 the Danish raids began again. Repeatedly the Danes were bought off but they always came back for more. In 1016 the Witan, the Supreme Council of England, chose Canute, the king of Denmark, to succeed Ethelred on the English throne.

Canute at that time was a savage pagan who consolidated his election to the throne by many murders. He was also the ruler of a great empire which included England and Denmark and was soon to conquer Norway. However, this powerful monarch became a Christian and married Emma of Normandy, the widow of Ethelred. He began to build monasteries instead of burning them and went on pilgrimage to Rome. He also supported the missionaries working in Norway and Sweden. But the North Sea made it difficult to keep his lands together and after his death his empire fell apart.

While these events had been happening in England, other Vikings had been settling in northern France. In 911 they made a settlement in the valley of the Seine which eventually developed into the Duchy of Normandy. This dukedom soon grew to be as powerful as the early French kings. But just as the strong kings of Wessex were found to resist the Danes in England, the house of Capet arose to serve the same purpose in France against the Normans. The Normans were contained and they expanded overseas. Normandy was a land of horses and the newcomers loved a horse as much as they loved a ship. The headlong challenge of the tournament ideally suited their temperament and once they had been converted the Normans became the most feared knights in Christendom.

The Norman Knights

The strong rulers of Normandy held both Church and State in their iron grasp. In the eleventh century they conquered England and Sicily. The recovery of Europe from the chaos of that age was led by such small strong feudal states as Normandy. Returning from pilgrimages to Jerusalem the Norman knights noticed the inviting weakness of Italy. Consequently they carved out for themselves a kingdom which included all southern Italy and Sicily. In 1058 the Normans made a treaty with the papacy which once again strengthened the Church with new soldiers to fight for the faith.

Stores are unloaded from a ninth-century Viking ship.

Alfred's England

From the extreme edge of utter defeat at the hands of the Danes, Alfred fought back to a position of strength. He was the first western ruler to turn back the tide of Scandinavian invasion. The royal house of Wessex did not enjoy good health and, at the age of twenty-three, Alfred was the fourth of his brothers to come to the throne. By his early fifties he too was dead but in that time he had transformed the kingdom which he had inherited. Later writers have every reason to call him 'Great' for much of what is valued today in Britain dates from Alfred's reign.

The Treaty of Wedmore

In 878, Alfred forced Guthrum, the leader of the Danes, to accept the Treaty of Wedmore. It was agreed to divide the country between Saxon and Dane, roughly along the line of Watling Street which ran from London to Chester. This division brought about half Mercia under the control of Wessex. The future of the Saxons was now centred on Wessex. Alfred was never to be king of all England but his grandson ruled from the Channel to the Lowlands of Scotland, and England was never divided again. A further treaty gave

end of his reign, this new English navy defeated and captured a Danish navy hear London. The fyrd, as the Saxon army was called, also came in for re-organisation. Alfred divided it into three parts and only one-third was called to serve at a time. The other two-thirds had to stay at home to keep the farms going and thus guarantee the food supply.

Law and Learning

Alfred's claim to greatness did not rest solely on his marked ability in war. As a child he had been taken to

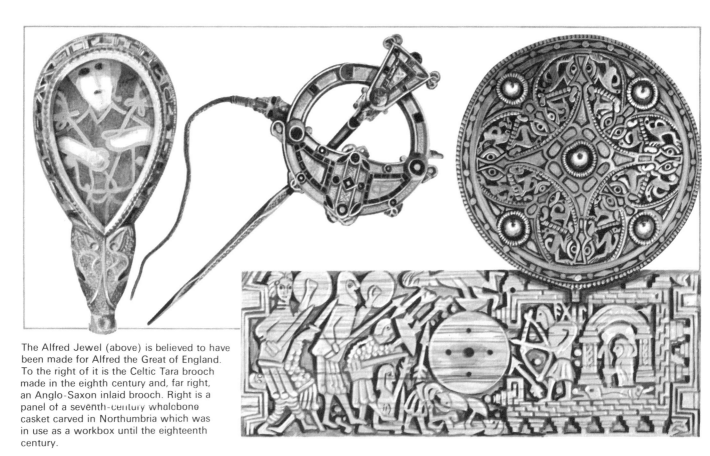

The Alfred Jewel (above) is believed to have been made for Alfred the Great of England. To the right of it is the Celtic Tara brooch made in the eighth century and, far right, an Anglo-Saxon inlaid brooch. Right is a panel of a seventh-century whalebone casket carved in Northumbria which was in use as a workbox until the eighteenth century.

In the three hundred years which separate Alfred from the arrival of St Augustine, the work of the Church and the warfare of the Saxons went on side by side in the greatest contrast. Monasteries grew up as retreats for quiet and thoughtful men while the small Saxon kingdoms fought each other for supremacy. Apart from rivalry with each other, they had to keep the lively Celts pinned back in the west and to fight against the arrival of Scandinavian pirates in the east. It was Alfred who started the English tradition of never acknowledging defeat and of surviving to win the last battle, for this is what he did in his fight against the Danes.

Alfred more control of the south-east, including London which he rebuilt.

Guthrum was forced to become a Christian by treaty and his people, as was the custom in those days, were compelled to follow suit. The sword brought defeat, the monks brought conversion of the ruler, and the whole people came into touch with Christian civilisation. Afterwards there were lapses but the process had begun.

Alfred realised the value of the Danish ships in moving troops in those days of swamp and thick forest. He therefore used a Danish ship as a model and improved it. Then he built the first English navy. Near the

Rome on pilgrimage and his respect for the learning and influence of the Church remained high. Despite all the distractions of war and serious ill health, Alfred not only restored learning but improved it in his own day. He founded monastic schools and he himself learned Latin late in life in order to help with the work of translating great books into English. Before invading Danes destroyed Northumbria, the great monasteries there had produced men of the quality of Alcuin and Bede.

Like all Saxons and Danes, Alfred had a great interest in law. This necessary branch of government was undertaken when he issued his own code of laws based on the custom of the past. This building up of law on the basis of past cases has remained a feature of Anglo-Saxon law in Britain and America to this day. In fact, the adventurous colonisation by the later English of large areas of the world was to give many of the early Saxon legal customs world-wide importance.

Church Records

After the time of Augustine, the dark mystery which shrouded the first hundred and fifty years of Saxon occupation begins to clear as Church learning starts to preserve records. At that stage the land was roughly divided between the Celts and the Saxons. The Celts had been pushed into the higher ground all down the western border. The rivers were not under control, there were vast areas of swamp, and forests were dense and difficult to pass through. Often a short voyage by ship was quicker than travelling by land. Many of the early settlements were simply clearings in the forests.

All life was based on agriculture and the Saxons were good farmers. They used large open fields divided into narrow strips. Each man owned a number of scattered strips which probably gave him a share of good and bad soil. The division and sharing of the strips were rigidly controlled by custom. There were three large fields in each village. One grew wheat for bread, another barley for drink, and the third was left empty, or fallow, in order to rest it. Today at Laxton in Nottinghamshire, one village has been preserved which still has strip fields owned by people in the village.

The village was the basic unit of Saxon life and the Church also adopted it under the name of the parish. In this form it has remained the foundation of rural society. Villages were formed into 'hundreds', which held regular courts, and the hundreds were formed into 'shires'. (County is the Norman-French word for the Saxon shire and it is the same thing.) The king appointed a shire-reeve, or sheriff, to look after the shire and the shire-moot met twice a year. At the head of this chain of representatives stood the powerful Witan, the wise council which advised the king. In bad times, the Witan deposed and appointed kings. Canute the Dane was chosen by the Saxon Witan. The Saxons possessed some slaves taken in war and they themselves were divided into simple and noble classes.

Anglo-Saxon Literature

During Alfred's reign great care was taken to gather together and preserve Anglo-Saxon literature, which is now called Old English. The long poem of Beowulf tells the story of heroic deeds done in Scandinavia. It was brought to England in the memories of the Saxon invaders and preserved by word of mouth until, centuries later, it was written down. Much of this literature is concerned with religion and the rest with war and the sea. *The Battle of Maldon* tells the story of heroic loyalty to a defeated leader in a famous last stand. *The Dream of the Rood* shows the tender piety which, by contrast, was stirring in some Saxon hearts. The rood is the cross. This mixture of great valour and simple piety demonstrates the two main influences on the people of those days. By this time also, the Saxon writers were keeping a yearly record of events called the Anglo-Saxon Chronicle, which is our main source of knowledge about those days.

The structure of society in feudal times was based on service by the ceorls, or freemen, to men of noble birth who in turn gave allegiance to the king.

The Norman Conquest

The conquest of Saxon England by William, Duke of Normandy, was efficient, cruel and permanent. England was taken out of the sphere of Scandinavian influence and brought back into the mainstream of civilised Christian Europe.

William had already had great success in France before he undertook his long-planned attack on England. Maine and Brittany were added to Normandy and he wisely married Matilda of Flanders to secure his eastern flank. In England, by contrast, there was hopeless confusion at this period. The last years of Edward the Confessor were dominated by the quarrels of the powerful earls who were jealous of each other's power. In this unsettled situation William, who was related to Edward, managed to get himself recognised as heir to the English throne. This arrangement was later confirmed when Harold, Earl of Wessex, was shipwrecked on the Norman coast and made to swear loyalty to William's claim. But when Edward died in 1066, Harold denied his enforced oath and became king.

Battle of Hastings

Trouble broke out both north and south. Harold Hardrada, who is said to have been over two metres tall, invaded Yorkshire with his Norwegians. He was helped by Harold's treacherous brother Tostig. The invaders defeated the Earls of Northumbria and Mercia near York on 20th September. Earl Harold hurried north with his army. The Norwegian king and Tostig were defeated and killed at Stamford on the 25th but William landed at

Pevensey in Sussex three days later. Again employing forced marches, Harold hurried south to find William dug in at Hastings, safely protected by the surrounding swamps.

Harold occupied the hill now known as Battle and the struggle began which lasted all day and finally settled the rulership of England. The weary axe-men of Wessex locked their shields in a solid wall around their king, supported by other lightly armed soldiers. The Normans were only a few thousand strong but they had mailed cavalry and archers. Two entirely different methods of war met that day.

Throughout the long day the axemen stood firm against all the Norman charges until a trick was tried. A pretended retreat drew the Englishmen down from the advantage of high ground. A hail of arrows over the shield wall killed Harold and two of

his brothers. The fyrd were scattered but the axe-men of Harold's household died heroically to the last man. It was the end of an heroic age brought about by new methods of war.

At first there were a great many revolts against William. But a fresh Danish invasion was bought off and William crushed and destroyed the country north of York, which had rebelled. The Domesday Book simply records three words—'here is desert'. The Saxons soon saw reason and William was crowned in Westminster Abbey on Christmas Day. The last show of defiance was made by the English patriot Hereward the Wake in the marshes of Ely but it ended when a great causeway was built.

William's Rule

If William was cruel, he was also exceptionally efficient and England

Reconstruction of a scene during the Battle of Hastings in 1066. The Norman cavalry charge up Senlac Hill in an attempt to dislodge the English forces from their defensive positions.

soon began to feel the benefits of strong, united rule. The thoroughness of the Domesday commissioners demonstrated the capable nature of Norman administration. The Church was brought under the control of law. No one escaped William's all-seeing eye. But he looked on himself as the rightful successor to the throne of England and he maintained Saxon customs where they were applicable.

Ever since the break-up of the Roman Empire the feudal system, as it is now called, was developing in western Europe. Men found it necessary to acquire protection from a local leader because of the prevailing dangers. They promised loyalty and yielded up the ownership of their land for the right to work part of it in peace. The lords in their turn owed loyalty and military service to the great barons and they in turn to the king. At every stage from the king down to the peasant each level had both rights and responsibilities. William saw to it that the great tenants-in-chief, his possible rivals, had their lands scattered throughout England so that they could not easily mobilise their power against him. He reserved about a quarter of England for his own share.

The Church in England
When William invaded England, he did so with the papal blessing, partly because of Harold's broken oath and partly because the Saxon Church was opposing the Pope. The European Church was undergoing a thoroughgoing transformation at the hands of the reformers coming from Cluny.

Hildebrand became Pope in 1073.

The Domesday Book was the name of the remarkable survey of England which William I caused to be made in the years 1085–6. It covers most of the country and gives very exhaustive details of land ownership and the numbers of people and their social condition. This thorough record of what England possessed became the beginning of local history. Most of the information exists in the form of a summary but a full survey is available for south-west England and East Anglia. The main purpose of the work was to assess taxation and the value of the great barons' lands.

Summary of key dates
    862 Rurik founds Viking state in Russia
    871 Accession of Alfred the Great
    878 Treaty of Wedmore
    911 Vikings settle in France
c. 1000 Leif Ericsson lands in America at
            Nova Scotia
   1016 Danish king Canute becomes king
            of England and Norway
   1066 Battle of Hastings. Coronation of
            William I
   1086 Domesday Book
   1115 Peter Abelard teaching in Paris

On the eve of the Norman Conquest England was divided into various kingdoms of which Wessex was the most powerful.

The Church in England profited by his reforms and received the gifted Lanfranc as the new Archbishop of Canterbury. Nearly all the Saxon bishops were changed and the Church came under strong European influence. William, however, was the strongest ruler of the time in the west and he utterly refused to submit any real power to the mighty Hildebrand. Lanfranc was his friend, some said his only friend, and the tactful Lanfranc softened the demand for unmarried priests for a time. But England was now increasingly a Norman land.

Norman French was the language of the new rulers and became the language used in the law courts. Latin was the universal language of the Church. Thus English disappeared from official use and from polite society and remained underground for nearly three centuries.

Asia and Africa

The great continents of Asia and Africa contain some of the oldest civilised societies the world has known. Most important are those of India and China whose origins stretch farther back in time than their recorded history can tell. But in other parts of the world outside Europe and the Americas there existed human societies about which very little is known, although in modern times more and more attention is being paid to these 'vanished civilisations'.

India after Asoka

When Alexander the Great's armies swept across the borders of India they had very little clear idea where they were going. Alexander himself knew nothing of the world outside the lands already mapped by Greek geographers. Possibly he believed that beyond India was an unknown stretch of water which separated them from the western seaboard of Europe. It was natural enough that, having come so far, he should wish to round off his conquests and bring the few remaining areas of land in the east under his control.

In India, Alexander's men did not find the savages they expected. They were confronted by an old and settled civilisation with a strong religious belief binding it together. But the Indians could not resist the greater fighting skill of the Greeks, and Alexander occupied Afghanistan and north-west India. He would have gone on but his men rebelled and the Greeks left the sub-continent, having erected temples to their gods and done their best to persuade the population that theirs was a superior way of life. But the Indians were unimpressed, content with their own gods and their ancient traditions.

It would be wrong, however, to say that India was unaffected by the Greek occupation, for it inspired a wave of unity and nationalist feeling that resulted in the Mauryan empire. Its first ruler was Chandragupta Maurya (c.300 B.C.) who took over the areas vacated by Alexander. Chandragupta's grandson Asoka extended the empire's rule over the whole of India except for the southern-most peninsula. It is from this time that India began to grow in importance internationally and to carry her ideas into other countries.

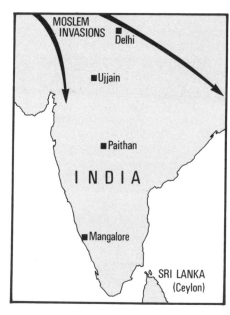

The Gupta Dynasty

The empire which Asoka forged did not survive his death. India fell into a period of civil wars between small states, as she was so often to do throughout her history. The 'unity' of the Mauryan empire was shown to have existed in name only. From time to time a new ruler emerged to give his name to a dynasty of kings, each as short-lived as the next. Not until the Gupta dynasty, founded by another Chandragupta (known as the First) in A.D. 320, were the territories of India again brought together and extended. The Guptas forced the petty princes to acknowledge them and took regular tribute from each as a token of submission.

During the Gupta dynasty Hinduism became politically supreme, and the period is notable for great advances in science and art and for the expansion of trade. India led the world in mathematics and astronomy at this time, and much of what the Arabs brought to the western world, such as 'Arabic' numerals and the decimal system, was derived from Indian sources.

The Hindu Gods

When Asoka was converted to Buddhism he allowed the greatest freedom of religious thought to others. Brahminism, the earliest form of Hinduism, flourished and held its own, even benefiting from Buddhist influence.

This tolerance is typical of the Hindu and illustrates the vital point that Buddhism and Hinduism are not separate and rival religions. It is wrong to think of Hinduism as a

Bronze sculpture of Siva,
the Indian god of the dance.

religion at all in the same sense as Christianity or Islam. Hinduism embraces many religions, for the Hindu is allowed a wide choice of thought and belief, so long as it does not conflict with the system of caste and other social customs which are also meant by the term.

The worship of Brahma and other Hindu gods continued throughout the partial conversion of India to Buddhism. In the end it not only survived but kept its position at the heart of most spiritual belief in India until the present day. The other great religious belief which remained dominant in India was not that of Buddha but of Mohammed.

The Moslems in India

By about the year A.D. 1000 Buddhism had almost disappeared from India. When it seemed that the whole of the country would come together in the Hindu faith, a new and shattering force crossed the boundaries of northern India. This was the 'cleansing sword' of Islam, brought by the Moslem invaders who gradually took over India during a long period which lasted about 300 years.

India was no stranger to occupation by foreign peoples: Scythians, Parthians and Huns were only a few of the different races who, at one time or another, had brought a temporary foreign rule to parts of India. Temporary, because the Hindus, with their unique ability to bend before the storm and absorb the best of other people's beliefs, invariably ended up by converting the newcomers, befriending, marrying and absorbing them.

The Moslem invasions were a different matter, for Mohammedanism and Hinduism could never be reconciled. The complete domination of India by Moslem rulers, which was achieved by the middle of the fourteenth century, left an indelible mark on India's history. As Moslems were outside the caste system, Hindus regarded them as unclean, whereas the Moslems, who were forbidden by the prophet to look up to any form of imagery, despised the Hindus as idol-worshippers.

The richest period of the Moslem presence and the one which brought most benefit to both sides occurred during the best period of the Mogul empire, which was founded in 1526. The Arab/Persian influence on language, art, architecture and music was of lasting beauty.

The Taj Mahal at Agra in India was built by the Mogul emperor Shah Jehan as a mausoleum for his wife. Perhaps the most famous building in India, its architecture has a grace and simplicity which is very unlike the style of most Indian buildings.

One of the twenty-four wheels on the temple at Konarak in India, built in the form of a chariot.

A painting in the Mogul style of the sixteenth-century Indian emperor Akbar.

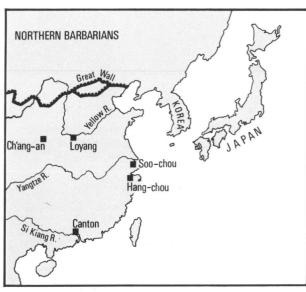

NORTHERN BARBARIANS

Great Wall
Yellow R.
Ch'ang-an   Loyang
Yangtze R.
                Soo-chou
                Hang-chou
Si Kiang R.   Canton

KOREA
JAPAN

A Samurai warrior of medieval times (left). The Japanese characters in red alongside the map of the Far East mean 'the source of the sun', a Chinese phrase from which the Japanese took the name of their country.

China

The Han dynasty which ruled in China from 207 B.C. to A.D. 221 was the first to have real control of the whole nation. Its emperors were very popular and even today people in northern China are proud to call themselves 'the sons of Han'. During this time when China was becoming united, she was cut off from the developing civilisations of the west. Almost her only contact with other people was with the barbarians who surrounded her. In the same way that people in the west grew up in ignorance of the east and regarded Europe as the centre of the world, so China, with its ancient traditions and little knowledge of the western world, held the opposite view and thought that China was the only civilised place on earth.

After the Han dynasty there was a long period in Chinese history called the Age of Confusion covering civil wars, rebellion and the breakdown of central government. It lasted until the time of the T'ang dynasty, whose second emperor T'ai-tsung is rated in China as the greatest ruler ever to have sat on the imperial throne. The T'ang dynasty is also the golden age of Chinese literature. T'ai-tsung himself was its greatest patron, and so fine an exponent of the art of handwriting, which the Chinese have always admired, that his writing is still used in schools today as a model for children to copy.

Chinese vase of the Ming dynasty (sixteenth century) bearing the dragon of the Imperial porcelain factory.

When the Han family died out there was the usual period of internal squabbling between rival factions before the Sung dynasty was founded in A.D. 960. In its turn it lasted until the thirteenth century, when the growing power of the Mongols finally overwhelmed the country and the great khans became emperors of China. The Mongols ruled until 1368, when the Ming dynasty began and took the Chinese nation out of the Middle Ages into the modern world.

Japan

Sometime in the fourth century A.D. the Japanese kingdom came into being with authority over a limited part of the islands which make up the present nation. One of the earliest influences upon Japan was Buddhism, brought to the country via China and Korea. The Buddhist faith had already captured China some 200 years earlier and it was to become the major religion of the Far East, although it is now more or less extinct in India, the country of its origin.

In A.D. 645 government on Chinese lines, with an absolute monarch, was introduced. The real power, however, was vested in the hands of a remarkable family called the Fujiwaras. From behind the figurehead of a succession of royal emperors, they controlled the affairs of Japan for over 500 years. The Fujiwaras and the families who succeeded them were like the dynasties of Chinese emperors, but they never sat on the throne. Instead they organised and directed the country by careful control of all high offices.

When the Fujiwara family finally expired it was replaced by the equally strong Minamoto clan, whose leader Yoritomo was the first to be given the title of Shogun by the emperor in A.D. 1185. Around the central figure of the Shogun, a position which became hereditary in Yoritomo's family, a new feudal and military society was created. This military emphasis came at the right time for Japan, for it enabled her to resist the two major attempts by the Mongols to invade the islands. The second invasion in fact was wrecked by natural causes, since a violent typhoon blew up and destroyed a large part of the Mongol fleet. Ever since, the Japanese have called such winds *kamikaze*, or the divine wind; a word which was later used to describe Japanese suicide pilots who deliberately crashed their planes on enemy targets in the Second World War.

The Feudal Age of Japan lasted until well past the middle of the nineteenth century. The most colourful figures of this time were the samurai, the professional soldiers raised from the ranks of the peasant class. It is estimated that at one time they numbered one-twentieth of the whole population. The samurai were probably the finest professional soldiers the world has ever seen, with a fanatical code of honour and devotion to their profession. They guarded their employer and his lands efficiently, their only reward being food and shelter and the privilege of bearing arms. The samurai's sword was never drawn for any petty quarrel, but once out of its scabbard the blade was not put aside until it had performed its task of killing or its owner was himself dead.

South-east Asia

The term south-east Asia covers a number of countries which lie in the area between China, India and Australia, and includes Vietnam, Laos, Cambodia, Malaya, Thailand, Burma, Indonesia and the Philippines. They are widely different places and there is no real justification for trying to link them together historically. Each developed in its own way at its own pace, although most came under the influence of China or India in their early years. Such independence as they had in the Middle Ages was soon exploited by European people between the sixteenth and eighteenth centuries. Nearly all knowledge of them before the period of European penetration comes from Chinese sources.

This Fijian sailing canoe is typical of the very seaworthy outriggers which were capable of long ocean voyages. Some of the bigger craft were a hundred feet long and could carry as many as forty or fifty people.

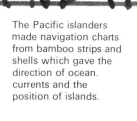

The Pacific islanders made navigation charts from bamboo strips and shells which gave the direction of ocean currents and the position of islands.

91

The Mongols

The steppes of central Asia cover a vast area of many thousands of square kilometres. Even today, it is a bleak and mysterious part of the world which has not been properly explored. For hundreds of years this inhospitable land supported wandering tribes of herdsmen. There is very little archaeological evidence for the existence of these roving people. Whatever is known about their early history has come down to us from the records of those unfortunate neighbours who suffered from time to time their fierce, plundering raids.

One of these tribes was the Mongols, whose name first appears in the annals of Chinese history in the sixth century A.D. The history of all early settled communities is known to us by the material objects which people leave behind them. The nature of the Mongols' life, as with all nomadic people, was such that it left to posterity few things for the archaeologist to dig up in modern times.

Living from the Land

Buildings, towns and any form of settled agricultural life were unknown to them. They were constantly on the move, living from the land as best they could but depending chiefly on their animals for all the basic necessities of life. Sheep, cattle, camels and horses provided food, clothing, transport and even the coverings for their mobile, tent-like homes.

Unlike the Aryan tribes of Mesopotamia, the original people of Mongolia were short and squat with characteristic yellow skins, slanting eyes and almost hairless faces. As time passed they mixed with other races and as a result of intermarriage the peculiarities of the Mongoloid physique were changed or modified.

The climate contributed to their appearance. Their almond-shaped eyes may well have come from generations spent peering through half-closed lids at a horizon swept by wind, dust and snow. Their thick, tanned skins were covered with grease in the winter to protect them against the bitter cold. When they were not sleeping or eating they spent most of their time on horseback, a fact which may have contributed to their general broadness of shoulder and narrowness of hip.

The early Mongols formed themselves into unions of small tribes, held loosely together without ever becoming properly organised into

Marco Polo (1254–1324), the Venetian traveller, first went to China in 1271 with his father and uncle. The journey from Venice to the court of Kublai Khan took over four years and the party crossed lands previously unknown to Europeans. Kublai Khan took a great liking to young Marco. He was made a special envoy to the Mongol court, and travelled in many parts of Asia on missions for the great Khan. Marco did not return to Venice until 1295. Three years later he was taken prisoner during a war between Venice and Genoa. The record of his travels may have been written while he was in captivity, from notes taken during his long stay in Mongolia.

Marco Polo, and a map of his travels in Asia.

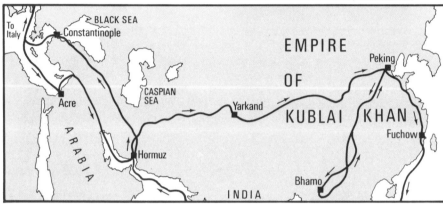

social groups. They spent a good deal of time fighting among themselves over the possession of good grazing land. They seemed to have none of the ambitions which man normally developed as he emerged from a primitive existence. They remained content with their narrow lives, absorbed by the physical demands of a hard life, their interest centred on the animals they herded, the horses they rode and their weapons. They never sought to conquer anyone or call themselves masters of any particular area of land. Their only contact with civilised places was when they swept down on some border town to plunder it, stealing the animals, burning the houses and simply slaughtering anyone who got in the way. The Mongols were superb horsemen, ferocious fighters, could ride for days on end in the worst conditions and were quite impervious to cold.

Genghis Khan

Not until the thirteenth century did a Mongol leader of extraordinary ability come to the fore. This was Genghis Khan, who was to lead his people to great conquests and the control of an empire bigger than any the world had ever seen. Son of a local chieftain, he was originally called Temujin. Only when he became

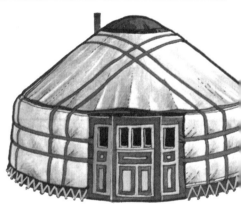

the undisputed leader of the Mongol people was he given the title Genghis Khan (which means the great or perfect prince). The best stories of his life are written in Persian but the earliest sources are Chinese, notably *A Secret History of the Mongols* written about 1250.

Genghis Khan was the first man to unite the Mongols and lead them to planned victory against other peoples. He was a master tactician in the art of war. He had the great gift of being able to sum up a situation quickly and of taking instant action. By that mixture of good fortune and judgement which so often attends the bold, it was invariably effective. Although he could neither read nor write he always prepared his battle plans in advance and studied the strength and position of the enemy carefully. Genghis Khan ranks with Alexander and Napoleon as a great soldier and world conqueror. When he died in 1227 he left to his heirs an empire which stretched from the far shores of China to the Black Sea. More than this, he bequeathed to his successors by his example the will and unity to extend Mongol power even further.

Mobile Columns

The strength of the Mongol army lay in its strict discipline and the speed with which it attacked. The success of its mobile columns of horsemen was in a way similar to that of the swift-moving German armoured columns in the Second World War. There was the same element of surprise and the same ability to strike quickly in one place and then make a rapid move to strike again in another direction. Wherever the Mongols went their enemies fell before them, unable to resist the powerful bows of the Mongol archers and the wily tactics of their generals. The Mongols were a race of soldiers,

The yurt is a circular tent used by nomadic tribes in Mongolia. It has a collapsible lattice framework and is covered by layers of felt, thin in summer (left) and thick in winter (right).

tough, ruthless and without fear—perhaps the most terrifying fighting force of the whole Middle Ages.

The great khans who succeeded Genghis, notably his son Ogadei and his grandson Kublai, led their armies successfully against Russia and those parts of China which so far had managed to remain independent. The Mongol empire was also stretched westwards by further conquests until it reached the forests of Germany. The only place where the Mongols were not triumphant, through the intervention of natural forces and the determination of their opponents, was in Japan. By this time the empire was so vast that it took a man on horseback two years to cross it from east to west.

After the death of Kublai the empire fell into some disorder. To control so vast a territory and so

The horse was probably the most important thing in the life of a Mongol warrior. He spent many hours each day riding, in pursuit of an enemy or hunting animals for food.

many people with differing traditions and ways of life required a genius and strength which the later khans lacked. Under the Turkish chieftain Tamerlane, who claimed to be related to Genghis, the empire was again united under a strong hand. Then, when it seemed that Tamerlane might revive full Mongol greatness, he died as the result of a battle wound.

Sculptured heads in bronze from Benin in Africa.

Africa

Although Africa is thought to be the original home of early man, for centuries great areas of the 'dark continent' remained untouched and unaffected by events in the rest of the world. The north coast of Africa, from the Nile to Morocco, was included in the early story of civilised man. Under the influence of the Egyptians, Greeks, Romans, Phoenicians and others, this strip of the continent facing the sea became part of the Mediterranean culture.

Inland, in the great Sahara desert, and in central and southern Africa, there was no contact with the European world until the beginning of the sixteenth century. At this time the first explorers were seeking a sea route to the East and began to probe their way around the coasts of Africa.

The Portuguese traders and missionaries were among the first white men to make contact with the black men of the interior. Before this the greatest outside influence on African people was that of the followers of Mohammed, who travelled in many parts of east Africa persuading the local inhabitants to take up the Islamic religion.

When the Europeans penetrated the interior of Africa they were astonished by the richness of the art and the organisation of some of the societies they found there. In particular, the Yoruba culture at Benin in southern Nigeria produced many beautiful objects some of which resembled the finest work of Greek sculptors. But Europe did nothing to help or preserve these civilisations.

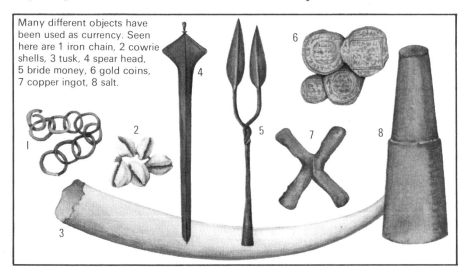

Many different objects have been used as currency. Seen here are 1 iron chain, 2 cowrie shells, 3 tusk, 4 spear head, 5 bride money, 6 gold coins, 7 copper ingot, 8 salt.

As the plantations in America and the West Indies demanded more labour the forests of Africa were stripped of their human inhabitants. The terrible story of the slave trading of black people by white Europeans, in which many of the African rulers co-operated, created a division of hatred and resentment between the races which has not been healed in modern times.

Lost Peoples

It is only in recent years that the discoveries of archaeologists have placed the existence of several early African tribes and kingdoms beyond doubt. Half a million years ago the Sahara desert itself is thought to have been a fertile area with primitive creatures living on river banks.

At Zimbabwe in south-east Africa the ruins of a settlement exist which have been the cause of much discussion since their discovery in the 1860s. The word Zimbabwe means 'stone houses' and it is the nature of the extraordinary stone buildings, erected on a central mound or acropolis, which has caused so much interest. They were built over a long period extending from the eleventh to the nineteenth centuries.

The walls of Zimbabwe are man's greatest surviving achievement in southern Africa. They were built from roughly shaped stones laid at first in irregular courses without foundations and without the use of mortar. There are no straight lines or angles in the construction and the face of the brickwork is decorated by the use of carefully executed patterns in herringbone and chevron designs.

Despite its character, Zimbabwe is not unique. It is one of a series of centres all of which belonged to the same culture. The people who lived there and their society were extinct before European travellers made their main explorations of Africa in the nineteenth century.

Knight, Priest and Peasant

The long struggle against the barbarian invaders brought about great changes in the daily lives of the ordinary people. What has since been called feudalism had grown up of necessity but now it became the basic framework of everyday life. In times of great danger the terrified peasant had been glad to place himself under the protection of a fighting lord. Gladly he accepted duties and services to repay his protector. But when the danger passed, the lord still required the peasant to do him service. In Norman England his grip was severely tightened and the precious freedom of the people was seriously reduced.

Wealth in those days was based on the ownership of land. If a man was wealthy, then he was the lord of great lands. All the basic necessities of life were produced locally from the crops and animals raised by the peasants. There were no man-made fibres and clothing came from the wool of the sheep and the furs and skins of animals. Building materials were rarely moved very far and gave a local character to all forms of housing.

Master and Man

There was now a wide gulf between the armed knights who owed military service to their king or baron and the humble peasants who provided the necessities of life. On the one hand were men of noble birth and on the other simple peasants who were in no position to dispute their lot with mounted knights, clad in armour and living in fortified houses. It was not until the rise of trade that a bridge began to be built across this gap. In Norman England the gulf between master and man was more marked because of the differences of race and language.

The Church also owned much land and many of the peasants had an abbot or a bishop for their master. When conditions improved for the peasants in the fourteenth century it was often possible for them to pay money instead of services to their lord and thus gradually buy freedom. Many an impoverished knight was glad to do this for money, and economics were poorly understood in the Middle Ages by the arrogant military man. The Church, however, was an institution and could always afford to wait. There was usually a competent man to succeed every abbot and bishop and their organisation rarely broke down. Consequently, peasants found it harder to free themselves on Church land.

The parish priest was a much more significant figure to the villager in his parish. Although he had to be supported by tithes, a tenth of everything produced, he baptised the people, married them, and brought them the consolation of the Church when they died. When Langland or Chaucer wrote with contempt of rich unfaithful churchmen, they spoke only with the highest admiration for the poor and faithful priests. The tremendous fatality among parish priests in the Black Death shows how faithful most were to their ministry. By comparison the knight did very little to justify his privileged position.

Detail of a tapestry from the Duke of Devonshire's collection at Hardwick Hall in England, made in Belgium in the fifteenth century and now in the Victoria and Albert Museum, London.

The Medieval Knight

The most glamorous figure of feudalism in the Middle Ages was the knight. Clad in armour from head to toe and mounted on his great warhorse, he was a magnificent sight when he rode forth to battle or challenged a fellow knight in the tournament. Knighthood came to the highest development about the twelfth century, especially in France and England whose kings were linked. For some time the king of England ruled more French land than the French king.

Originally the knight was simply a tenant who held land in return for military service to his superior lord. But as the gulf between lord and peasant widened, the knights became a privileged class. Eventually far more was expected of a true knight than mere military service. A code of chivalry was drawn up which made the training of a knight long and arduous. Even then the reception of the coveted honour of knighthood was by no means easy or certain. It was finally bestowed after a man had distinguished himself in great feats of arms and proved himself a leader among his fellow warriors.

Courtly Life

The distinction of knighthood was the ambition of every highborn youth. Such a boy had military training almost from birth. At the age of seven or eight he was sent to live with the family in a castle with the idea of learning 'manners'. This meant the

The full coat-of-arms of Edward the Black Prince (1330–76), son of Edward III of England, at the time of his death. The shield and the crowned lion crest carry the silver label of an eldest son.

proper way to carry himself in all the requirements of courtly life. He received regular training in the use of weapons and took part in the hunting and hawking parties which kept knights fit for more serious killing. At about the age of fifteen the young page became a squire which made him an assistant to one of the fully fledged knights. He was his personal servant and eventually was allowed to ride out to battle with him when fully trained. It was now for him to prove himself worthy of the honour of knighthood. The method of making a knight is still followed today by the British monarch in exactly the same

The joust was a mock combat between mounted knights armed with long lances. It was the principal feature of medieval tournaments.

way as in the past. The one to receive the honour kneels before her and she 'dubs' him by touching his shoulder with the flat of a sword.

In the great age of faith, the knight had also to undertake a spiritual preparation for the honour of knighthood and to swear important vows which should make him 'a true and gentle knight'. The night before his investment he spent in prayer before the altar until daybreak. In this frame of mind he swore to defend the weak and the Christian faith with his life. The next day he was dubbed and received a sword, spurs, and a coat of mail. Despite their cruelty and love of war, the knights always seemed to retain some respect for the Church and their knightly vows.

Some of the most colourful events of the Middle Ages were the great tournaments where famous knights from near and far took part in friendly but dangerous contests. These exciting fights between famous knights for the sheer love of fighting were called jousting. The ladies were enthroned on the dais to see their champions fight for them and a large excited crowd watched the keen and fierce rivalries. The contestants were sometimes killed and often seriously maimed but the danger appealed to the daring spirit of the age. Nevertheless violence as the solution to all problems was uppermost in the minds of these knights, and the chivalry of the Middle Ages finished in the suicidal Wars of the Roses which destroyed the great houses of England.

An illumination from the fourteenth-century Luttrell Psalter shows Sir Geoffrey Luttrell, an English knight from Lincolnshire, leaving for war, attended by his wife and daughter-in-law.

Orders of Knights

More interesting are the great knightly orders which were formed by soldier monks who wanted to fight the battles of the Cross against the heathen. The two most famous orders were the Knights of Malta and the Knights Templar, both of which date from the days of the Crusades. The Knights of Malta began in the Holy Land when some merchants from Amalfi in Italy sought permission to run a hospital for sick pilgrims in Jerusalem. The hospital was supervised by Benedictine monks. They wore black habits with an eight-pointed white star. Later, a French noble, Raymond du Puy, became the first Grand Master and they became the Knights of St John of Jerusalem. They were now Augustinians. Their vows required them to be chaste, obedient and to fight to the last drop of blood for Christ. Charles V gave them Malta and here they lived on, patrolling the Mediterranean against pirates and caring for the sick until Napoleon brought their work to an end.

The Templars were started, with the help of St Bernard, as the Poor Knights of Christ and acquired their name of Templar from association with the Temple of Solomon in Jerusalem. They wore white robes with a blood-red cross. Their recruits, drawn from noble families, became very wealthy and powerful. They were far more military than the Knights of St John and their wealth made them into bankers. In 1312 the order was suppressed by the Pope.

The Order of the Garter is the highest order of chivalry in England. There are twenty-seven true members including the reigning monarch and the Prince of Wales. Certain special additions are permitted to allow royal princes and foreign sovereigns to become members. The order was founded in honour of the Virgin Mary, St Edward the Confessor and St George. The motto *honi soit qui mal y pense* means 'may he be shamed who thinks evil'. The order uses St George's Chapel in the grounds of Windsor Castle as its chapel, where the Garter Knights' banners are hung.

Longbow and Gunpowder

In eastern Europe, there was a great deal of exciting knightly activity which drove the frontiers of Christendom across the north German plain and converted the Baltic lands. This was the work of the Knights of the Sword and the Teutonic Knights of Prussia. Henry IV of England took part in some of these campaigns. This Germanisation and conversion of the east paved the way for the rise of the Hanseatic trading towns of which more will be said later.

Men fighting on foot had no answer to the mounted knight until the coming of the English longbow and gunpowder. The heavy horses were also protected by full armour, and with the mounted knight they formed one-man tanks which no foot soldier could withstand. So heavy was the knight in his armour that a rope and pulley had to be used to crane him from the ground into the saddle. His shield bore his personal coat of arms by which he was identifiable on the battlefield and when travelling along the roads of Europe. With the castle and the cathedral he was part of the majesty of the Middle Ages.

The *Krak-des-Chevaliers* (above) is a fine example of a heavily fortified crusading castle where each section is a fort in its own right. The Templars (left) were a military order of knights founded at the time of the crusades. A Saracen (right).

The Crusades

Christianity was triumphant in the west in the eleventh century and a series of great statesmen-popes rejoiced over the downfall of all the enemies of the Church. The ideal of a united Christendom under the leadership of the Pope was becoming a reality. Suddenly pilgrimages to Jerusalem were forbidden. The more tolerant Moslems had been replaced by the Seljuk Turks. These uncivilised barbarians accepted the faith of Islam and turned fanatically against all unbelievers. They soon attacked the eastern empire and took Asia Minor.

The Christian knights had also taken a vow to defend their faith to the death. To these warlike knights Urban II proclaimed a Holy War under the banner of the blood-red cross to deliver the Holy Places from the infidel. The response to his call was wildly enthusiastic. The flower of French chivalry and an unorganised mob rushed to arms. Many could not wait to head east and they met their fate disastrously at Turkish hands. All were ignorant of the countries and climate they were going to experience.

Surprisingly the First Crusade was the most successful. Clad in leather and heavy armour, the Crusaders penetrated Syria and took Jerusalem in 1099. They acted with exceptional brutality and rejoiced in slaughtering the heathen. Five feudal states were carved out of their gains and many superb castles were built.

Saladin Attacks

All this success was very short-lived. The Turks counter-attacked and took Edessa, one of the five states. St Bernard raised a second crusade but it achieved little. Then in 1171 Saladin, ruling from Egypt, banded together the independent Moslem states and re-took Jerusalem, which the Moslems were to hold until 1918. His humane conduct to the defeated was an example to Christian knights.

The Crusades proved the strength of the appeal which the idea of a united Christendom had to medieval men and women. Many of them were ready to die to defend Christ's kingdom on earth. But deep-seated rivalries caused failure. The rivalry of England and France was too much for the Third Crusade. The eastern empire and western Christendom were also rivals. The Normans who had taken south Italy and Sicily from the Greeks were distrusted by Constantinople, and very little help

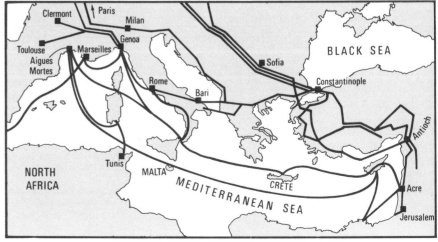

Crusading routes across Europe to the Holy Land

was given to the Crusaders once the Turkish danger had been removed.

The sea-going republics of Italy, particularly Venice, obtained most benefit from the Crusades. They secured ports in the Near East and established those connections with the luxury trade of the caravan routes which brought them immense wealth and power. Their true interest was revealed when they managed to turn the Fourth Crusade against Constantinople. The city was taken and ruled by the Latins for fifty years. After that temporary occupation, there was never again a hope that the breach between the western and eastern churches would ever be healed.

Church and State

The Church was now very powerful and her extensive lands gave her great wealth. The reforms coming from the Abbey of Cluny had revitalised the Church and two new orders, the Carthusians and the Cistercians, further increased the amazing number of monasteries in Europe. In the eleventh century reforming popes soon made their strength felt by contesting the leadership of Christendom with the Emperor and the leading kings. Hildebrand, Pope Gregory VII, was the greatest of these statesmen popes. In the struggle which ensued, both Anselm of Canterbury and Hildebrand himself preferred exile to defeat. St Thomas Becket endured both exile and death in the fight for papal supremacy.

The lands under the control of a bishop or an abbot made him a very powerful man in this life as well as in the next. Such a man had a double hold on the people and could be a serious opponent to the king. Churchmen represented a state within the state in each country, owing their first loyalty to a foreign pope in Rome.

Summary of key dates

This early picture of the martyrdom of St Thomas is based on eyewitness accounts.

There was bound to be a collision of interest. William I was strong and founded church courts to bring churchmen within the English law. He also utterly refused to hold England as an overlord approved by the Pope. The battle was fought out over the appointment of bishops. Strong kings refused to surrender the right to invest bishops in their own lands but the weaker ones were overawed. The struggle, known as the Investiture Question, went on for two centuries.

Becket and Henry II

It came to a head in England between Becket and Henry II. Henry wanted to bring the clergy under the control of the ordinary courts. Becket refused and the dispute led to the martyrdom of the archbishop. Later, in the reign of King John, the whole of England was excommunicated for a year, and Innocent III interfered with the terms of Magna Carta. Such was the power of these mighty popes.

Thomas Becket

Henry II chose Becket to serve him when he was a man of no importance, and made him Chancellor of the Exchequer. The two men were friends and at this stage Becket lived luxuriously. But later, when he was made the archbishop of Canterbury, his whole manner of life changed and he took up the cause of the Church. The king was resolved that the tradition which laid down that it took two crimes to hang a priest should be abolished. Becket was equally resolved that every claim of the papacy should be obeyed. Four of Henry's personal knights, knowing of the king's fury against Becket, came to Canterbury and murdered the archbishop in the cathedral. There was general horror at the deed and Henry had to undergo public flogging by the monks as a penance. The pope created Becket a saint and Canterbury became a shrine for pilgrims from all over England. Chaucer's pilgrims were on their way to Canterbury in his famous Tales.

Peasants and the Land

The three-field system which the Saxons used to work their land continued with very little alteration until the eighteenth century. As only two of the fields were used at a time while the third rested, this meant that one-third of the farming land of the country was always idle. The value of root crops as feeding stuff for stock had not yet been discovered and the farm animals were then much smaller and fewer in number.

Towards the end of the year most of the animals were killed off and salted down so that to eat no meat in Lent was often making a virtue of necessity. Additional items to the sparse diet of the time were eagerly sought. Fish was an important food and giant dovecotes maintained a

Magna Carta, the Great Charter of England which the barons forced King John to sign in 1215. It protected the rights of the Church and of all freemen under the feudal system.

In the Middle Ages protection, called sanctuary, was given to criminals who took refuge in holy places. By this means, they could escape summary vengeance and hope for a fair trial at the hands of the law. In some churches there were special symbols of sanctuary, such as the sanctuary knocker which the fugitive grasped, or the frithstool in which he sat.

supply of winter meat. Beekeeping was understood and the honey was used to make monotonous food more pleasing. Geese were kept on the village green but all the wild life was the property of the lord. From the earliest times, however, poaching was common and savagely punished.

The Manor

In England, the lord's estate was known by the French word, manor. The manors varied in size and by no means corresponded with the parish

or village. There was no true freehold in those days for even the barons, the great tenants-in-chief, held their land from the king. In the same way, whatever rights he might have, the lesser occupier of the land was only a tenant, the word we still use. The Domesday survey caused what had been done 'time out of mind' to be set down in a written record. A manor court was appointed to handle all disputes, and its doings were recorded in the manor rolls.

The lot of the peasants was extremely hard. The great castles and cathedrals remain but the miserable hovels, in which the peasants lived, have long since been swept away. These humble dwellings usually had two rooms, one for the beasts and the

Sanctuary knocker from Durham Cathedral and a frithstool from Hexham Abbey in England.

other for the family. Very little money was in use at that time. The peasant paid for his land in goods and services. Roughly speaking, he was obliged to spend about half the week on the lord's demesne, or home farm round the manor house, and the rest he could spend on his own land.

At the busiest periods of the year, such as spring and autumn, when the sowing and harvesting had to be done, he was required to do more. This extra labour was called boon work. There were also further levies for special expenses which the lord had

to meet when his eldest son was made a knight or his eldest daughter required a dowry. Should the lord have the misfortune to be captured in war, the ransom for his release could reach a staggering sum. And it would have to be provided by his tenants. A form of death duty, called a relief, was also charged when a man succeeded to his father's holding, so that very little was overlooked.

Ownership of Land

Most of the Saxon thegns, or freemen, lost their special status at the Conquest. The term 'villein', which once meant simply a villager, now meant a man 'bound to the soil'. He could not leave his land or change his work. He required his lord's permission to be married. Apart from the labour which he had to provide personally or by substitute, he also had to send much of his best produce for the upkeep of the manor.

The total holding which a man held, made up of separate strips of land, varied, but it was normally about twelve hectares. In this time of change there were various types of villagers. Some were called freemen and had more legal rights against their lord and more power of movement. Others, known as bordars and cottars, had less rights than villeins. But all these classes had some land which they could call their own. There were no dispossessed landless labourers as there were later in English history.

There were some serfs who were bondmen and had no land. These people worked directly for the lord's household. The keepers of pigs and the bees, the hewers of wood and the drawers of water were the lord's serfs. Later on some of them progressed to become manor officials and earned a wage.

The working of the land was more organised than the separate scattered strips would suggest. It was agreed, for example, to grow the same crop on the same acre plots. Ploughing was a job for co-operative effort. The ploughs were wooden and pulled by a team of oxen. Normally eight of these weak, bony creatures were needed to draw one plough. Horses were seldom used on the land. Apart from the fields, there were many additional rights which helped a balanced agriculture. There was common grazing land for cows and geese. Certain rights of cutting wood and feeding pigs in the woodland

were granted. The village greens and 'commons' are survivals of those days but very few any longer offer rights to the local inhabitants beyond a pleasant stretch of grass which cannot be built on.

The Peasant's Lot

The literature of the Middle Ages consistently describes the lot of the peasants as hard almost beyond endurance. Despite the undoubted truth of these complaints, the people then had certain advantages. Society was much more settled and people were born, grew up and died in a close-knit community. There was one Church with a single faith which all men and women believed. The feast days of the Church were the only holidays (holy days) the people had but they were celebrated with tremendous enthusiasm. Unemployment was something unknown to that age.

The manor house, with its great hall, tithe barn and chapel, was the central point around which the life of the people revolved in feudal times. Also important were the giant dovecotes, one of which is seen in the drawing, where doves were reared to be killed for meat when there was a shortage of other food in winter.

By the fourteenth century in England the ordered state of society had begun to break up. The growth of the wool trade and the French wars had brought fresh sources of wealth to the country and the idea of belonging to one English nation. Money now entered much more freely into everyday life. Peasants were allowed to buy their freedom from compulsory work and lords found it more convenient to hire workers. A kind of early socialism was preached. 'When Adam delved (dug) and Eve span, who was then the gentleman?' asked John Ball, one of the leaders of Wat Tyler's rebellion against the King of England in 1381.

Medieval wagon drawn by oxen

A plan of strip cultivation of the land on a three-field system in which each field was rested in yearly rotation.

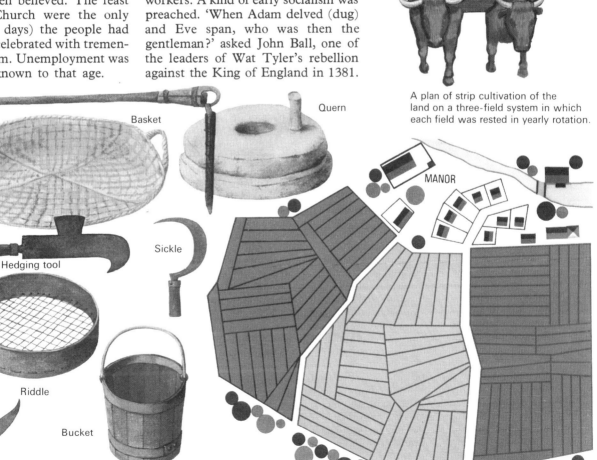

Flail

Basket

Quern

Hedging tool

Sickle

Riddle

Scythe

Bucket

MANOR

Towns and Trade

The growth of trade was the new factor which changed feudalism into modern society. The merchants and craftsmen represented a new middle class which bridged the gap between the lord and the peasant. The Church was no longer the only road to improvement for the poor boy. The knight, with his contempt for useful work and real ignorance about money, was now surpassed and outdated by the vigorous merchants who began to control the growing towns. Towns understood each other and soon worked together to make an international network of trade. The two supreme examples are the Hanseatic League in northern Europe and the part the wealth of the Medici played in the Italian Renaissance.

The Growth of Towns

It is not at all clear why towns were permitted to start in the first place or how they obtained the necessary permission. The sites were due to geographical position or custom. A port, a river crossing, or a mountain pass caused routes to focus at one point and there a town grew up. Sometimes a fair or a famous shrine brought traders and pilgrims.

These points where many people met brought the opportunity of a second income in trading goods and caring for travellers. Money as a means of exchange was increasingly used and the townsmen, banding together, could offer the overlord a fine sum for a charter giving them rights of self-government. In this way the towns were important in the

early fight for freedom. They were governed democratically in the general interest and many useful institutions were developed.

Commutation, which was the payment of money instead of performing feudal services, made money readily available to the nobility, who found taxes difficult to collect when they dwindled so surprisingly as they passed from hand to hand. Thus the whole situation was more fluid and once the towns had begun they flourished very quickly and trade began to be a rival to agriculture.

Merchants and Craftsmen

The charters once granted were rarely lost. The London apprentices were foremost in the fight for freedom as early as Magna Carta. When the early parliaments were summoned, they found it necessary to invite two burgesses from each large town in order to communicate the king's will to the people. Not only did the townsmen unite to deal with their overlord or king but they also worked out their own self-government very carefully in two types of guilds.

The merchant guilds were responsible for a whole trade, such as the

Carcassone (top) is a medieval walled town in south-west France. Built on the site of an old Roman city, parts of the town date from the seventh century. In the late 1800s the walls and towers were restored. Above is the ground plan of a typical medieval walled town and a section of a town house.

Heraldic arms of the Company of Merchant Adventurers of England, who ruled the export trade of England and held court in European towns.

The Company of the Merchants of the Staple of England. Their trade was the purchase and export of wool to the European continent.

The Company of Merchant Taylors in the City of York. This was made up of three craft guilds, the Tailors, Drapers and Hosiers.

The Hanseatic League was a powerful confederation of cities in North Germany. Shown here is the Hansa seal and flag, and a cog, a type of ship which originated in northern Europe.

goldsmiths. They organised themselves as a monopoly to keep all the business of their trade in their own hands. But within the trade their influence was very moral and just. The quality of goods and workmanship was guaranteed and a fair price was fixed for the product. The hallmarks used for gold and silver are still maintained today.

The craft guilds when they started dealt with very small units. The master was a man who knew his own trade thoroughly and taught it to apprentices and when they were fully skilled they became known as journeymen. Often they all lived together in the same house. The training and conditions of apprenticeship and the terms of employment were all set down in detail in the guild records and obeyed by master and man. But as the size of the trading unit grew larger, the interests of master and man drew apart. Today owners and trade unions sometimes have great difficulty in co-operating.

Civic Pride

The towns showed tremendous civic pride. Churches, hospitals and schools were endowed by the rich merchants. Almshouses were built and charity work of all kinds was sponsored in a fine community spirit. In England,

the rich wool villages of East Anglia and the Cotswolds still show how beautiful were the merchants' houses at the time. In Italy the wealth of the great banking families was enormous, particularly the Medici family who did so much for the Italian Renaissance, including the rebuilding of St Peter's Church in Rome. Church festivals were the only holidays then and they were enjoyed to the full. The guilds put on gorgeous pageants which included the production of early plays on a procession of carts.

In Europe the rise of the town was even more important, because in the torn and disrupted countries of

Germany and Italy the main progress of civilisation took place in the towns and cities with their superior political organisation. Florence, Milan and Venice are brilliant examples in Italy. In the north, many leading German and Baltic ports banded together to form the Hanseatic League. For two centuries before the great voyages of discovery, this league dominated trade in northern Europe. It had its own navy to defend its ships against pirates and once fought a war with the king of Denmark. Such leagues of merchants could dispute their rights with powerful rulers. The supremacy of the knight was over.

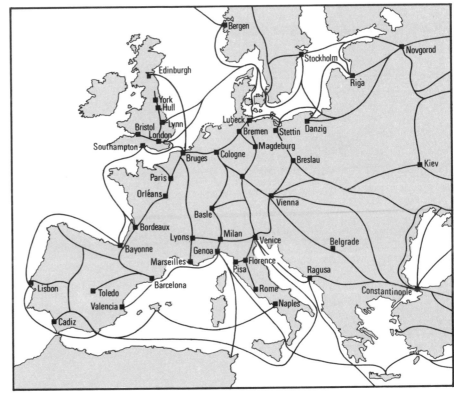

The network of trading routes between towns in the Middle Ages.

Cathedrals and Universities

The magnificent cathedrals of western Europe are the highest achievement of the medieval builder. In the twelfth and thirteenth centuries the Catholic Church was supreme. The Pope could challenge the Emperor and excommunicate kings. Under the papal banner, quarrelsome warriors rushed to fight for the cross against the heathen. New orders of monks and friars served the Church with the offering of their quiet, busy lives. All men and women had the same faith. The parish priest taught and cared for them, and their moral conduct was sternly supervised by church courts. The great cathedrals express the devout offering in stone which this Age of Faith made to the glory of God.

The cathedral was and is the chief church of the area where the bishop or archbishop had his throne. Of the oldest cathedrals in England, about half were run by priests and half by monks.

The medieval builder built as if he were building for eternity. The finest cathedrals are centuries old and they will outlast by centuries most things built today. The first cathedrals followed Roman models. The Norman ones were solidly built with very thick walls and massive pillars as if they were castles for the Church. The Gothic cathedrals which followed used larger windows with a pointed shape and less solid materials. This tendency was carried on in the Perpendicular cathedrals which are full of light and air. Ribbed vaulting for the high ceilings and buttresses to support the slender walls enabled the builders to use enormous windows and less and less stone. Beautiful stained glass was used of a quality later ages could not repeat.

Some cathedrals were built and rebuilt over a long period and have many styles while others, like Salisbury, in England are completely in one style. The superb cathedrals of Chartres, Rheims, Amiens and Paris in France were all built within a century. In those days, no other evidence of the force of religion in men's lives is needed than these magnificent churches raised lavishly by a small population.

Hunger for Knowledge

Another development of the Age of Faith was the university. The basic questions of existence seemed to work on men's minds like a ferment: which was most important—Church or State, this life or the next? There was a hunger for knowledge which broke out all over Christendom, particularly among the young. A new type of pilgrim thronged the roads in search of great teachers, passing from city to city and country to country. Latin was the universal language. Teaching was done without books and there were no grants. So the students were a law unto themselves, always arguing and fighting with authority. 'Town versus gown' riots were common but the sudden thirst for knowledge was deep and genuine. The rowdy poverty-stricken students were the sons of the middle class and the poor. The nobility disregarded learning and became cut off from the new influences.

The Friars were the new teaching orders who went out into the highways and byways to preach. Consequently they were often far more in touch with the ordinary people and they had a great deal to do with the founding of the universities. The Dominicans were founded on the need for learning and the Franciscans, after the death of St Francis, followed their example. The poverty of

St Francis of Assissi was a gay, rich young man who turned to the religious life after a severe illness. He believed in helping the poor and unfortunate. All his own money he gave away. He worked with his own hands to repair a ruined church which became the centre of his order. Simplicity and love formed the basis of his teaching. But so many men came to join him that against his wishes an order had to be formed to organise them. The later Franciscans grew wealthy and powerful and became famous for their learning.

This is the coat of arms of Walter de Merton who founded the most important of the first three colleges at Oxford. He was twice chancellor of England.

both orders recommended them to the half-starved students.

Origin of Universities

Universities originally were just groups of teachers and students in one place who organised themselves in order to teach and learn. The centre where such activity first took place was called a *studium generale* and at first was completely under Church control. The first charters licensed teachers and permitted schools to be formed which were not attached to cathedrals.

The study of Roman law had never quite died in Italy and the university of Bologna became the leading authority on law. Salerno had long studied medicine and had received great benefit from Jewish influence. Medicine and science at this time were a mixture of genuine knowledge and curious superstition. But the quality of the best minds of the Age of Faith cannot be doubted.

The university of Paris was born in the twelfth century and had the greatest influence throughout central Europe and Britain. The dazzling Peter Abelard did much to make Paris famous. The subjects taught concerned religion, law, medicine and the arts. It is thought that Oxford started as a university after an influx of students from Paris. Shortly afterwards, during the Becket dispute, a similar migration from Oxford started Cambridge. These universities had halls of residence which became the basis of modern colleges. Merton College (1264) was the first to use the now familiar quadrangle design. Central Europe and Scotland followed this early lead and the university became the centre of education for the future.

The earliest ceilings were based on a simple barrel vault designed from Roman models. When two vaults crossed at right angles, groin vaulting resulted.

In the next stage the ribbed vault and the pointed arch combined to form a new type, the Gothic arch. Durham Cathedral is a fine example of this type.

Further development led to an excessive degree of decoration. Some sections of the ceiling bays were cut away, leaving only the skeleton of the ribs.

Representation of a typical rose window, a feature of many of the cathedrals. The finest stained glass was produced during the twelfth and thirteenth centuries. Chartres Cathedral in France has some of the best examples.

This cut-away drawing illustrates the main features of a cathedral of the thirteenth century. The building is in the shape of a cross set out according to the four main points of the compass. The altar is placed against the east window, which looks towards Jerusalem where Christ died. The length of the building is divided by the rood screen into the nave and the chancel. The congregation sits in the nave before the pulpit and the choir on both sides of the chancel, facing each other in special stalls raised on steps. The chancel is subdivided by the altar rails which separate the altar area from the rest of the cathedral. In this building there is a central tower which carries the spire.

Nations at War

The Hundred Years War is the name given to the long struggle in the late Middle Ages which ended by separating the French and English peoples into two distinct nations.

One result of the Norman Conquest was that French kings sat on the throne of England. They had great possessions in France, often owning more land than the king who ruled from Paris. In England the Conquest had been efficient and permanent but in France the position of the king was very weak. He was surrounded by great dukes who were his rivals and who had no thought of loyalty to France as a country. When the English armies invaded France, they did so as allies of one or other of the great dukes. War for the English meant an exciting invasion abroad and the horrors of the Black Prince's campaigns were never experienced in England.

Although their rulers had much in common, France and England were already very different countries. France was much more feudal and very civilised. She had given the lead to Europe in chivalry and in the

reform of monasteries. But in both the arts of war and peace her leaders were curiously blind to the changes that were going on. The knights who fought for France at Crécy were feudal nobles who belonged to one privileged class. The English armies had knights, yeomen and archers who represented the whole nation. The French knights were easily brought down by the English archers or they impaled themselves on the stout stakes the archers had driven into the ground as a protection against cavalry charges. In this war, the English forces used artillery a hundred years before the French learned to copy them.

The Cost of War

The cost of these long campaigns was greater than the old manorial resources could support. Appallingly heavy taxes were laid on the long-suffering French peasants but they were collected so badly that only a fraction of the total sum ever reached Paris. In England, where the merchant class and important country

people were represented in parliament, taxes were collected more efficiently. Surprisingly, although the taxes were grumbled about, the war itself was popular with the people.

In order to build up their own kingdom, the French kings were obliged to attack lands owned by the English. Tension could not be avoided and the French aim was to drive the English out of their country into the sea. At this point, the royal house of Capet in France failed to produce a male heir for the first time for over

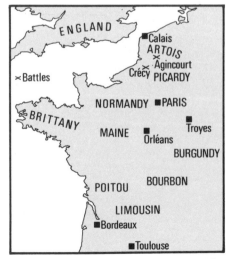

France during the Hundred Years War.

300 years. There was a serious dispute as to who should be king. Philip of Valois, a cousin, eventually came to the throne but the English king, Edward III, also claimed to be the true heir. These claims were based on the medieval custom of transferring a noble lady's land to her husband on marriage. But this typical medieval quarrel was strengthened by an economic one.

Philip was trying to bring under his control the rich province of Flanders and he made its count ban the export of finished cloth to England. Edward III replied by stopping supplies of raw wool. The power of trade was shown when the Flemish merchants preferred alliance with the English king to obedience to Philip.

Sluys and Crécy

The war started triumphantly for England. The first action, the battle of Sluys, took place at sea and gave England total command of the English Channel for thirty years. The wool trade flourished once more and wine was again imported from Bordeaux. France was invaded and at Crécy the lesson of the longbow was ruthlessly demonstrated to the French nobles. The military glory of France was overthrown and Petrarch, who visited the country at that time, was appalled at the extent of the destruction wrought by the English armies. The French king was captured and his ransom set at an enormous sum. The suffering was so great that even the French peasants revolted, only to be brutally crushed.

But the tide began to turn for France. Paris held out. The Treaty of Calais gave them a few years of peace and Bertrand du Guesclin, constable of France, avoided pitched battles with the English. Gradually he stripped them of all French territory except for three ports. But the French threw the victory away. Burgundy, which controlled Flanders, became the ally of England.

At this time, both France and England stood badly in need of peace, but Henry V came to the English throne full of military ambition. At Agincourt, the French were again defeated, but Henry was able to prove that he was a knightly hero. He married a French princess and was recognised as the heir to the French throne.

Fleur-de-lis means lily flower and is a well known heraldic emblem associated chiefly with the French monarchy. It is made up of three leaves banded together. In the centre is a large spear-like leaf and turning away from it, to the left and to the right, are two smaller leaves balancing the design. There are several variations but the emblem is easily recognised. It has been used widely in heraldry and for general ornamentation in France and England, but it is most famous for its connection with the royal arms of France. An old legend connects the lily of purity with Clovis, the fierce leader of the Franks, at a time when he was baptised and forsook his pagan past. Certainly it was adopted by the French kings in the twelfth century for use on coins, clothes and arms. Later the number of *fleur-de-lis* in one design was limited to three in honour of the Holy Trinity.

At last fortunes changed for the French. Burgundy changed sides and Henry was never crowned at Rheims. Soon he died, to be succeeded by the infant Henry VI. In France, Joan of Arc gave a moral upsurge to her country's flagging cause. The French king, Charles VII, was better served by his administration. In the field, his armies now used artillery. By 1453 the French forces were finally triumphant and the English adventuring in France was over. Henceforward the two countries, now fully conscious of nationhood, were to pursue separate and often hostile paths.

Castles and Weapons

The castles built by the kings and great nobles of the Middle Ages are as magnificent as the cathedrals. Starting from simple beginnings they grew larger and more complex until they became great stone structures. If these castles were defended by determined men, who had plenty of supplies, they could defy all besiegers.

The Normans increased their strong grip on England by building castles throughout the land. Apart from the White Tower of London, these first castles were not built of stone. They were called 'motte and bailey' castles and were fairly simple and easy to build wherever digging was possible. A high mound of earth was thrown up and a wooden fortification was built on top. The deep ditch left by the digging made the earth hill more difficult to attack. Round the foot of the mound a good-sized area, usually rectangular, was enclosed by another ditch and a stout fence. This area was known as the bailey. Under pressure, these small defensive forts could be constructed in a few weeks but they were sufficient to hold down the local inhabitants.

Stone Castles

Stone castles required much stronger foundations. Their sites were carefully chosen on hard rock, cliffs or natural hills which could take the great weight of materials. The walls of these castles could be nine metres (thirty feet) thick. Not only were they much stronger than the wooden ones but they could resist fire. The stone keep housed the defending garrison and was the place where the lord and his lady could live in some comfort. Communication between the floors of the keep was made by a narrow spiral staircase. In the event of an attack, each step had to be won against a defender occupying higher ground.

Castles grew steadily larger and more impressive. The four-square tower gave way to the stronger round one. Edward I of England built a chain of magnificent castles in north Wales which had strong walls with defensive towers at regular intervals. Within was another complete ring of walls. These walls within walls caused these castles to be called concentric, which means 'having a common centre'.

The sea coast was often used as a site for castle building. This gave added protection and enabled the castle to be supplied by ships in the event of a long siege. Farther inland, castles often had an artificial lake, or moat, around them. The attackers had to cross the water under severe fire and scale the walls or rush the gate. Should the first ring of walls be breached, the attackers were caught in a murderous crossfire between the two rings of walls.

The favourite method of attacking a castle had been to undermine it. Both fire and explosives could then be used to cause part of the wall to collapse. A great rush of soldiers would swarm through the breach. But the moat foiled attempts to undermine the castle and there could be no element of surprise when wall after wall had to be breached. From the safety of a great height, boulders and burning pitch could be hurled down on the attackers far below. Even much later castles were able to withstand siege artillery for months.

The Art of War

But the art of war was changing. The old method of raising an army for part-time service as a feudal duty did not meet the needs of a long campaign. Money was increasingly in use and soldiering became a separate paid trade. Mercenary leaders and their men became the first professional soldiers. Two new weapons had changed the balance between ordinary men and the armed knight. These were the longbow and the pike. Later the cannon and the hand-gun completed the new techniques by which the castle and the knight became outdated.

The longbow from the time of its

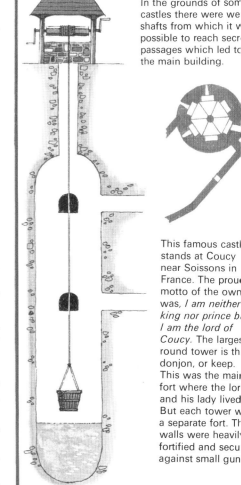

In the grounds of som castles there were we shafts from which it w possible to reach secr passages which led to the main building.

This famous cast stands at Coucy near Soissons in France. The prou motto of the own was, *I am neither king nor prince b. I am the lord of Coucy.* The larges round tower is th donjon, or keep. This was the mai fort where the lor and his lady lived But each tower w a separate fort. Th walls were heavil fortified and secu against small gun

discovery remained the most deadly hand weapon until the invention of the modern breech-loading rifle. The fully trained archer could send his heavy arrow 100 millimetres (4 inches) through an oak door. Plate armour reduced the risk to a knight but could not withstand a point-blank shot. To use horses against such fire-power was suicidal. Charges of cavalry were also hopeless against a solid wall of Swiss pikes. These weapons were not expensive, whereas the best armour required long and careful workmanship. The knights were now compelled to dismount in order to fight and the weight of their armour on wet ground made them dangerously clumsy.

Cannon were used as early as the fourteenth century. At first large missiles were fired but they were difficult to propel. As soon as it was learned that a much smaller ball moving very rapidly was more effective, the cannon became superior to the fortified place. A siege, which was once a matter of starving out the defenders for months, became a matter of days.

Early medieval cannon.

This drawing reconstructs the castle at Coucy as it appeared during the Middle Ages. At that time it was one of the most highly developed castles in France. On the left is a ground plan which shows the layout of the castle in more detail. Until heavy artillery was developed in the fourteenth century, such a castle was able to withstand normal siege tactics. A moat protected the outer walls from the tunnelling work of miners. The effect of battering rams and siege engines against the towers was greatly reduced by making the towers round instead of square. It was more difficult to strike an effective blow against a round surface than against a square one. When castles were well stocked with provisions and efficiently manned, attacks on them were almost always unsuccessful. Sieges could last for many months.

The Rise of Nations

By the thirteenth century it was clear that the dream of a united Christendom was not to be realised. Germany and Italy, the countries which had most to do with the Holy Roman Empire, were sadly disunited and played no part in the new movement towards nationhood. The Electors, or princes, of Germany did not use their position to appoint a true German emperor but always chose a ruler whose main territories were not inside the German Reich.

In 1273 they chose Rudolf of Habsburg, a Swiss noble, to be emperor and thereby laid the foundations of two European nations. He was not interested in Italy but preferred to use his power in the conquest of Austria, which he made the centre of a mighty empire that lasted until the present century.

Swiss Rebels

The Swiss people at this time were oppressed by their local feudal lords and totally ignored by their distant emperor. They decided to resist and by so doing became the first free people in Europe. The Habsburgs hated the Swiss rebels but failed to tame this hardy race. For two centuries the Swiss fought on until their late masters decided to leave them alone. Thus they became the first country to be free from kings and nobles. They used this political liberty wisely and became a refuge to which the less fortunate could run from their oppressors.

There was a great German achievement to the east at this time. The Baltic nations were being brought into the European community by the work of the Hanseatic League, which

banded together all the great ports of the north in common trade. Also, Prussia was conquered by the long service of the Teutonic knights and added to the west. But the main benefit of these extensions of German influence was to be felt in the future. Nationhood was to be denied to the Germans until the nineteenth century.

Moorish Spain

In the west the old Roman province of Spain was divided between the small string of Christian kingdoms in the north and the Moslem territory in the centre and south. Until the eleventh century, the Emirs ruling from Cordova had a much superior way of life to the poor Christian kingdoms in the north. The Moors had learned from the civilisation of the Arabs much of the science and knowledge of the past, combining it with what remained of Roman tradition. Irrigation made agriculture prosperous and the dry land was decorated with fountains. The Moors were very tolerant of other faiths. Jews and many Christians preferred to live in the south. Suddenly strife broke out among the Moors, and the Emirs disappeared in favour of a republic. This change occurred at the time of the Crusades and the knights of Spain were inspired to make a great advance southward into Moorish territory.

Spain is a difficult country to unite because of its mountainous and forbidding terrain. But Pope Innocent III managed to persuade the proud knights of the small kingdoms of Portugal, Castile, Navarre and Aragon to fight together against the heathen Berbers. Within fifty years the Berbers were driven back into Granada where they managed to maintain a small kingdom safely behind the mountains.

The unity of Spain progressed no further at that time until the discovery of the new world brought her new wealth and great power.

Early Russia

Far to the east the experience of the vast empty land of Russia had been very different from the lands of Christendom. The Norsemen, who had come with Ruric and his successors, remained fighters and traders and had no time for agriculture. They made Kiev the chief centre and brought the Russians into touch with Constantinople. Consequently, the ruler at that time, Vladimir I, became a Christian of the Greek Orthodox type about the year 1000. Fortunately the Greek Church used the native language in its services and introduced some learning and knowledge of law to the Russians. But the Principality of Kiev was weakened by family quarrels.

This early Russia was overrun by

Alexander Nevsky (1218–63) Russian prince and hero in battle.

The rise of Russia as a nation in the sixteenth century.

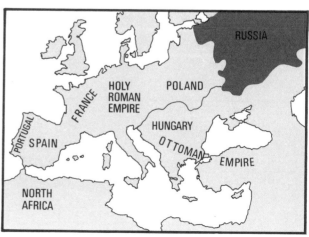

King Richard II of England confronts the rebel Wat Tyler. The Lord Mayor of London feared for the king's safety and killed Tyler. The young king then rode out to the peasants and offered himself as their leader.

the Tartars, a Mongol people led by the terrifying Genghis Khan. The country was saved from extinction only by the harsh extremes of climate. A faction of these invaders broke away from the main body and ruled the Russian steppes for 200 years, as the Golden Horde. Even the great ruler Alexander Nevsky, who prospered against Russia's enemies in the west, could not withstand these Mongols.

The Grand Dukes of Moscow now rose to importance. They served the Tartars abjectly, but cunningly used their masters' power against their fellow Russians. Moscow became the head of Church and State. The city was founded on agriculture by those refugees who had trekked into the deep forest for safety from invaders.

In the fourteenth century Russia was attacked and dominated in the west by Lithuanians with Polish help. This conquest had an important effect on later Russian history. Little Russia in the west had different ideas and ways of life from Great Russia in the east. Holy Moscow was the link in between. At this point, Tamerlane broke the Golden Horde and soon afterwards the Turks took Constantinople, making Russia the leader of the Greek Orthodox Church. The way was now prepared for Ivan the Great (1462–1505) to become the first Czar.

The British Isles

In the British Isles, Wales gradually became more firmly united with

The German Order of Teutonic Knights was created by the crusades. Some merchants from Bremen and Lubeck were appalled by the sufferings of the crusaders at Acre. They decided to found a hospital for their care. This new monastic order adopted the same rules as the Knights Hospitallers of St John and soon obtained the support of emperor and pope. A Polish duke then invited them to assist in the struggle against Prussia and they began the work for which they have become famous. They linked with the Brethren of the Sword and the two orders were responsible for the conversion of Prussia and the Baltic states. These states soon asserted themselves and only the support of the King of Poland allowed the knights to hold their position. Later their power declined.

England. Welsh archers fought with the English armies in the French wars. But the demands of the French campaigns allowed the Scots to keep their independence, so dearly won by William Wallace and Robert Bruce. Ireland, even then, remained subdued but unconquered.

In the fifteenth century, the nobles of the houses of York and Lancaster fought for the succession to the throne until they had virtually destroyed themselves. This fortunate deliverance paved the way for the great Tudor line.

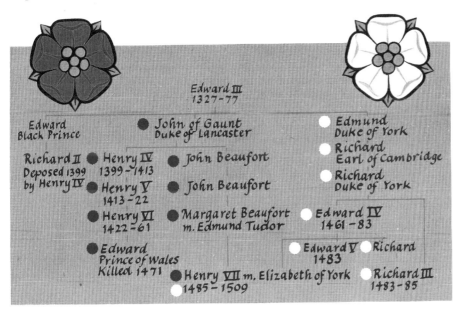

Edward III 1327-77

Edward Black Prince

John of Gaunt Duke of Lancaster

Edmund Duke of York

Richard II Deposed 1399 by Henry IV

Henry IV 1399-1413

John Beaufort

Richard Earl of Cambridge

Henry V 1413-22

John Beaufort

Richard Duke of York

Henry VI 1422-61

Margaret Beaufort m. Edmund Tudor

Edward IV 1461-83

Edward Prince of Wales Killed 1471

Edward V 1483

Richard

Henry VII m. Elizabeth of York 1485-1509

Richard III 1483-85

The Black Death

The growing number of people who lived in towns in the Middle Ages brought new hazards to the health of the community. Plague was a constant visitor to the narrow streets of medieval towns, with their primitive sanitary arrangements. Plague was dreaded by all for no one knew how to contain its ravages. But an epidemic in the fourteenth century, called the Black Death, was of such crisis proportions that it shattered the western world.

The plague came from China along the medieval trade routes and attacked the whole of Europe from Scandinavia to the Mediterranean and from Constantinople to Britain. Accurate figures are hard to give for those days but it is estimated that twenty-five million people died in Europe. Ships floated helplessly at sea without crews. Animals wandered untended in neglected fields. Monasteries and similar institutions, where many people were herded together, suffered most severely.

The plague manifested itself in black spots and boils, and seemed to prefer the young and the strong. It struck most severely in the years 1347 and 1348 but recurred twice more before the end of the century. Both in England and France it caused so great a labour shortage that the decay of the old feudal system of agriculture was hastened. The panic which swept the afflicted countries took wildly exaggerated forms. Some people were convinced that the end of the world was at hand and scourged themselves publicly for their sins so that they might be saved. Others decided to make the most of things while life lasted and lost all they had in riotous living. But when the plague had spent itself and passed on, life resumed its normal, steady pattern.

The English Parliament
The French wars brought many benefits to England indirectly. The nation had found itself in the long struggle and was now proudly English. The excellent legal system begun by Henry II and Edward I was firmly established and accepted by all the nation. The wars had been very expensive and Parliament had to be called frequently to vote supplies. When the wars were over the voice of Parliament could no longer be ignored. Those who paid taxes in England could now expect to have some say in the running of the country.

Edward III was as careful for English trade as he was eager for success in war. England was the greatest producer of wool in Europe but the manufacture of finished cloth was very slight. The great mass of raw material was exported to the Low Countries for manufacture. But now the king took advantage of the war situation to invite Flemish weavers to come to work in the British Isles.

One famous weaver, John Kempe, brought his workmen from Flanders across to Norwich and set up his business there. The cloth trade, with plentiful supplies of raw wool ready to hand, flourished marvellously. Many of the beautiful houses built by the wool merchants, and the churches which they endowed, still grace the old wool towns of East Anglia and the Cotswolds. They prove how prosperous the new merchant class had become.

Geoffrey Chaucer
The wave of patriotism which swept England caused all things French to become unpopular. Thus after three centuries of underground existence the native English language once again rose to the surface and became the tongue of the whole nation. The royal court, the law courts, and the schools now spoke English from choice and there was an outburst of fine literature which produced Geoffrey Chaucer as its most famous representative. Chaucer enriched the English language with French words but the main part remained firmly English. His greatest work was *The Canterbury Tales*. The tales are a convenient framework to give a vivid picture of social life in fourteenth-century England.

A new feature of international life at this time was the rise of banking. The medieval knight considered arms

as the only fitting profession for a gentleman. He had no interest in trade. Consequently, he had no understanding of the way in which money worked. When he needed to finance a new castle or a long war, he had to place himself in the hands of others. The position was made more difficult by the teaching of the Church.

With the best of intentions, the Church had forbidden Christians to lend money to their fellow Christians in order to gain interest. On a small scale the teaching no doubt worked well. But now large sums were required and no one was prepared to lend so much without some reward for the risk and the service. The Jews and the Lombards took advantage of their religious freedom to offer this service and so became the masters of early banking.

Italian Bankers
Italy was the first country to challenge the Jewish supremacy in international money and all Italians in banking were likely to be called Lombards. This was the way in which the famous banking street in London received its name. Several of the great city states of Italy became famous for banking but none more so than Florence. The

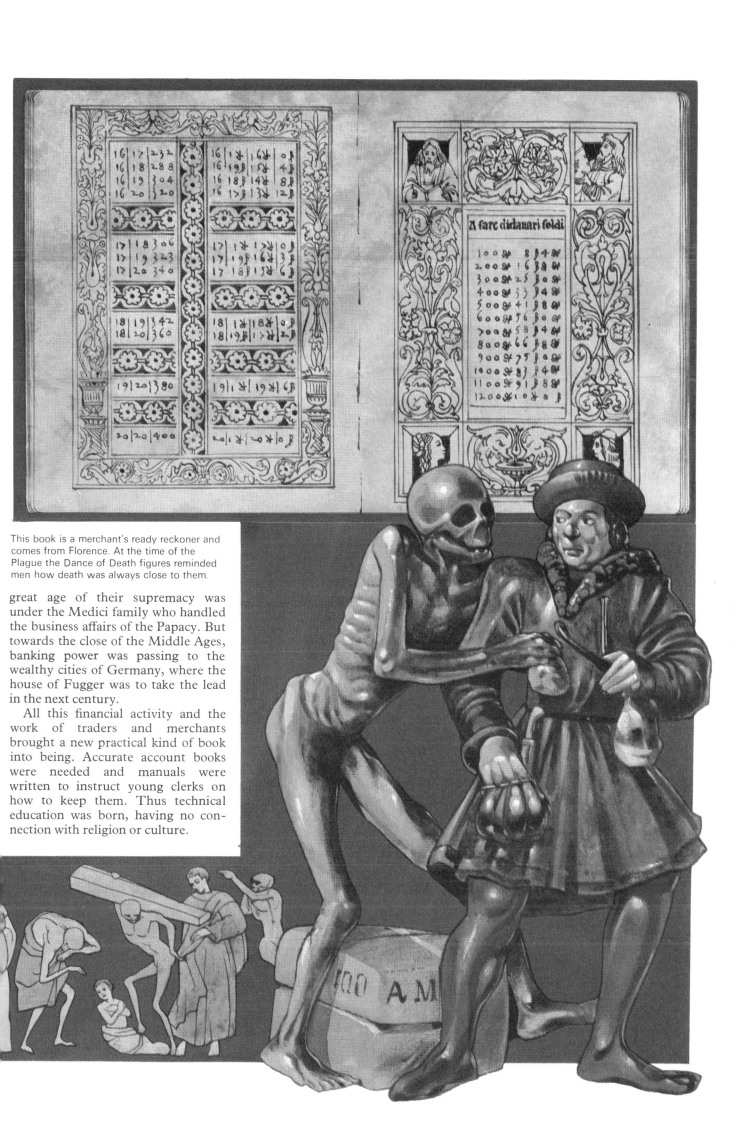

This book is a merchant's ready reckoner and comes from Florence. At the time of the Plague the Dance of Death figures reminded men how death was always close to them.

great age of their supremacy was under the Medici family who handled the business affairs of the Papacy. But towards the close of the Middle Ages, banking power was passing to the wealthy cities of Germany, where the house of Fugger was to take the lead in the next century.

All this financial activity and the work of traders and merchants brought a new practical kind of book into being. Accurate account books were needed and manuals were written to instruct young clerks on how to keep them. Thus technical education was born, having no connection with religion or culture.

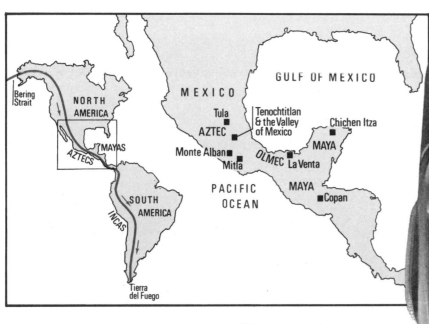

Early American Peoples

No traces of primitive man have been found in the New World of the Americas. There are no remains of the ape-like ancestors from which man probably developed. The earliest traces of human occupation there date from Neolithic, or New Stone Age, times about 12,000 years ago, although many scientists think that settlement was much earlier, possibly 40,000 years ago.

If man in the New World did not evolve there, where did he come from? It is believed with some confidence that groups of human beings crossed from Asia into America at a time when the waters of the Bering Strait, which separates Alaska from Siberia, were covered with ice. Another theory about the geography of the area is that there may have been an actual land bridge between the continents. Other people from Mongolia may have crossed the sea in boats to land at various points lower down the coast. Over a long period these pre-historic people moved gradually southwards, some settling at different places along the way and others pushing on until they reached the central areas of South America. The earliest civilisations grew up in the warm regions of southern Mexico, Central America and Peru.

Early Migrations
The first people to live in the Americas left Asia before any of the great civilisations of that continent had developed. So, naturally, they came without knowledge of the later

This stone head made by the Olmec people, the first major civilisation of the New World, has a mask-like expression typical of their sculpture.

achievements of those civilisations. They were perhaps weaker tribes who had been pushed up into the in-hospitable top corner of Asia by their enemies. Seeking new and better lands, or because they were forced to do so, they made the journey from one continent to the other with no idea of where they were going.

The many and varied types of people that developed in the Americas are probably an indication that migration from Asia was gradual, taking perhaps 20,000 years or more, and that successive waves of differing Asian types entered the continent. This length of time, the changes wrought by mixed breeding between races, the natural survival of the fittest and the effects of environment, account for the distinction between, for example, the American Indian and the Eskimo. The other great racial groups which make up the American people today—the European and the African Negro—came into the country as immigrants or as slaves.

It was Christopher Columbus who first gave the people of the Americas the name 'Indians'. When the great explorer landed on one of the Caribbean islands in 1492 he thought he had found his way to the eastern shores of the Asian sub-continent of India, and so he called the people he met 'Indians'. Other early explorers

called the Indians 'redskins', because of their reddish-brown skins; but they are not really red, nor do they have anything to do with India. In the languages of the American Indians there is no word which describes all of them collectively, since they never thought of themselves in this way but only as people split up into lots of different tribes.

Two Main Societies
The two main societies of early American people, one in Central and the other in South America, grew up independently from the Old World, and from each other. In Asia there were always links and some inter-change of ideas between the different civilisations. But in America the people of each group did not even know that the rest of the world existed. Many of the things which seemed to evolve naturally in the Asiatic civilisations did not come to light in America. There was no domestication of large animals, crops were different, and there were no wheeled vehicles—for no one had invented the wheel, or at least found a use for it.

At Labna, once a major city of the ancient Mayas, the most imposing relic is this arched gateway.

When the Spanish *conquistadores* of the sixteenth century made their separate ways to confront the Aztec and Inca civilisations, men of two entirely different cultures with no previous knowledge of each other met face to face. It had never happened before and could never happen again. The result, unhappily, was a tragedy for both Aztecs and Incas. Within a few years their empires were destroyed. Millions of people died, in battle, or from starvation and disease, or as captive slaves.

The Olmecs

One of the earliest civilisations in America was that of the Olmec people, whose origins are uncertain. They settled in lands facing the Gulf of Mexico about 1000 B.C. They worshipped a jaguar figure, which was apparently regarded as the dread spirit of the jungle.

At different places near Mexico City the Olmecs built the first crude pyramid structures which were to become the typical temple buildings of the whole area. On one of these sites the great city of Teotihuacán grew up between A.D. 300 and 700. Much of it remains as well-preserved ruins and the eighteen square kilometres (seven square miles) of pyramids and avenues form one of the most spectacular sights in all America. The city was carefully planned, dominated by the Pyramid of the Sun, 210 metres (700 feet) square at its base. All the ceremonial buildings were grouped around the broad three-kilometre (two-mile) long Avenue of the Dead. The larger pyramids were earth mounds, covered with sun-dried bricks and smooth lime plaster.

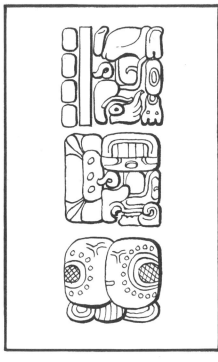

Maya hieroglyphics were an ancient form of writing which has been only partly deciphered. They combine a system of dots, bars, faces and hands and were used to record events and their dates. On the right is a Maya date stone erected to mark the passing of time.

The Mayas

Occupying a large area of Honduras and Guatemala were the Mayas. They have been called the Greeks of Middle America for they were skilled above all others in arts, crafts and mathematics. The classic Maya period was between A.D. 300 and 900 when hundreds of pyramid buildings were erected in the jungles of the district. Their most characteristic building is the steep-sided thirty-metre (hundred-foot) high temple at Tikal.

Many Maya cities have been cleared of undergrowth and restored, particularly at such places as Copán in Honduras and Chichén Itzá in Yucatán. Their culture, hieroglyphic writing and magnificent carved statues inscribed with mathematical calculations, are still a puzzle to archaeologists. They were a highly intelligent, peaceful people with a respect for customs and tradition. When they collapsed, their reasoned society was to give way to one that was more powerful, harsh and vigorous.

Aztec noblemen dressed in splendid costumes to take part in ceremonial processions in honour of the emperor Montezuma.

Central America

The fall of Teotihuacán was violent. The barbarian Chichimec tribe looted and burned the city and massacred its people. For the next 300 years there followed a Dark Age, out of which sprang the most famous and feared people of ancient Mexico—the Aztecs. They were descended from the Chichimecs, as were the Toltecs, an earlier race.

About the year A.D. 970 the Toltecs rose to power and dominated the valleys of Middle America from their capital city Tula. By the end of the tenth century they had taken control of most of Mexico. They revived the old Maya centres of Yucatán and Chichén-Itzá and turned them into beautiful cities.

Topiltzin's Prediction

One of the first Toltec leaders was responsible for the prediction which contributed to the fall of the vast Aztec nation before a handful of Spanish soldiers. He was Topiltzin, who changed his name to Quetzalcoatl when he came to power. This has led to natural confusion between Topiltzin/Quetzalcoatl the man and Quetzalcoatl the Mexican god, particularly after Topiltzin's death, when the two figures became merged in legend.

Quetzalcoatl, the Feathered Serpent, was on the whole a kindly and benevolent god and was worshipped as the bringer of civilisation. But the fierce Toltecs introduced other gods and turned away from Quetzalcoatl. The gentle Topiltzin was forced to abdicate and he spent twenty years in

exile. The pattern of his later life is lost in legend. There are many romantic versions of his end but all are agreed on one thing. Topiltzin vowed to return to his people in the form of the god Quetzalcoatl—coming from the direction of the rising sun—and even specified the exact year in which this would happen. In terms of the European calendar this was 1519—by an extraordinary coincidence the fateful year in which Cortés and his troops landed in Mexico. The Aztecs were used to complete submission to the traditional utterances of their religion, and many regarded the Spaniards as gods, with magic powers that could not be resisted.

The Aztecs

The Aztecs made their first appearance about the beginning of the thirteenth century after the fall of the Toltec empire. They were wandering tribes who roamed across the plateau of Anáhuac, now the Valley of Mexico. In 1325 they founded a permanent home at a place called Tenochtitlán. This was to become the capital city of the Aztec empire and later the site of present-day Mexico City. Tenochtitlán was built on land

reclaimed from the shallow waters of Lake Texcoco. It consisted of canals, aqueducts and raised streets of hard earth—a Venice of the New World. The Aztecs chose this unusual spot because their chief god Huitzilopochtli had decreed that they should build their new city at a place marked by a cactus plant growing from a rock on which an eagle was perched with a snake in its beak. Unlikely as it may seem, this weird assortment of omens is said to have been found in the middle of Lake Texcoco.

At first the Aztecs were a subject race, employed as mercenary fighters by the Nahua people. But the newcomers were so savage in battle that everyone soon learned to fear them. By the middle of the fifteenth century they controlled the whole Mexican valley and beyond. The Aztecs were people of quite unusual ferocity, with a genius for organisation which enabled them to knit together and rule all the independent tribes of Mexico.

The Aztecs were dominated by their religion and the hunger of the god Huitzilopochtli for human sacrifice. The sun, which Huitzilopochtli controlled, would not rise unless a

Summary of key dates
c. 496 Settlement at Chichen Itza
970 Toltecs rise to power
c. 1000 Second Mayan empire
1325 Tenochtitlán founded
1502 Montezuma II becomes emperor of the Aztecs
1520 Cortés conquers Mexico
1526 Pizarro reaches Peru
1531 Death of Atahualpa, Inca chief

regular diet of human hearts was offered up afresh each day. The fervour with which the Aztecs served the god's wish was seen in the grim towers of skulls which stood beside their temples. The religion of the Aztecs was the bloodiest and most terrible ever devised by man. When the Aztecs went to war, their chief aim was to take prisoners who could be offered as sacrifices to the gods. Tens of thousands of victims were killed each year. When human hearts were offered to the gods the Aztecs were rewarded with fresh victories, which led to more sacrifices and more victories. It was a vicious circle of death. The Aztecs were efficient farmers and good governors, but they ruled against a background of slaughter in their magnificent city of Tenochtitlán.

A reconstruction of the Temple of Quetzalcoatl, the Feathered Serpent, at Teotihuacán, the great Aztec city in central Mexico planned by master architects.

The metal figure of an alpaca, the animal which the Inca raised for wool, and a stone head of a god.

The Inca Empire

In South America lay the empire of the Inca built on the ruins of earlier civilisations. It had existed for only about a hundred years before Pizarro and his invading Spaniards smashed it in 1533 and killed its leader Atahualpa. The traditional legends of the Inca only begin with their own history and go no further back than the eleventh century A.D. But Peru has a long history, about which very little is known. As the Peruvians had no written language their history can only be pieced together by the archaeologist as he examines ancient sites and the objects found in them.

The figure on this Inca plaque holds a bolas, a missile which was hurled to trap an animal

Even here, there are no monuments with carved inscriptions to decipher, no clay tablets, no records of any kind, only stone buildings, pottery and textiles.

The Inca empire at its greatest extended from the north of present-day Ecuador 4,000 kilometres (2,500 miles) to the south and included parts of Peru, Bolivia, Chile and Argentina. Its people lived on a strip of land which followed the line of the Andes mountains and bordered the Pacific Ocean. Geographically it was a land of enormous contrasts, ranging from hot, waterless deserts near the sea to the snow-capped, 6,000-metre (20,000-foot) high mountains which enclosed fertile valleys and supported high, arid plains. People settled there about 11,000 years ago and well organised villages existed by 1500 B.C.

Village Communities

These early people lived by fishing and cultivating grain and other crops. Unlike their counterparts in Middle America, the Peruvians had tame, domesticated animals at some stage in their development. The alpaca and the llama were carefully bred from wild stock; the alpaca for its woolly fleece and the llama as a pack animal. It is also of interest that there appears to have been a jaguar-god cult in South America which some archaeologists have seen as an historical link with the Olmecs of Middle America, although there is no real evidence that the two races had any contact with each other.

Before the Inca there existed many individual civilisations over this vast and varied land. The remains of their buildings still exist and many objects in a remarkable state of preservation have been dug up. Two of these peoples were the Nazca and the Mochica, who made beautiful pottery vessels and built great ceremonial pyramids. They are believed to have died out about A.D. 600 to be replaced by a new culture centred on Tiahuanaco, near the borders of Peru and Bolivia. This city is now an enormous ruin but from it ruled the first people to have power over the whole of Peru. Their empire is believed to have lasted until the eleventh century.

Pachacuti

The true founder of the Inca empire was Pachacuti, who came to the throne in 1438. The authority of the Inca was based on a strong army. Their rule was humane and their method of conquest was by persuasion, although those tribes who refused to co-operate were treated savagely enough. Religion was not the supreme authority in Peru, but good government was. It was well organised and supported by a complex system of communication, with trained teams of relay runners who carried messages and instructions to every corner of the land. Perhaps the most remarkable thing about the Inca empire during its greatest period was the fact that it functioned efficiently for over a hundred years without either of the two things which other societies found they could not do without: for the Inca had no system of writing, and money, or any other conventional system of exchange, was unknown.

Renaissance and Reformation

As the Middle Ages drew to a close in Europe, the spirit of change invaded every corner of men's lives. Already the rise of trade and nationhood had shattered the old feudal framework. Now new ideas began to alter the way in which men thought and even what they believed. The shape of the earth, man's position in the universe, and the truth of the teaching of the Catholic Church were all challenged at the same time. The age-old certainties suddenly became a matter for agonising doubt. The result of all this mental turmoil gave birth to the thinking of the modern world and our present way of life.

Since Roman times, education had been in the hands of the Church. In the face of great difficulties and constant danger the servants of the Church preserved learning and taught the barbarians how to read and write. Without that essential basis, little could have been done. But the Church kept study within strict limits. Religion dominated all that was done and any questions from inquiring minds, which threw doubt on existing ideas, were sternly repressed. The Renaissance and the Reformation between them changed this constricted world for ever.

Greek began to be taught in fourteenth-century Italy and that spirit of free inquiry which had led Athens to the heights of mental daring was once more free to influence the minds of the West. Soon the number of people who wanted to know the answer to everything that they could not understand was vastly increased. Where no answers were immediately

forthcoming, they determined to search for truth by study and experiment until they had unearthed it. This new spirit of inquiry, together with its wonderful achievements, is called the Renaissance. The word means re-birth. It is fair to the inquiring minds of earlier days to point out that many isolated figures, such as Peter Abelard in the twelfth century, had pointed the way.

Church Reform

The ideas of the Church were not the only matters under attack. The enormous power of the Church in the Age of Faith had led to the amassing of great wealth. Slackness and corruption had crept in with a long period of easy living. Those Christians with stricter views pointed to the simple life as lived by Christ and his apostles in the gospels, and demanded reform. Some of these devout people wanted to reform the old Church, which they loved, from the inside. Others thought the position so hopeless that only a fresh start could return Christianity to its original simple path. In a way both had their will. The Protestants, who were making a 'protest' against the Church and all her ways, broke away and formed their own independent churches while the reformers, who wished to remain Catholic, worked to restore the shattered Church to its former standards.

The men and women who found themselves in this new world of a divided Church were, of course, also the men and women who experienced

all the other changes going on at the time. A wealthy trading class now had independence and alertness of mind. New-fledged nations found it to their advantage to side with Catholic or Protestant to serve their political interest. Bitter warfare broke out, and the nations who had remained Catholic sought unsuccessfully to reconquer the Protestants by force of arms. From all this confusion, a remarkably clear pattern emerged. The line of division between Catholic and Protestant followed roughly the old frontier of the Roman Empire. The north of Europe became Protestant and broke away, following its racial and language grouping. The south, the original lands of the western Roman Empire, remained true to the Catholic Church and the Latin language. The division has remained decisive ever since.

Men of Imagination

The Renaissance had a more unifying effect. The new scientists and scholars made truth their only standard. What was not known had to be discovered. Men of great imagination suggested possible explanations but these were then tested by practical experiment and only those which stood up to this rigorous test were accepted. Personality, liking and prejudice did not come into it. Their early apparatus showed the simplicity of genius. Galileo dropped weights from the leaning tower of Pisa to study the acceleration of falling bodies. Copernicus cut slits in the walls of his house to mark the swing of the stars.

Three leading figures of the colourful and dramatic years of the Renaissance. In turn, they represent outstanding beauty, political intrigue, and great artistic achievement.

Isabella D'Este

Cesare Borgia

Michelangelo

The Italian Renaissance

The Renaissance was one of those great flowerings of the human spirit which have occurred only a few times in the whole history of civilisation. It began in fourteenth-century Italy and flourished for some two hundred years. The Renaissance was essentially a rediscovery of the traditions of Greece and Rome. But the intense intellectual activity it created invaded every department of life. There had been earlier revivals in the days of Charlemagne and again in Abelard's Paris, but they were as nothing to the broad flood which now swept Italy. The old world of Latin Christianity in France, Spain and South Germany was the most strongly influenced by the Renaissance. In the succeeding years, the new spirit also crossed the Alps and influenced countries in the north but there the full impact of new ideas was lessened by the puritan spirit of the Reformation.

Italy was a divided land at this time. The Papal States lay across the middle of the country cutting it in half. Four other rich cities contended with Rome for supremacy in Italian affairs: Venice, Milan, Florence and Naples. Although Milan in the north and Naples in the south threatened to become dominant, Florence was to become the very heart of the Renaissance movement, a city of unparalleled beauty and great wealth.

It was not a peaceful time although there were no major conflicts. But the condottieri, mercenary professional soldiers, fought each other in the interests of the rival states. Even the Papacy of those days, under the Borgia popes, sought to extend its territory by war. Danger and cruelty went hand in hand with an acute love of beauty and extreme sensitivity.

Grandeur of Rome

It was fitting that Italy should be the leader in the Renaissance for the remains of the grandeur of Rome were to be seen all over her land. But the renewed interest in Greek had most to do with the new spirit of free inquiry. The pressure of the Turks on eastern Europe was building up to the final destruction of Constantinople, the last bastion of the eastern Roman Empire. It was not difficult to persuade Greek teachers that they had a brighter future in Italy and they came in increasingly greater numbers.

Suddenly the view of life became outward-looking and expansive. Man himself became important, not the poor sinful creature of the Middle Ages but a being with the possibility of power and dignity. The confident

Andrea Verrocchio's powerful statue of Bartolommeo Colleoni, the captain general of the Venetian armies, stands in St Mark's square in Venice.

men of the Renaissance were attracted to personal glory and expected to receive the reward of their labours in this world. This robust, aggressive spirit was very different from that of the generations of nameless craftsmen who had built the great Gothic cathedrals.

The merchant princes of this age brought a new figure into existence, the patron. No longer did the noble disdain art and science, instead he was eager to use some of his wealth to sponsor the work of genius. The Church remained the greatest patron and, despite the worldly outlook of Renaissance men, the majority of the works of art have a religious subject.

Universal curiosity about everything produced a new kind of all-round genius, the man who could do almost everything. Three men,

Alberti, Leonardo and Michelangelo, were so gifted in many directions that we can only stand in awe at their achievements. They embrace so much of the ideals of the age.

Alberti was a fine athlete and horseman. He also wrote extensively on architecture and built churches. He was distinguished as a writer, musician and painter. Practical engineering and science also engaged his attention.

Leonardo was the Aristotle of his time. In the front rank of world artists, he was a painter, sculptor and architect. His interest in everything is recorded in notebooks which survive. They are curiously written from right to left, in shorthand and without punctuation. In these secret notes he shows his interest in anatomy, the movement of planets,

One of the many fine Renaissance palaces in Rome, the Palazzo dei Conservatore.

fossils in rocks, mechanics, perspective, and the principles of flight. He was a famous engineer both for military matters and civil needs, such as canals and irrigation. This brief list gives some idea of the towering ability of this one Renaissance figure. He worked under the patronage of both Lorenzo the Magnificent of Florence and Ludovico Sforza of Milan.

Michelangelo

Michelangelo did most of his work in Florence and Rome. He painted the Sistine Chapel and designed the dome for the new Church of St Peter. His sculptures are magnificent portrayals of human power and splendour. During the last years of his long life he produced tender madrigals and sonnets.

Renaissance costume for both men and women was rich and colourful. At the foot of the page is a sixteenth-century Italian lute.

The beginnings of the Italian Renaissance are often considered to start with the painter Giotto and the writers, Dante, Petrarch and Boccaccio. Giotto painted religious pictures but made the people in his work natural human beings and thus pointed the way to a more humanistic art. Dante wrote the greatest religious poem of the Christian era, the *Inferno*, but he also had a major share in forming the new melodious Italian language from the various dialects of Italy.

121

The Spread of Learning

The restless curiosity which was so marked a feature of the Renaissance affected every branch of human activity. There was now a compelling need to know. The first Greek and Roman books to be translated were concerned with the way gentlemen lived in classical times. When that aspect had been satisfied, the reading of the old books did not stop. Greek mathematics and science were taken up just as enthusiastically by the lovers of culture. As a result, the old Greek spirit of free inquiry was once again applied to the physical universe and to man himself.

Man became the centre of attraction and the head of creation. The sculptors turned to living models of youth and power. Attractive women were used by painters as models for the Virgin Mary. The Greek care for the body on equal terms with the mind brought a renewed interest in sport.

Libraries

As a symbol of the new thirst for learning, libraries became fashionable in the homes of the wealthy. Cosimo de' Medici invited Greek scholars to settle in Florence and his grandson, Lorenzo the Magnificent, spent £60,000 a year on his library. Rare manuscripts were rediscovered and collected. What was now needed was a method by which this valuable information could be distributed and shared. The need brought its solution in the invention of printing.

The first printers tried to imitate the writing of the manuscripts which they were copying. They were conscious of the beauty of these early books and they sought to make their own work comparable. They succeeded so well that many of the first printed books are works of art by reason of their fine craftsmanship. The Aldine Press, founded in Venice by Aldus Manutius, issued a series of reproductions of the classics which were of a handy size, cheap, pleasing to the eye, and accurate in their scholarship. The day of the great, cumbersome folio volume had passed in favour of the portable book.

The optimistic and confident ideas of the Renaissance which made man once again a figure of power and dignity are called Humanism. Looking back to classical times, men now had a strong sense of history, of belonging to what had been done in the past and of responsibility to carry it forward into the future. The city-states of Greece in many ways were not unlike the city-states of Renaissance Italy. It was fascinating to read how the Greeks had run their affairs so differently and how they had solved their problems. The study of politics, which means strictly the way in which cities are governed, was renewed with keen interest. Such studies led Machiavelli to write his book *The Prince* which coldly analyses, but with approval, the methods of gaining and holding political power in the days of the ambitious Borgias.

The Humanists believed that man could be improved by reason and therefore they gave great attention to education. Latin and Greek were the central core of their studies and the necessity to master these difficult tongues required many teachers and grammarians. Hence the foundation of grammar schools to meet the need. The other chief subjects studied were history, the lessons of the past, and ethics, the great debate over what is right and what is wrong in human conduct. These liberal studies, designed to produce the best type of free man, have dominated education until the present century.

The best examples of this thinking, both in Renaissance Italy and later in Tudor England, were very impressive. These 'all-round' men were physically well trained and proficient

Johann Gutenberg
1397–1468

Aldus Manut
1450–1575

quē prōiat furgūt iūip ho uſtoꝫ·

fer boiem fignificās uiuere qu

Jo in V tention mation

in arms and horse-riding. They were highly educated for the business of the state. In their private lives, they were cultured to a high standard in the writing of poetry and the performance of music. There seemed to be no end to their ability. But these outstanding human beings were exceptional and few people had the ability or the leisure to perfect themselves so far. In that way the ideas of Humanism increased the distance between the gentleman and the ordinary man and prepared a formidable class distinction.

The Universities

The enthusiasm for libraries and culture which now possessed the wealthier classes caused the universities to become more attractive. A period at a university, followed in many cases by a tour of Italy, became part of the liberal education of a young gentleman.

Greek was now being taught at Oxford by men of the stature of John Colet, the friend of Sir Thomas More. But the Netherlands was set alight by the great Erasmus of Rotterdam. This tireless scholar, whose riches were in his mind and heart, had enormous influence on the educated world of his day. He remained a convinced

Thomas More's map of Utopia

No more attractive figure appeared in the tragic Reformation period than Sir Thomas More, the godly man who rose to be Chancellor of England. His opposition to both Henry VII and Henry VIII on matters of principle cost him his life on Tower Hill. His writings include two important works, *Utopia*, which describes a perfect country, and *History of Richard III*, which set new standards in the writing of history. More was always inclined to become a priest. He was canonised in 1935.

The art of printing was known in China long before it appeared in western Europe. It is possible that this useful knowledge was transmitted from east to west but so far no direct connection has been traced. The first books were printed by carving a whole page from a block of wood. This block printed one page at a time but a separate block was needed for each page. Printing with moveable type appeared in Europe about 1450 and the name usually credited with the lion's share of discovery is that of Johann Gutenberg of Mainz. He produced the 42-line Bible, which has that number of lines on each page. Moveable type depends on a separate piece for each letter. When a page is finished, type can be broken and reset for another page. With a basic stock of alphabet a book can be printed from an economic quantity of type. Each letter type was carved in wood which could then be used as a pattern for making moulds to cast more type in metal. The craftsmanship of the first printers, such as Aldus Manutius, who produced the famous Aldine editions of Greek and Roman classics from his press in Venice, was exceptionally high. These printers made the first printed books objects of great beauty.

a

forza, e dico s' ci fo senza cres

Some examples of letter forms from different periods in history. From left to right, Gutenberg's black letter, a half Roman/half Gothic letter, a Roman letter and an italic letter.

An early wooden hand printing press. On the right three pieces of printing equipment. The forme for holding type, the tympan on which sheets of paper are placed for printing, and the frisket which holds the paper in place.

Seen below is a sixteenth-century woodcut of printers at work using the forme, tympan and frisket.

Catholic and studied the original Greek of the New Testament, but he wanted the man at the plough to read the scriptures in his own language. He hated vice and ignorance and attempted to show the true direction of Christianity by his own life.

Secular learning, that is learning connected with the matters of everyday life, began in earnest at this time. The merchant class and their employees needed instruction in order to run their expanding businesses properly. Books on banking, book-keeping and navigation appeared. Applied science and technical education followed the rarer lines of thought.

The first voyages of discovery were beginning to take place around the coast of Africa as part of the Renaissance activity. They are so important to the future development of Europe that their full treatment follows in the history of Modern Europe. Nevertheless, the necessary knowledge which made the ocean voyages possible had long been in preparation. In the Spanish peninsula there had been an Arab civilisation for centuries which was far more advanced in science and mathematics than its Christian rivals. When Prince Henry of Portugal founded his observatory and school for navigation on the Atlantic coast, he was able to draw on this fund of advanced knowledge for the training of his explorers and seamen.

A further barrier to communication among the different countries of western Europe was broken down by the use of Latin as the language in which the educated people wrote and often lectured. The Renaissance love of decoration made the Latin very involved and difficult for a plain man to follow. However, growing national pride caused the local languages of the separate countries to thrive. Attractive literature became available in English, French, Italian and German. At last the mother tongues of ordinary people were coming into their own.

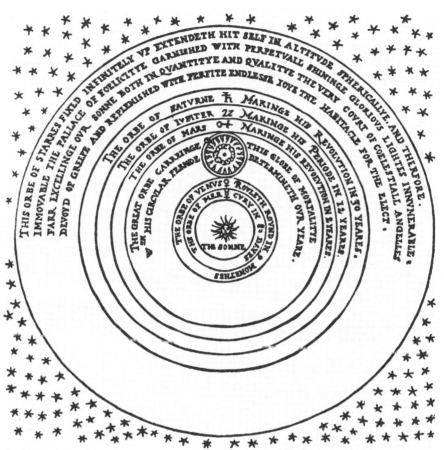

The diagram around the circles reads (from outer to inner):

THIS ORBE OF STARRES FIXED INFINITELY VP EXTENDETH HIT SELF IN ALTITVDE SPHERICALLYE. AND THERFORE. IMMOVABLE THE PALLACE OF FŒLICITYE GARNISHED WITH PERPETVALL SHININGE GLORIOVS LIGHTES INNVMERABLE. FARR EXCELLINGE OVR SONNE BOTH IN QVANTITYE AND QVALITYE THE VERY COVRT OF CŒLESTIALL ANGELLES DEVOYD OF GREEFE AND REPLENISHED WITH PERFITE ENDLESSE IOYE THE HABITACLE FOR THE ELECT.

THE ORBE OF SATVRNE ♄ MAKINGE HIS REVOLVTION IN 30 YEARES.

THE ORBE OF IVPITER ♃ MAKINGE HIS REVOLVTION IN 12 YEARES.

THE ORBE OF MARS ♂ MAKINGE HIS REVOLVTION IN 2 YEARES.

THE GREAT ORBE CARRYINGE ⊕ THIS GLOBE OF MORTALITYE DETERMINETH OVR YEARE.

THE ORBE OF VENVS ♀ ROVLETH ROVND IN 9 MONITHES.

THE ORBE OF MER ☿ CVRY IN 88 DAYES.

THE SONNE.

The Scientific Revolution

Science as we know it today began in Renaissance Italy. It was a practical world in which financiers, merchants and craftsmen had a very strong influence. There was far less division then between the artist and the craftsman. The technical problems which arose were a matter for general interest. The artist studied anatomy and met the doctor on common ground. The banker, in search of new supplies of bullion for his expanding trade, became involved in the practical problems of deep mining for precious metals. This intelligent approach to man's limitations was more than half the battle in overcoming the difficulties. Science applied to useful ends and the making of apparatus by gifted craftsmen followed in the wake of the cultural revolution. The wide range of activity which the Renaissance felt was necessary to develop the fully rounded man produced men who could link different branches of knowledge in coming to solutions.

The Italian universities expanded greatly at this time and to them came brilliant young men from all over

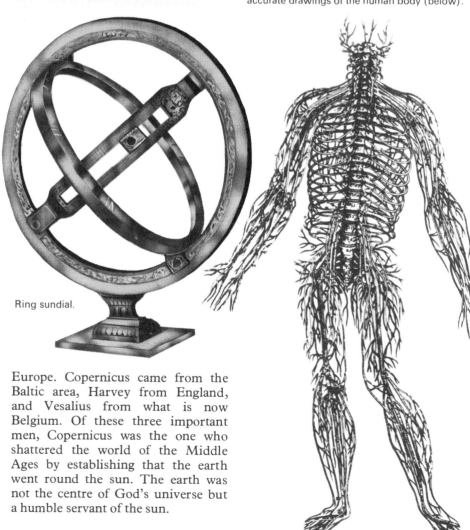

Ring sundial.

Europe. Copernicus came from the Baltic area, Harvey from England, and Vesalius from what is now Belgium. Of these three important men, Copernicus was the one who shattered the world of the Middle Ages by establishing that the earth went round the sun. The earth was not the centre of God's universe but a humble servant of the sun.

Copernicus was born into a prosperous merchant family but orphaned as a boy. Fortunately for him his uncle, the bishop of Varnia, was an important statesman who arranged for him to follow in his own footsteps in the universities of Cracow and Bologna. At Cracow, Copernicus learnt Greek and mathematics and followed these studies with more mathematics and astronomy in Italy.

The New Universe

Near the end of his life, in 1543, Copernicus published his great work *Concerning the Revolution of the Heavenly Spheres*. He not only realised that the position of the sun and the earth was reversed but he also realised that the unchanging stars must be an immense distance away. Suddenly the universe was enormous and man and the old world of the Middle Ages were very small indeed. The old world of

The diagram (left), drawn by an English scientist named Digges, illustrates the ideas of Copernicus. Vesalius personally carried out dissections on the bodies of criminals, and great artists helped him to reproduce accurate drawings of the human body (below).

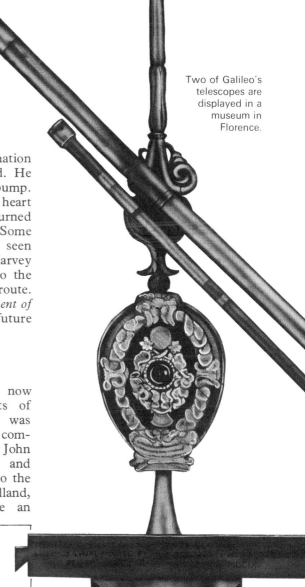

Two of Galileo's telescopes are displayed in a museum in Florence.

astrology and blind faith was now doomed. Following the Dutch invention of the telescope, later astronomers carried on the careful work of observational proof until it was brought to a conclusion by Newton.

Both Leonardo and Michelangelo, at great risk to themselves, had secretly practised dissection in order to further their knowledge of anatomy. The beautiful and accurate drawings in Leonardo's notebooks are a result. Then a medical work appeared, written by Andreas Vesalius, which was illustrated by fine accurate drawings to show the working of the human body. It appeared in 1543, the

before into an organised explanation of the circulation of the blood. He realised that the heart was a pump. The blood went out from the heart through the arteries and was returned to the heart through the veins. Some of this system could not be seen without a microscope but Harvey used colour traces injected into the bloodstream to discover the route. His book *Concerning the Movement of the Heart* became the basis of future progress.

The Modern Approach

Logic and experiment were now established as necessary parts of scientific method. To these was added mathematical proof to complete the modern approach. John Napier invented logarithms and Henry Briggs converted them to the more useful basis of ten. In Holland, Simon Steven proved to be an

Tycho Brahe gave his life to recording accurately the movements of the sun and stars for future use.

Kepler was a poor German scientist who continued the work of Copernicus and assisted Tycho Brahe.

Galileo checked his work by experimental and mathematical methods similar to those used today.

same year as the revolutionary book by Copernicus, and was called *The Fabric of the Human Body*. This work displaced Galen as an authority and paved the way for Harvey's later work on the behaviour of the blood.

Medicine had already been put on an improved basis in England when Thomas Linacre, the physician to three kings, was allowed to found the Royal College of Physicians in 1518. In the next century, William Harvey appeared. He studied at Cambridge and at Padua. Doctors had been working on the problem of the bloodstream for years and made intelligent guesses at the truth.

Harvey united all that had gone

engineer of genius in the application of mechanics. Trained as a clerk, he composed the first interest tables and understood that the movement of tides was due to the moon.

Meanwhile the astronomers were using mathematics to check the new telescopes. Tycho Brahe employed his power and wealth to build a huge observatory and research institute in Denmark, known as Uraniborg. From Augsburg he obtained far better instruments than had been used before. Then he persuaded the brilliant young Johann Kepler to continue his work. Tycho suspected that the path of the planets was oval and not round as Copernicus had

thought. But Kepler worked out the true laws of planetary movement.

The world of science was becoming international. William Gilbert's ideas on magnetism influenced Kepler and Galileo and leading scientists were increasingly in touch with each other.

The clear mind of Galileo drew all these threads together. He learnt from Archimedes how to use mathematics to make experiments more precise. He investigated the problems of mechanics and devised accurate apparatus to measure his results. An improved telescope enabled him to discern the separate stars of the Milky Way and to reveal the moons of Jupiter. This magic window which Galileo threw open on the heavens made him lose all caution. He gave enthusiastic support to the ideas of Copernicus and found himself in trouble with the Inquisition. Consequently he was obliged to spend the last years of his life under house arrest but still he experimented and secretly published his findings.

The Reformation

The unity of Christendom which had been the dream of the great popes in the Ages of Faith was now to be shattered permanently by the forces of the Reformation. In the past, when abuse cried aloud for reform, a new wave of enthusiastic servants of the Church arose who set the Church's house in order and all was well again. When reformers again cried aloud against new abuses, the Church took the view that the trouble would pass. But the fundamental changes brought about by the Renaissance added to the normal pressures. This time the fabric of the Church could not stand the strain and the western Christian world became divided between Catholic and Protestant.

Catholic and Protestant

There were many new factors in the situation at the time of the Reformation. The idea of nationality was gaining ground and obedience to Italian priests was far from acceptable to the northern nations. Both merchants and rulers of the new seagoing nations felt independent and economically secure. The old dislike between German and Latin was just beneath the surface. As the use of national tongues grew in importance, foreigners were more resented. The

cost of the new St Peter's Church in Rome caused the papal revenue collectors to be too reckless and the wealth going from the north of Europe to Italy became a very sore point. All these influences helped to increase differences in religious ideas and to bring Catholic and Protestant to a sad and bloody parting of the ways.

During the fourteenth century disputes within the Church led to the Great Schism and the establishment of a second papacy at Avignon where these French popes were under the influence of the French crown.

The false political position of these popes was generally resented outside France, particularly in England. There the great reformer, John Wyclif, attacked Church abuses. Fortunately

he had the protection of John of Gaunt who had his eye on the wealth of the Church.

Wyclif went further and challenged the teaching of the Church, refusing to believe in the central miracle of the mass. He appealed to the scriptures and, having had the bible translated into his native English, he sent his poor preachers throughout England to spread his ideas. These ideas also spread to Bohemia where John Hus took them up with great fervour. After Hus had been burned for heresy, there was a great popular revolt in Bohemia.

Martin Luther

The main attack of the Reformation came in Germany in the fifteenth

Martin Luther nailed a document, containing his ninety-five points of protest against the sale of indulgences to raise funds for the Church, on the door of the Castle Church in Wittenberg in Germany. On the right is the title page of the pope's bull, or edict, against Luther, which ordered the burning of all his books.

Bulla contra errores Martini Lutheri z sequacium

century. Martin Luther condemned the sale of indulgences which were being offered for cash without repentance or confession. His stand against the friars made Luther a national figure. But Luther went on to attack Church doctrine and papal methods in general. In 1520 he was excommunicated but found safety in the castle of the Elector of Saxony. The university of Wittenberg also supported Luther and from there the university of Cambridge was to be influenced.

Luther was a violent man and easily quarrelled with friend and foe.

The beautiful stone tracery of the roof of Henry VII's chapel (c. 1512) at Westminster Abbey in London is a fine example of Gothic fan vaulting. From the roof are suspended the banners of the Knights of the Bath.

He failed to agree with Zwingli, the Swiss reformer, and so the two new Protestant churches went their separate ways. However, the Lutheran Church won the approval of the Scandinavian countries. In Geneva, John Calvin organised a stricter form of puritanism. The divisions within Protestantism, which have gone on from the days of the Reformation, were already evident in the early days.

At this point of indecision, events were brought to a head by the king of England's difficulties over a legal heir. Henry VIII was only the second king of a new dynasty and needed a son to succeed him on the throne. It is one of the ironies of history that one of his daughters became England's greatest queen, worth many kings who have sat on the English throne. But when the king learned that his wife Catherine could not give him the wanted child, he sounded out the papacy for the necessary divorce. The matter was referred to Rome for decision, where the emperor Charles

V, the nephew of Catherine, was undisputed master. Coldly the divorce was refused and the furious Henry resolved to act for himself. The result was that England left the Catholic Church never to return and the king of England was made head of the Church by Act of Parliament.

The New Princes

It is clear that many critics of the Church acted purely from envy of her wealth. The princes of Germany and the new men of the Tudor monarchy were anxious to secure the transfer of that wealth to themselves. Some of the proceeds went to good purposes but most acted as a colossal bribe for the revolutionary changes in church and state. In the mixed motives of politics and genuine belief, Protestantism and Catholicism were born. For good or evil the breach was made permanent.

The literary ability of the great reformers was very high. The Catholics, More and Erasmus, have their honoured place in European thought while the Protestants, Luther, Tyndale and Cranmer, were all wonderful prose writers who added much to both German and English.

The Modern World

In the fifteenth century the countries of western Europe took to the sea and drastically altered the shape of the known world. Until that time the heart of Europe was around the shores of the land-locked Mediterranean Sea. Now new lands were discovered across the vast wastes of the oceans.

Progress in mathematics and engineering at the end of the Middle Ages had made possible the building of ocean-going ships with better navigational instruments. Prince Henry of Portugal led the way by sending his sailors south along the African coastline until they gained the prize of the sea route to India.

At the same time Columbus and his fellow seamen sailed westwards and found the Americas and the mighty Pacific Ocean beyond. Tiny ships sailed right round the world with Magellan and Drake, and power passed to the sea-going nations. Five of these, Portugal, Spain, France, Holland and England, disputed the ownership of the sparsely populated lands to the west. The struggle dominated the naval wars for the next three centuries until Nelson finally gave the command of the seas to England by his victory at Trafalgar.

The rush to colonise these new lands and to exploit them for the benefit of the home countries led to a mixed record of success and failure. The early colonists set patterns which decided the future. Our modern world has the task of solving the problems brought about by those days of wild expansion.

The first wave of colonists went for a quick profit and used slaves from Africa to work the tropical lands. The modern world is still trying to heal that social disaster. But good men also accompanied the adventurers. In the west the Jesuits went with Columbus, and later, men like David Livingstone opened up the darkness of Africa. Christianity and education worked the same miracle in these new lands as they had done with the barbarians in Roman times.

The religious wars which followed in the wake of the Reformation did little to alter the position. When peace at last came the division between Catholic and Protestant was final. In England there was a bitter struggle between King and Parliament

Magellan's *Victoria*

Map showing the circumnavigation of the world by Francis Drake, engraved by Jacob Hondius c. 1590

for power, which resulted in a working compromise which has stood the test of time. Other nations delayed their solutions and in France this led to the Revolution from which most of our political unrest and progress has stemmed.

If France made little headway under her autocratic kings, it was compensated for by the cultural lead which the Sun King, Louis XIV, gave his nation. For diplomacy and culture, French became the key tongue for educated Europeans.

In the eighteenth century there was a renewed interest in ideas and science among the gentry. Much valuable work was done by gifted amateurs and they gave great thought to improving their estates. This encouragement led to a tremendous advance in agricultural methods which increased the food supply and improved the quality of stock and crops. In England this was followed immediately by the development of the textile industry which began the Industrial Revolution. Other western European nations followed suit, with the result that our modern society began to change swiftly from agricultural to industrial and city life.

Political Changes
This basic change in economic life led to great political changes. Men living in cities could organise much more easily than scattered farm workers. Political and moral reform went hand in hand. The right to vote was spread wider and wider until all men and eventually women obtained it. The trade unions were formed and proved able to argue on equal terms with the captains of industry.

Transport, which had made little progress from ancient times, was now revolutionised. Steam power heralded the way in which machinery was to dominate the lives of modern men. It had scarcely begun to be used when Faraday invented the electric motor, generations ahead of his time.

During the early days of industrial development there was room for all to expand but soon the western industrial nations began to compete for world markets. Germany and Italy, who were late on the colonial scene, were handicapped in obtaining raw materials and equal trading opportunities. These pressures led to war in the twentieth century, with terrible booms and slumps in their wake which put millions out of work.

World Powers
In Russia a long-delayed revolution violently brought that sleeping giant to the front of world politics, there to confront the United States which had enjoyed the exceptional advantages of developing in peace. Today these two late arrivals in world politics dispute leadership with the colossus of China. Only big units can have an effective voice in the modern world and western Europe is uniting into one community to make a fourth great power.

Atomic power has at last caused man to look at the problem of war with sane eyes. No longer can anyone afford to face the powers of destruction which we now possess. Clumsily but surely the world is feeling its way towards a form of world government through the work of the United Nations. Already some conflict has been avoided by sensible discussion.

Drake's
Golden Hind

Discovery and Exploration

The rapid changes which marked the close of the Middle Ages brought swift alterations of fortune to the sea-going nations of Europe. The growing power of the Turks in the eastern Mediterranean made them masters of all the land routes to the East, from which alone silks and spices could be obtained. The luxury trade of wealthy

The portable astrolabe was an instrument used by mariners to determine the altitude of the sun, moon or stars, thus enabling them to fix the position of a ship when at sea.

Venice was cut off from easy access to the old supply lines. Slowly but surely the magnificent city began the steady decline from which it never recovered.

Another route to the mysterious East was needed which avoided the lands held by the Moslem Turks. The rich prizes which awaited successful explorers now urged the sea-going nations to brave the terrors of ocean voyages in their tiny ships.

In every way it was a new departure. Before 1500 Europe had relied on the past for knowledge and had remained set in its outlook and ideas. Now Europe was to lead the world in technology and political ideas. Explorers and colonists were to take these ideas with them to the four corners of the earth as forerunners of European leadership in world politics. Looking back from our own day we can see these developments clearly, but at the time the true significance of the first ocean voyages was not realised.

The African Coast

The Portuguese took the lead in ocean navigation by occupying Ceuta in Morocco as early as 1415. This Moslem port thus became Christian, but of more importance was its connection with the African gold trade. Gradually the Portuguese ventured farther and farther southwards along the African coast, building forts and founding trading stations. Gold was in short supply in Europe, so Portugal soon became prosperous by conveying supplies home directly by sea. Another source of wealth revealed itself when the Portuguese began to deal in slaves. As the western colonies were developed, this horrible trade was to become more important than gold.

Progress along the African coast reached its climax in 1487 when Bartholomew Diaz reached the Cape of Good Hope. He realised that Portuguese ships would be able to round Africa and sail eastwards towards India. Ten years later, Vasco da Gama reached the coast of India at Calicut. This long sea route round Africa to the East became the normal trading route until the Suez Canal was cut in the late nineteenth century. The Portuguese possessions in the East soon extended to the Malay Archipelago and the spice trade was in their hands.

Meanwhile, three small Spanish ships under the command of Christopher Columbus sailed west with incredible daring across the vast empty wastes of the Atlantic. His flagship was only ninety feet (twenty-seven metres) long. No one expected to see him or his men again. Columbus had complete self-confidence, however, and an unshakable faith in God's blessing on his voyage. Italian by birth, he had served for many years in Portuguese ships and was acquainted with all the new developments in ships and navigation. The geographers of that time, as may be seen from Martin Behaim's famous globe, under-estimated the size of the world. They thought that it was about a third smaller than it really is. Columbus was as ignorant of the existence of the Americas as everyone else; he was seeking a route to Asia.

Columbus Sails West

After taking his plans around the courts of the sea-going nations for years, Columbus at last received the necessary support. Isabella of Castile was persuaded to provide the ships and Columbus finally sailed under the Spanish flag. He left Spain on 3rd August 1492 and after a five weeks' voyage made landfall on an island of the Bahamas group. He called it San Salvador in honour of Christ and it is generally thought to be Watling Island.

He went on farther to find Cuba and Haiti, and in later voyages he was to visit all the West Indies and a good deal of the Central American coastline. To his dying day Columbus thought the lands which he had discovered were the coasts of Asia with their offshore islands.

Columbus, partly because of his own difficult nature, had a very mixed reward for his great discovery. He was

These four men, all Portuguese, made Portugal the leading country for oceanic exploration. Prince Henry the Navigator (1) gave all his energy and influence to supporting Portuguese seamen. He founded a school of navigation which profited from the advanced knowledge of the Jews and Moors, and which learned the art of shipbuilding from Genoa. Vasco da Gama (2) followed in the footsteps of previous navigators when he successfully reached India in May 1498. Later in life he was viceroy of India. Ferdinand Magellan (3) captained the first ship to go round the world, although he did not live to complete the voyage himself. Bartholomew Diaz (4) paved the way for da Gama by rounding the Cape of Good Hope.

at first loaded with honours but later carried back to Spain in chains to answer charges brought against him. He then had a second period of royal approval but died in poverty in 1506.

Spanish Adventurers

In his wake came a rush of Spanish adventurers drawn by the discovery of gold and silver on the American mainland. One of these explorers was Amerigo Vespucci who made a long voyage down the South American coastline and thereby gave his name to the new continent which was being discovered. A greater figure was Ferdinand Magellan who rounded the fearsome Cape Horn and sailed his ship the *Victoria* successfully across the Pacific Ocean. The daring Magellan was killed in the Philippines, but the surviving members of his crew brought their ship safely home to Spain and thus completed the first voyage round the world.

Meanwhile a Portuguese captain, named Cabral, was blown off course

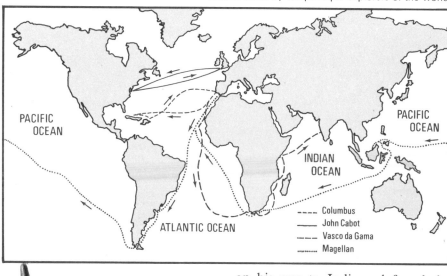

PACIFIC OCEAN

PACIFIC OCEAN

INDIAN OCEAN

ATLANTIC OCEAN

- - - - Columbus
———— John Cabot
— — — Vasco da Gama
.... Magellan

on his way to India and found the coast of Brazil jutting out into the Atlantic. He claimed this new territory for the crown of Portugal.

These voyages had the conversion of the heathen to Christianity as an important part of their mission. They sailed with the pope's blessing and he laid down the area of Spanish and Portuguese influence by direct command. Both countries accepted his decision, so when the later challenge of Drake and his fellows came, it was against both the Spanish rulers and

Columbus and his men made their first landing in the New World on an island of the Bahamas group. The crusading cross reminds us that winning souls for Christ was part of the mission.

It was the marriage of Ferdinand and Isabella which united Castile and Aragon and brought about the unity of Spain.

the Catholic Church. In Drake's day Portugal was under Spain's control.

Now that the true sizes of the world and of the Pacific Ocean were known more exactly, it was clear that the riches of India were not to be tapped by the western route. But a rich compensation was found in the mines of the New World which were exploited ruthlessly.

Cortés and Pizarro

Soon after they had established themselves on the mainland of America, the Spanish *conquistadores*, as these daring adventurers were called, came into contact with the two fascinating civilisations of the Aztecs in Mexico and the Incas in Peru.

Hernando Cortés, the conqueror of Mexico, was educated for the law but preferred the excitement of the New World. After some years in the government service, he was chosen by Velasquez, the governor of Cuba, to lead the expedition against Mexico.

Hernando Cortés, conqueror of Mexico

He had barely seized bases on the coast when he was recalled; a command which he ignored.

At this point Montezuma, the emperor of the Aztecs, unwisely sent envoys with gifts to Cortés, which proved the amazing reserves of Aztec wealth.

The fighting was hard and desperate. Montezuma heard that Cortés was a rebel disowned by his masters, and his hopes rose. But Cortés was equal to every demand. He not only burnt his own ships at Vera Cruz so that his men could not retreat, but also had new ones built in sections which were carried overland so that the capital, set in its defensive lake, could be stormed. Montezuma was tricked into becoming a hostage and in the later confusion lost his life.

The force which had been sent to relieve Cortés of his command arrived at the coast, and Cortés left the main fighting to deal with it. He sent the leader back in chains and added the new men to his own. But when he returned he found that his men in the capital had been cut to pieces by a terrible defeat which is still remembered as 'the night of sorrows'. But Cortés gathered himself for a final effort and took the city in the lake, which was utterly destroyed by fire.

The Aztecs were wise in irrigation and astronomy and had built up a fine civilisation over the centuries. Their art, particularly sculpture, was highly developed but now their immense treasure was looted for the benefit of Spain. Like Columbus, Cortés received an indifferent reward for his labours at the hands of the government at home.

The conquest of Peru was even more remarkable. Francisco Pizarro,

Aztec stone calendar

who discovered and conquered Peru, was never able to read and was driven on by a devouring greed which made him able to surmount all fears and scruples. Pizarro's first attempt to find the land of the Incas was a failure. The next attempt was undertaken with only a handful of companions, but he found the Incas and later conquered them with less than two hundred men. At this time there was a civil war among the Incas which Pizarro exploited. He also used blatant treachery and Atahualpa, the unfortunate Inca ruler, was strangled. But the main factor of Pizarro's easy conquest was the curious way in which the Incas ruled their land.

Inca was really the name for the small ruling caste who had complete control of the whole empire. They ruled it in the interest of all the people but there was no questioning their absolute commands. Consequently, when this small group of all-powerful rulers had been seized there was no one left to dispute the newcomers. There was simply a transfer of power to the Spaniards. However, these fortune hunters quarrelled bitterly among themselves over the riches of this unbelievable land.

The discovery of so much easy wealth at a time when the nature of true wealth was not understood, corrupted Spain and led to her decline after the first burst of temporary advantage. The sudden arrival in the Old World of great quantities of bullion caused inflation and a sharp rise in prices. The lot of the poor was grievously worsened by all this new treasure.

The Northwest Passage

Meanwhile, far to the north the English and French were making a small beginning on the exploration of North America. As the eastern routes were dominated by the Spanish and Portuguese, John Cabot, who like Columbus came from Genoa, had persuaded Henry VII to support him in finding a Northwest Passage to India across the North Atlantic. He was the first of many brave men who failed to find the non-existent channel.

Aztec sacrificial knife

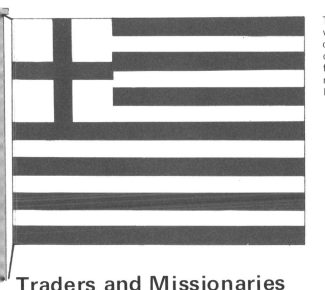

The East India Company was the most successful of the early trading companies. It had its own flag (left) and a fleet of merchant vessels which led the world in design.

Traders and Missionaries

The exciting deeds of the *conquistadores* and the glittering treasure of the New World briefly dominated the attention of Europeans. The future, however, lay with the quieter but more solid achievements of the traders and missionaries. The original intention of the ocean voyages was to reach India and open up the rich spice trade. John Cabot took bales of cloth with him to Newfoundland, although he found no one with whom to trade.

To many, and certainly to Isabella of Castile, the winning of new souls for Christ was of more account than the gaining of earthly treasure. The

age-old work of the Church in converting and civilising heathen peoples was continued in the newly discovered lands by dedicated missionaries from Christian Europe. By these two channels of trade and religion, many of the benefits of European life were transmitted to the lands now about to be colonised.

The division brought about by the Reformation had caused the Catholic Church to lose control of the north of Europe to the new Protestant churches. But the Catholic missionaries now compensated the Church for that loss by gaining millions of converts in Asia and the Americas.

This new wave of missionary activity was mainly the work of the Jesuits, or the Society of Jesus. The founder of the order was Ignatius Loyola, a Spanish soldier who suffered crippling wounds while fighting in Navarre and was caused thereby to reflect on the course of his life. After long years of preparation of the severest kind, he banded together with six companions of like mind in Paris. The great St Francis Xavier was also one of these original seven Jesuits. The Jesuits decided to make

Detail from a Japanese painting showing a party of Jesuit traders visiting Japan.

themselves intellectual soldiers of Christ by education, and to rebut all heresy and to promote the true faith wherever the need arose. They placed themselves without any reserve whatsoever at the absolute disposal of the reformed papacy which was now leading the Counter Reformation.

The full training of a Jesuit takes about thirteen years and has altered little in its severity or thoroughness over the years. The detailed plans made by Ignatius Loyola have stood the test of time amazingly well. The Jesuits were free of other Church ties but were committed to go wherever the pope required them to serve. Loyola became the first general of the new order and a remarkable degree of power was centralised in his hands.

The Jesuit missions sailed east and west with equal success. Xavier became the 'Apostle to the Indies' and converted thousands in India, Ceylon, Malaya and Japan. In China he met his death near Canton but Matteo Ricci continued his work and brilliantly adapted his message to the Chinese way of life.

Some progress had already been made in the Americas in preaching Christianity but the Jesuits sent their missions farther afield. The greatest success of all was the magnificent work done by the Jesuit mission to Paraguay, which lasted for two centuries and became a model to all other missions.

Chinese porcelain, such as this early Ming flask, was much admired by western craftsmen when brought to Europe in the 1800s.

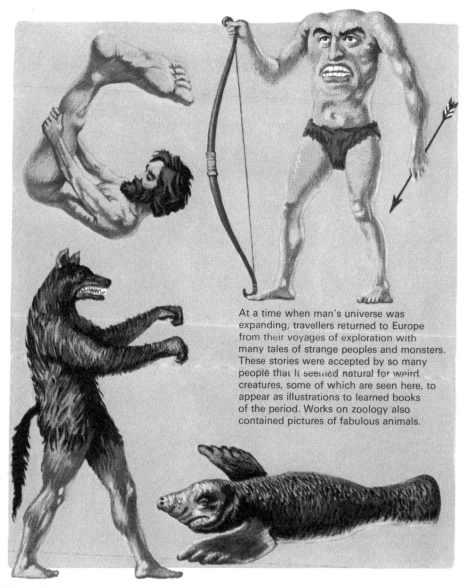

At a time when man's universe was expanding, travellers returned to Europe from their voyages of exploration with many tales of strange peoples and monsters. These stories were accepted by so many people that it seemed natural for weird creatures, some of which are seen here, to appear as illustrations to learned books of the period. Works on zoology also contained pictures of fabulous animals.

Merchant Adventurers

The Merchant Adventurers of England had been formed for the defence of English trade as early as the thirteenth century but had made little headway against the powerful Hanseatic League. But with the coming of the enterprising Tudors to the throne, all this was changed. Nations now began to compete for trading advantages, and the Merchant Companies were formed to finance the great expense of fitting out expeditions for long and dangerous voyages.

One daring voyage was made by Willoughby and Chancellor to the north of Russia, using the Arctic sea route. Willoughby and his crew perished in the ice but Chancellor finally reached Archangel and was taken on to Moscow. The result was the Muscovy Company which traded for many years between England and Russia.

Spain absorbed Portugal in 1580 and this act gave the English the opportunity to challenge Portuguese supremacy in the East. In 1600 the famous East India Company was formed to support the English sea captains who were sailing Indian waters and attempting to seize the Portuguese spice trade. The remarkable history of this company, which eventually led to the establishment of British rule in India, makes it the most important of all the companies which were formed in the Tudor age.

Summary of key dates	
1487	Diaz rounds Cape of Good Hope
1492	Columbus sails for the New World
1497	da Gama reaches India by sea. Newfoundland discovered by John Cabot
1513	Balboa discovers the Pacific
1519	Magellan's *Victoria* sails round the world
1534	Jacques Cartier discovers St Lawrence river in Canada
1549	Francis Xavier begins Jesuit mission to Japan
1580	Drake completes voyage round the world
1600	East India Company formed

The Wars of Religion

The Château Chambord in France was built for Francis I in 1519.

The success of Protestantism continued and the Catholic Church prepared itself for its great offensive known as the Counter Reformation. A new spirit was seen in the papacy. At the Council of Trent (1545–63) the teaching of the Church was defended and laid down for the future. Abuses were reformed and a new order of popes rose up to give the Church a positive lead. The Jesuits, committed to the defeat of heresy and the defence of the papacy, threw their iron will and great learning into the struggle.

Austria, Spain and France, the three greatest powers of the day, were Catholic, and it should have been easy for the Catholic powers to overrun the Protestants. But national rivalries were stronger than religious loyalty. The House of Valois, ruling France, preferred to work with Protestant or Turk to outwit the House of Habsburg, which ruled Austria and Spain. To persecute Protestants at home but to ally with them abroad was standard French policy. This disharmony was most helpful to Protestant survival. On the other hand, the Lutherans and the Calvinists were quite unable to work together. There was much confusion in the situation on both sides.

The Thirty Years War

In France, during the religious wars, the struggle was very violent but the country emerged from the experience stronger than it had been formerly. In Germany, however, the Thirty Years War tore that land to pieces and set back the clock of progress two hundred years. The only result was a permanent frontier between Protestant and Catholic which differed very little from the position when the fighting had started. The bitterness of the war made it impossible for the two sides to come together again in the future.

The Jesuits, however, had considerable success. They concentrated on gaining the support of important and powerful people who had political influence. Higher education passed

By inheritance, Charles V of the House of Habsburg became the most powerful monarch in Europe, and he was duly elected Holy Roman Emperor. His rivalry with Francis I of France led to wars both in Italy and Burgundy and, at one time, the French king was captured and had to accept humiliating terms. Henry VIII was an exact contemporary of both kings, as was Martin Luther. The church struggle in England caused Henry to change his alliances with the two kings according to the demands of the home situation.

into their hands and they infused their determination into the Catholic leaders, particularly in Vienna. At that time, Poland was full of refugee Jews and Protestants of every kind, but the Jesuits slowly but surely increased their grip until the whole country became an enduring outpost of Catholic Christianity in eastern Europe.

The Huguenots

The wars of religion in France occupied the second half of the sixteenth century and were very bitter. The treachery, constant assassinations and frequent changes of alliance very nearly destroyed the hard-won unity of France. Despite severe persecution, the French Protestants, who were called Huguenots, continued to make progress. Their cause was taken up by the Bourbon princes who were not convinced Protestants but who wished to oppose the Catholic party led by the Dukes of Guise. One Bourbon brother was the leading archbishop and the other the foremost soldier of France. A third party, led by the Duke of Montmorency, tried to act as a balance between the two hostile parties. In fact, at a later stage one of the duke's nephews, Admiral de Coligny, became the greatest of the Protestant leaders.

This confused situation was made worse by the weakness of the French throne. The queen mother, Catherine de Medici, although a woman and an Italian, was compelled to rule the troubled country because of the feebleness of her three royal sons. The choice before her was whether to

135

act alone and be independent of the papacy, as Henry VIII of England had dared to do, or to accept the overlordship of Spain and make certain of a Catholic victory. Catherine decided to do neither but to use all her devious skill to work for a compromise. Unlike the crown, the Catholic party was willing to work with Spain and the Protestant party to work with England.

The first Catholic successes were halted by the assassination of Francis, Duke of Guise in 1563. La Rochelle was converted into a great naval fortress by the Protestants and Coligny took Paris. There was a period of peace and some Huguenot liberty was granted. Above all, Margaret of Valois, a daughter of the Catholic ruling house, was married to the Protestant Bourbon Henry, King of Navarre. French foreign policy also favoured Protestant allies so that France could attack Flanders.

This victory for the Protestants could not be accepted by the Catholic party, and the shocking massacre of St Bartholomew's Eve took place on 24 August 1572. Both in Paris and throughout the country the slaughter of Protestants was heavy. The head of Coligny was sent to the Pope and there was wild rejoicing by the Catholic party. But the third party and the queen mother were shocked by this event into trying to restore the balance. In 1588 Henry III, the last and worst of Catherine's sons, had the leaders of the Catholic party assassinated in the castle of Blois.

Henry of Navarre

The Catholic League, backed by Spain and the Pope, now seized Paris, deposed the king and ruled the city with an iron hand. The deposed king allied with his cousin, the popular Henry of Navarre, who was next in succession. When the king was assassinated, only Henry of Navarre was left to succeed to the throne.

The crisis was solved when Henry, a wise and able ruler, became a Catholic in order to succeed to the throne as Henry IV. He and his minister, the Duke of Sully, genuinely cared for France and for the good of the ordinary people. A long, hard bargain was worked out with the Huguenots which was signed as the Edict of Nantes in 1598. This Edict gave Protestants liberty of worship and considerable privileges. It was the first example of two rival religions

being given the right to co-exist in a modern state.

The resulting peace brought in a period of great prosperity for France, which laid the foundations for her brilliant future. The happy outcome of this strife in France was in marked contrast to events in central Europe where rivalry between Catholic and Protestant led to international war.

The Thirty Years War was one of the most destructive wars ever to be waged. In particular, it was a great tragedy for Germany, where the land was left exhausted and divided into some 350 states.

The quarrel came to a head in a situation already tense, over who was to be the King of Bohemia. A Catholic was chosen to be the next Habsburg emperor and thereby the new King of Bohemia. The Bohemian Protestants looked around for help and the two sides clashed in bitter fighting, supposedly under the banners of their respective faiths.

But there were few true religious loyalties in this ugly war. On one side, Catholic France sided with Protestant Sweden and Holland, while Lutheran Germany sided with Catholic Austria and Spain. Now Richelieu, the great French cardinal,

saved the Protestants in order to further French foreign policy. He financed the Swedes to come to the assistance of their fellow Protestants.

The Swedish king, Gustavus Adolphus, was a remarkable man in every way. He spoke eight languages and was a master of war. His men wore uniforms and were organised for lightning campaigns. For two years this brilliant soldier carried all before him. The Catholic leaders, Tilly and Wallenstein, were beaten, but the brave Gustavus, who endured every hardship which he demanded of his men, was killed at Lutzen. But he had defended the Lutheran faith for which he honestly cared and advanced Sweden's grip over the Baltic Sea where the power of the Hanseatic League had now crumbled.

Wallenstein, whose greedy and devious conduct had tried the patience even of his own side, was assassinated by his employers. Yet in 1635 the Lutherans of Germany sided with the Catholics of Vienna against the Swedish Lutherans in return for freedom of worship.

All pretence of true religious war now disappeared. The Bourbons of France were openly at war with the Habsburgs of Austria and Spain. The French generals were successful on land and the Dutch hit the Portuguese overseas possessions and defeated the navies of Spain and Portugal. Portugal, in disgust, tore herself free from Spain never to be united again.

Reason began to prevail. The Spanish and the Dutch made peace, and the Peace of Westphalia (1648) followed, giving some satisfaction to almost everyone. The Protestants as a whole were saved but Bohemia was lost to the Catholics for ever. The Swiss and the Dutch had their freedom confirmed. Germany was a mere shadow of the land that had seen the start of this war and two-thirds of her inhabitants are thought to have died at the hands of the heartless mercenary soldiers. At last, the other Protestant faith, Calvinism, was recognised together with the Lutherans and the Catholics. Sweden advanced her

The religious conflict in France between Catholic and Protestant came to a head on St Bartholomew's Eve in 1572 when nearly 2,000 Huguenots were murdered in Paris. The drawing on the left is a detail from a contemporary painting of the massacre.

The Inquisition was a special court organised by the Catholic Church to suppress heresy.

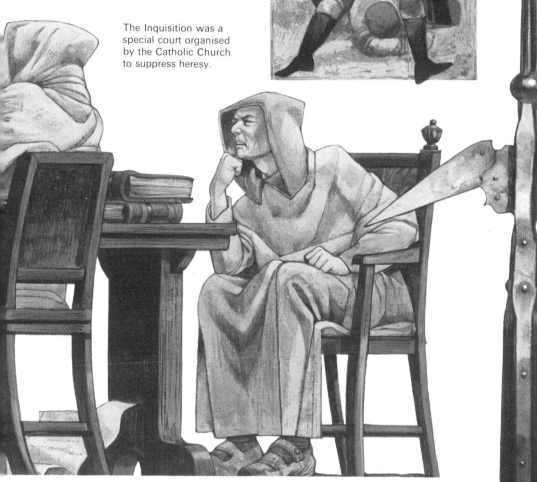

Sixteenth-century German halberds and partisans, a type of longer halberd

territories considerably and France gained the ominous possession of Alsace which led to much future trouble with Germany.

The Inquisition

The Inquisition was devised by the Catholic Church in the early thirteenth century to enquire into heresy at the time of the fierce crusade against the Albigensian sect in France. Local tribunals were set up. The names of informers were kept secret and torture was used, if necessary, to obtain confessions. If Church punishments brought no change of heart, the

heretic was handed over to the civil power for the death sentence, usually by burning at the stake.

The Spanish crown revived the Inquisition and used it at home, in the Americas and in the Netherlands. English seamen and Dutch burghers, who were Protestants, felt the full weight of this Spanish terror. In Spain, where there were secret Jews and Moslems, heresy was stamped out, but abroad the Inquisition awoke a fury of revolt which strengthend the Protestant resistance. In that fanatical age, neither Catholic nor Protestant paid much heed to the loving side of Christianity.

Elizabeth I and Spain

This portrait of Queen Elizabeth I, known as the 'Armada Portrait', is attributed to Marc Gheeraerts, c. 1588.

England was a weak and troubled land when Elizabeth, the daughter of Henry VIII and Anne Boleyn, came to the throne in 1558. Since her birth her position had been uncertain as the rival fortunes of Catholic and Protestant rose and fell. Her sincere and unwise sister Mary had permitted the public burning of Protestants during the last unhappy years of her reign and the religious tension had sharpened. Abroad the forces of the Counter-Reformation were growing in strength day by day. If France and Spain had ever agreed to work together, any hope of survival by the English and Dutch Protestants would have been over.

The character of the young woman who came to the English throne was in marked contrast to the hot-headed and violent spirit of the age. She possessed considerable political skill which showed itself in an untiring gift for compromise and endless ability to scheme her way out of dangers. She chose her ministers from men of like mind. William Cecil, later Lord Burleigh, was her leading adviser for forty years and he was succeeded by his able son.

Elizabeth was the child of Anne Boleyn so that in the eyes of Catholic Europe her mother was never truly married and she had no legal right to be sitting on the throne of England. This opinion brought the possibility of civil war nearer in the struggles between the Catholic and Protestant parties. There was also the danger of foreign invasion. The real danger of invasion by Spain later in the reign had the effect of keeping the religious dispute within bounds, for if the choice had to be made Englishmen chose to be loyal to their country rather than their faith.

Adventurous Seamen

Economic questions also helped to unite the Protestants. The land which Henry VIII had taken from the Church and transferred to his supporters was not going to be released willingly by the new owners. But above all else, the adventurous seamen of England wanted a share in the vast wealth which the Spanish and Portuguese had discovered in the New World.

The queen secretly encouraged her seamen while publicly disowning them. She refused an offer of marriage made by the all-powerful Philip II of Spain who had already been married to her sister Mary. But the queen used her position to keep trouble at bay. With England as her dowry, she appeared to listen to other offers of marriage from France. Her subjects wanted an heir for the throne. With outward playfulness but inner shrewdness, she used these offers to gain time for the safety of England.

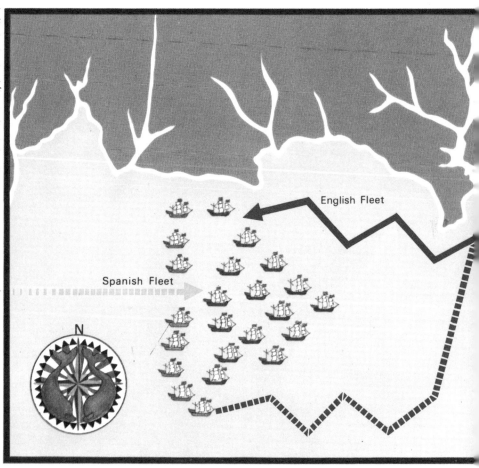

English Fleet

Spanish Fleet

N

While the possibility of her marriage seemed likely, she used the uncertainty to weaken any threat to England. In fact, Elizabeth was married to England and devoted her whole life to saving and strengthening her country.

Meanwhile, the English seamen, led by Francis Drake, the greatest privateer of them all, set out to harry and rob the Spanish in the New World. Their attacks were little short of open piracy but there was a colouring of patriotism in weakening the dangerous power of Spain. Also, the hated Spanish Inquisition made the Tudor seadogs determined to avenge their unfortunate fellows who had the misfortune to fall into enemy hands. It was only with the greatest difficulty and under heavy escort that the Spanish were able to bring their treasure fleets home when Drake and his men lay in wait. Spain had every reason to object and the strain between the two countries increased until war was unavoidable.

The Spanish Armada sailed slowly up the English Channel, harried by the English ships which came out from Plymouth and attacked from the rear. The Spaniards ran for home by sailing right round the coast of Britain but suffered heavy losses in the process.

Coruna

Cadiz

Mary, Queen of Scots
Other events increased the tension and brought matters to an open conflict. William of Orange, the heroic leader of the Dutch Protestants, was assassinated by order of the Spanish king. There was ceaseless plotting against the queen's life and finally Mary, Queen of Scots, was implicated. Reluctantly she was put to death by Elizabeth for treason. Spain was further strengthened at this point. The Portuguese royal line failed and Spain took over the smaller kingdom for sixty unhappy years.

Knowing that war could no longer be avoided, the English decided to strike some surprise blows. They had the best sailors and the best ships. They had also, in their new broadside mounting of guns, firing power which gave them outright superiority.

The Armada Medal

Drake was now the foremost English seaman. He had sailed round the world, losing four out of his five ships rounding Cape Horn. But undaunted he brought his *Golden Hind*, laden with treasure, safely home. Now that war drew near, Drake first raided the West Indies and then, in 1587, the port of Cadiz in Spain, where the great Armada was preparing. There, the devastating effects of the English broadsides finished the oar-driven galley as a ship of war.

The Armada
In 1588 the long-awaited Armada sailed. The Pope had given his blessing and the expedition was a crusade against heretical England. The plan was to sail to the Netherlands and carry the Duke of Parma and his

William Shakespeare was born at Stratford-upon-Avon in 1564 and died there in 1616. His father John was a prominent trader in the town and his mother belonged to an important local family. At eighteen he married Anne Hathaway and they had three children. About five years later he went to London and spent his time among actors and playwrights. Working in the theatre, he began to help in the writing of plays and achieved such success that he became a shareholder in the Globe theatre and finally retired prosperous and famous. Shakespeare's poetic drama has made him 'not for an age but for all time'. His sure reading of human nature has given him a universal appeal ever since. The range of his language is complete, from the tearing passion of the great brooding tragedies to the softest and most delicate lyrics of his love poetry.

forces across the Channel to invade England. Consequently, there were more soldiers than sailors with the Armada and an aristocratic landsman was in command. The Spanish had more ships but they were cumbersome and could not compare with the heavily gunned, highly efficient ships commanded by men like Drake and Hawkins.

The Armada crawled up the Channel for a week and reached Calais terribly weakened by the English broadsides from ships it could not engage. English ammunition was running low and Drake sent in fire ships. At Gravelines the Spanish fleet was pinned against the coast by an onshore wind and fiercely mauled. Damage was considerable but few ships were actually sunk. However, the Spaniards broke and decided to run for home right round the coast of Britain. But fierce storms wrecked the crippled ships on unfriendly coasts and only about a third reached Spain. The conquest of England had failed. Strong and confident, England was now free to colonise the world in the following centuries.

Summary of key dates
1520 Field of Cloth of Gold, alliance between England and France
1558 Accession of Queen Elizabeth I of England
1564 Birth of William Shakespeare
1571 Battle of Lepanto
1572 Massacre of St Bartholomew
1582 Gregorian calendar introduced
1588 Spanish Armada sails
1598 Edict of Nantes

The battle of Lepanto in 1571 was a crushing victory for the combined Catholic fleets over their Turkish opponents. It was also the last effective use of galleys in naval warfare.

Don John of Austria

The Ottoman Empire

While so much discord and strife raged in western Europe over the differences between Catholic and Protestant, the position of eastern Europe was even more perilous. The crusading period had weakened the eastern empire beyond repair and there was no hope of effective unity. The weak state of south-east Europe invited conquest and once again the forces of Islam attacked the west.

In the frontier province of Bithynia, in Asia Minor, there sprang up a new peril of the gravest kind to the Christians of eastern Europe. The Ottoman Turks were originally simple shepherds and herdsmen ruled by the Seljuks. But Othman, the founder of the Ottoman dynasty, decided to become independent of his masters. Early in the fourteenth century, he set up his own small kingdom and carefully built up his power. Education, trade, hospitals and, above all, the army, were the objects of his intelligent care.

The most famous of his creations was the Janissaries. These were new types of soldiers, originally Christian children who had been taken from their homes and brought up as fanatical Moslems. The trade of these slaves, indeed their whole life, was war. But so ruthless was their training and so effective its results that the Janissaries became feared on every field of battle on which they appeared. A constant supply of Christian children was exacted by the Turks as a tribute from all conquered lands.

Towards the end of the fourteenth century the Ottoman Turks crossed into Europe and defeated a composite army of Serbs, Bulgars, Albanians and Hungarians at Kossovo. They extended their sway westwards to the Danube and eastwards to the Euphrates. The eastern empire appeared to be delivered, however, when Tamerlane, with his even fiercer Mongols, erupted into Asia Minor and tore the young Ottoman power to pieces at the beginning of the fifteenth century. But eastern Europe was so disorganised that the Turks were able to recover in the Moslem city of Adrianople, their European base.

John Hunyadi
Slowly the Turks rebuilt their power but their oppression of Hungary was so severe that a great Christian hero arose, John Hunyadi. He routed the Turks decisively in 1444 and they asked for peace. Foolishly, Hunyadi granted their request and he was never again able to unite the Balkan peoples against their common enemy. Nothing now could save Constantinople and the last outpost of the empire fell in 1453. Thus the Turk bestrode the bridge between Asia and Europe and continued to advance his power.

The capture of Constantinople by Mohammed II encouraged the Turks to expand farther. The divided peoples of south-east Europe could find no answer to the fine guns and professional armies of the Moslems. Soon all Asia Minor was theirs and they swiftly advanced to the Adriatic coast, thus threatening Italy.

Mohammed's son, Bajazet II, ruled for thirty years but was forced to abdicate by his son, Selim, who carried on the conquests of his grandfather. Selim conquered Syria, Egypt and Arabia and took over the control of the Moslem world from the feeble Kaliphate. The old culture of the Arab world was lost and Istanbul, the new name for Constantinople, became the capital of Turkish power until this century.

The victories of Selim were followed by those of his son, Suleiman the Magnificent, better known to his

own people as 'the Lawgiver'. Suleiman was an intelligent and cultivated man as well as a great warrior. Under his long rule of nearly fifty years, the Ottoman Empire reached the zenith of its power. In swift succession, he captured Belgrade, compelled the Knights Hospitallers to leave Rhodes, and defeated and killed the king of Hungary at the decisive battle of Mohacs in 1526.

Hungary had been weakened by religious wars with Bohemia but its reputation was great. Hungary's defeat deprived the Christians of eastern Europe of their only able defenders. Austria was now exposed to Turkish threat and the burden of defence passed to the Habsburg rulers in Vienna.

Battle of Lepanto

In the Mediterranean Sea the Christian powers had more success. The Knights of Malta made a heroic defence of their island against the full weight of a Turkish attack and gave Suleiman his only serious defeat. The Turkish corsairs, sailing out of Algiers and Tunis, had preyed on Christian shipping for many years, causing great losses. Spain, with her long Mediterranean coast, was particularly troubled. She prepared a navy and under the leadership of Don John of Austria, Philip II's half-brother, the

Spaniards gained a great victory over the sultan's fleet at Lepanto in 1571. This battle saw the last use of the oared galley in war. On the tideless Mediterranean the galley was used to ram the enemy and thereafter to act as a platform for hand-to-hand fighting by soldiers. Drake's raid on Cadiz a few years later showed that the galley was useless for ocean warfare against heavily gunned ships.

After Suleiman the sultans became lax and a treaty was made with Austria which fixed the boundaries between the two powers. The training of the Janissaries was first softened and later abandoned. Christian subjects were allowed to follow their business in Turkish lands with the lazy consent of the Turks who had little interest in routine work. By contrast with the persecution in Christian lands, the Turks became reasonable and tolerant.

John Sobieski

Fortunately for Europe, the Turks were at a low ebb in the first half of the sixteenth century, while the Protestants and Catholics fought out the Thirty Years War. For a while the Turks were content to let matters drift until some remarkable leaders were produced in Albania by the Kiuprili family. In 1683 the Turks began to advance again. Vienna was

Suleiman the Magnificent

the immediate object of their ambition but Rome was also in their plans. Unexpectedly the Turks were halted in the north by John Sobieski, the king of Poland. The victories of Sobieski and the repulse of the Turks from the walls of Vienna marked the turn of the tide. The Austrian Empire began to spread eastwards, adding to its own territory the lands which it freed from the Turk. In this way the Austrians came to rule that extraordinary mixture of peoples and languages which made their empire vast and impressive but extremely difficult to manage.

The day of expanding Turkish power in Europe was now over. Gradually decay set in and Turkey degenerated to become the Sick Man of Europe. As the Turkish tide ebbed back on itself, the great powers dabbled in the control of the emerging lands in the interests of their own political advantage. Thus the Balkan area of south-east Europe became a powder keg of future trouble.

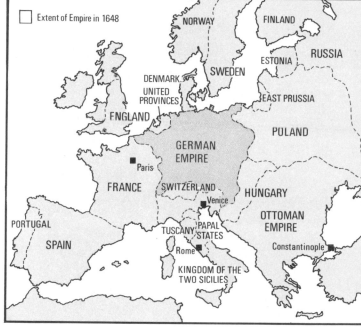

The Royal Standard of James I of Great Britain united the standards of England, Scotland and Ireland. It retained the lilies of France to signify the English claim to the French throne. On the left is a gold unite of James I, minted in 1604, the first coin to bear the legend 'Great Britain'.

Royal Houses of Europe

Now that the idea of nationhood was firmly established in western Europe, the person of the king became increasingly important. The untimely death of a king or the accession of a mere child to the throne of a troubled kingdom often gave the signal for civil war or invasion by an unfriendly neighbour. The marriage of a prince or princess had similar importance. A major transfer of power and territory could easily take place when a royal pair were united. The religion of the bride or bridegroom was also of paramount importance in those days of fighting hatred between Catholic and Protestant. The marriages of the royal families of Europe thus became a matter of most careful political decision and bargaining.

The rulers of the new kingdoms of Europe moved in the direction of absolute power over the peoples under their sway. At the end of the Middle Ages, the new trading classes had won many valuable rights of self-government from their feudal lords. These precious liberties were now challenged by the rising power of the kings. In England the struggle between king and parliament led to the Civil War and the death of the king. In France the monarchy was successful in destroying all its opponents and

the king became supreme. The French parliament was rendered weak and helpless.

Habsburgs and Bourbons

The main factor in the history of western Europe now lay in the rivalry of the two leading houses of Habsburg and Bourbon. Both sought to dominate Europe. At first everything went well for the Habsburgs but at the end of the struggle the Bourbons of France triumphed, in the person of Louis XIV.

France, Spain and Austria were the leading monarchies at the time and each of them courted the friendship of the rising power of England. Then a series of exceptionally fortunate marriages brought tremendous power to the Habsburgs. All the territories belonging to Austria and Spain were united under one ruler, Charles V. From Ferdinand and Isabella, his grandparents on his mother's side, he inherited Spain, the New World and the Spanish possessions in Italy. From Emperor Maximilian I and Mary of Burgundy, his grandparents on his father's side, he inherited Burgundy, all the Habsburg lands in central Europe, and the Netherlands. When he was Crowned Holy Roman

Henry of Navarre, who became Henry IV of France.

Emperor in 1520 he was the most powerful monarch in Europe.

France found herself hemmed in both to the west and to the east by the rival houses and desperately sought alliances. Although Catholic like Spain, France in her need willingly sought alliances with Protestant, German or Turk in order to be able to match the challenge of the Habsburgs. The power of Spain threatened the security of both France and England.

Dutch Independence

But the empire of Charles was made up of parts which could never agree. The Germans, the Spanish and the Italians had little in common. And a black side of his policy brought serious difficulties. Charles savagely persecuted his Protestant subjects in the Low Countries. In Spain similar ferocity had wiped out heresy but in the north such resistance was provoked that the Dutch rebelled and at the end of the struggle gained their independence. Meanwhile, in 1556, Charles retired from public life to spend his final days in a monastery, making his brother Ferdinand his successor as emperor and his son Philip the king of Spain and the Netherlands.

French Kings

France made little headway against the power of Spain under Charles. Then, in the second half of the sixteenth century she was torn by internal religious wars which nearly destroyed her. Eventually Henry of Navarre obligingly changed to the Catholic faith in the interests of peace and France became united again under its first Bourbon ruler. Henry

was succeeded by his son Louis XIII. During his thirty-year reign the great Cardinal Richelieu built up the power of France and securely laid the foundations on which the triumphs of Louis XIV were achieved.

Richelieu was appalled at the extraordinary privileges which had been granted to the Huguenots as the price of peace in the religious wars. He realised that the right given to them to hold fortresses made them an armed state within the state. They were a constant danger and a challenge to the king's authority.

Systematically the cardinal destroyed the political power of the Huguenots. He also moved against the proud nobility. Richelieu created an army and a navy paid by the state and began a civil service directly responsible to the crown. No great victories were gained by France in Richelieu's days but his subtle diplomacy gained many triumphs. By subsidising Sweden and bringing Gustavus Adolphus into the Thirty Years War, he prevented the Austrians gaining too much territory in Germany. Although the Austrians were the forces of the Catholic Counter-Reformation, country meant more than faith to Richelieu. He not only restrained his Austrian rivals but he started to make progress in France's extension towards the Rhine, which Louis XIV was to take much farther.

Meanwhile, under Philip II and his successor Philip III, Spain underwent a series of misfortunes. Her sea power was destroyed. Portugal, which had been added to Spain when her royal line failed, tore herself free in disgust. Her union with Spain had cost her the loss of most of her empire in the East. Philip II had continued his father's persecution of the Low Countries but the Dutch resistance grew ever sturdier and France lay between the king and his troublesome subjects. Finally, Spain was compelled to grant a peace treaty. At home the country was exhausted and in revolt. The mountainous, rugged nature of Spain made good central government difficult. The great days were over and the work of Richelieu had prepared France to take the leading role.

Summary of key dates	
1579	United Provinces of the Netherlands formed
1589	Henry of Navarre becomes Henry IV of France
1602	Dutch East India Company formed
1603	Union of English and Scottish crowns
1608	Irish rebellion. English and Scottish settlers sent to Ulster
1618	Beginning of Thirty Years War
1624	Richelieu first minister of France

Musketeers played a vital part in seventeenth-century warfare.

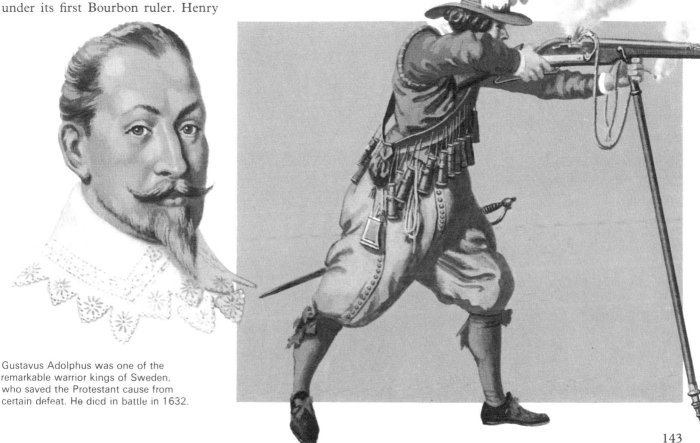

Gustavus Adolphus was one of the remarkable warrior kings of Sweden, who saved the Protestant cause from certain defeat. He died in battle in 1632.

The Sun King

When the French king Louis XIII died in 1643 he left a child of only five to succeed him. His mother, Anne of Austria, and Cardinal Mazarin became the real rulers of the country and they were both foreigners. The Italian cardinal was cordially detested by almost every section of the French people but he continued the work of Richelieu. The Treaty of Westphalia in 1648 was a triumph for France. Germany was kept weak and divided and very much under the influence of French culture and fashion.

Yet at this promising point in her history France was almost brought down by rebellion against the hated government of the cardinal. There was a general air of revolution in many parts of Europe, and the British had brought their king to the scaffold. The two risings which now troubled France are called the First and Second Fronde. They were caused by losses of civil liberties and the terrible burdens of a hopeless financial system.

The first rising was led by the magistrates of Paris, but they were really only interested in benefits for their own narrow class. The insurgents were united by a common hatred of Mazarin but there was no plan or long-term design such as guided the English parliament. However, the barricades went up in Paris and the mob seized control until an agreement was reached.

The second rising was occasioned by Mazarin's imprisonment of the prince of Condé, the aristocratic general of the French forces and supporter of the Fronde. For a time the position was serious; Condé was released and Mazarin had to flee. But once again there was no real unity in the popular movement. Condé was too autocratic to listen to other points of view. It was not difficult for the scheming Mazarin to detach his allies. The great soldier Turenne was bribed to change sides and Paul de Gondi, the accepted leader of the Paris mob, was bought for a cardinal's hat, becoming Cardinal de Retz.

Absolute Rule

By 1652 Louis XIV was in Paris where his young mind was deeply impressed by the events. He had witnessed the unpleasant union of nobles, clergy and mob against the throne and he decided then and there that his rule should be personal and absolute. Three years later he made his famous reply, 'The State? I am the State.'

The policy of France at this time was to make the great natural boundaries of the Alps, the Pyrenees and the Rhine her national frontiers. Mazarin successfully ended the troubles with Spain by a treaty which permanently made the Pyrenees the southern boundary of France. He also arranged the marriage of the young king to Maria Theresa, the daughter of the Spanish king and thus increased the likelihood of a union between France and Spain.

In 1661 Mazarin died and Louis seized the opportunity to become his own first minister. His power was to remain supreme until his death in 1715. The proudest nobles, who had now been rendered powerless, were drawn to the glittering court which surrounded the king. Instead of leading the affairs of the nation, they became idle and fawning courtiers. Despite his failings, Louis was a dedicated, hardworking monarch. Duty came first because it was all for his glory and the success of his land.

Brilliant Ministers

Louis had inherited from Mazarin a group of truly brilliant ministers who

Cardinal Richelieu (1585–1642) was born into a noble French family which had fallen on hard times. Trained as a soldier, he abandoned this to become a priest and was raised to the bishopric of Luçon when he was 22. He became a cardinal in 1622 and minister of state to the king. His main task in life was the destruction of the Huguenots and the glorification of his country. A man of immense ambition, he always wanted to be a writer. He founded the French Academy.

made France the best organised country in Europe. At the head of these stood Colbert. He believed in wealth based on hard work and praised the classes who were generally despised. Although France under her great generals was now established as the foremost military power in Europe, the French did not care for the sea. Colbert, however, saw the need for a good navy to rival the English and the Dutch. Every corner of France and her colonies came under Colbert's all-seeing eye, with great benefit to her prosperity. Finance and communications were immensely improved, but the unequal spread of taxation went on. Colbert shared the common view that international trade could flourish only at the expense of other nations. It was barely concealed warfare for money instead of a peaceful exchange for mutual benefit.

When the Spanish king died, Louis claimed the Spanish Netherlands by right of marriage to the king's daughter. He was temporarily checked by the alliance of Britain, Holland and Sweden. This was the first of the coalitions against his aggressive power which were finally to defeat France, but this one was broken up by Louis.

The great palace of Versailles, surrounded by magnificent gardens resplendent with fountains, was intended as a setting for the glory of the Sun King.

Louis XIV, the Sun King

The Protestant traders of England were business rivals to the Dutch and their Stuart kings became the paid allies of France. Sweden was similarly detached and the heroic Dutch were isolated. Louis advanced again and at the Treaty of Nijmegen he gained more land which took his frontiers to the French Alps. He also gained some important fortresses towards the Rhine. To these he added Strasbourg and Metz by peaceful intrigue.

Versailles

The king was now at the height of his power. He converted his father's hunting lodge at Versailles and made it into the magnificent palace which is a showplace of the modern world. Constantly throughout the palace the emblem of the sun disc is found, the symbol of the great Sun King who so outshone all his rivals. The nobility crowded into the surrounding villages, and the court and government were transferred from neighbouring Paris. At this high point of success the king made his greatest blunder.

Louis had always hated Protestants. Now he was influenced to complete the work of destruction against the

Huguenots by revoking the Edict of Nantes. The Huguenots had already lost their political power, now they had to lose their religious freedom. Hundreds of thousands of France's most gifted craftsmen left their country and took their skills to enrich England and other friendly countries.

The plight of the Huguenots hardened opposition to Louis, and the coalitions against him became more powerful. The unwise James II of Britain was soon a refugee at the French court and his Dutch son-in-law William III became with Mary ruler of England and led the opposition to Louis. Louis thought the

English rejection of James to be a local rebellion and he supported the Jacobite cause for many years. Under William he found England to be a strong Protestant enemy which would never be his ally.

After the death of William III, the brilliant and successful Marlborough continued the fight against France, and the Treaty of Utrecht in 1713 finally prevented France from linking with Spain and also from reaching the Rhine as her third natural frontier.

145

Civil War in England

The Civil War broke out in the reign of Charles I and cost that monarch his life. But the seeds of rebellion were sown in the days of his father, James I, who was utterly convinced that kings were responsible to God alone for their acts. He completely misjudged the English kingdom which he came from Scotland to rule upon the death of Elizabeth in 1603.

James was a man of contradictions. Henry of Navarre called him, 'the wisest fool in Christendom', for the new king was a good scholar but no judge of men. James met his parliaments only to quarrel with them. He did not understand that men like the Puritans, who at any cost intended to have their independence in religion, would also want it in politics.

In the reign of Charles I the fighting broke out and monarchy in Britain (as it now was) received a severe check just at the time when absolute monarchy in Europe was proceeding to its greatest triumphs. Charles was a better man than his father but he believed just as firmly in the Divine Right of Kings and was hopelessly influenced by his favourite, the Duke of Buckingham. Buckingham arranged Charles's marriage to a French princess and the Puritans rightly feared a strong Catholic influence on the royal family. For the first four years of his reign Charles tried parliaments, but the only result was the Petition of Right. In this parliament stated its terms for further business: no more improper taxation, no imprisonment without trial, and no compulsory billeting of troops except on inns whose owners must be paid. Charles dismissed this parliament and ruled alone for twelve years.

The personal rule of Charles was mild for that age and torture was abandoned, never to return in Britain. But two strong figures, Archbishop Laud and Thomas Wentworth, ruled the king. The Puritans, however, stood firm. Sir John Eliot died in the Tower and John Hampden led a revolt against taxation without representation. Laud's attempt to establish bishops in Scotland led to the National Covenant of 1638 which united thousands in Scotland against the king. The Covenanters formed their own army and Charles decided not to fight.

The Long Parliament

Wentworth was now recalled from Ireland and made Earl of Strafford. His gospel was thoroughness and his wish to see Charles an absolute king. Before Strafford could act, the Scots invaded England and had to be bought off. Without money or army Charles was compelled to recall parliament. Thus the famous Long Parliament met in November 1640.

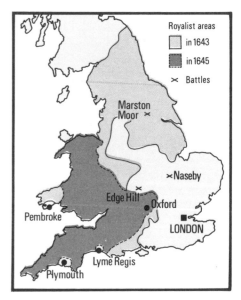

Charles I showed courage and dignity on his way to execution. The map below shows the areas of allegiance to King and Parliament during the Civil Wars.

Almost its first act was to arrest Strafford and bring him to trial.

The mood was now ugly. John Pym, the first great political organiser, worked up public opinion. Strafford was condemned to death by parliament and the king was frightened by the mob into agreeing. Parliament next abolished the special courts which had done Charles's bidding, and they were never restored.

But the fanatical Puritans were going too far, too fast, and there was a

split in the ranks of parliament which eventually led to the Roundheads and the Cavaliers. At this point a new rebellion in Ireland meant that the militia had to be called out. The question arose of who was to command them. Pym meant it to be parliament but he was compelled to flee. There was now no hope of a compromise, and the king left London to prepare for war.

Parliament's Victory

Parliament had the support of London and south-east England as a solid block. It also held most of the larger towns and the fleet, so the king could expect no help from abroad. In the main the nobility and the higher gentry were for the king, which gave him control of the countryside. Most of the population were not involved and the troops were very amateur. However, Pym made a treaty with the Scots, which contained the Highlanders who supported Charles. Oliver Cromwell, in charge of a troop of horse, soon showed himself to be a fine judge of horses and men, and after some local royalist success, parliament won the important battles. The first part of the war was over, but the problems of peace had just begun.

The Scots and the majority of the members of parliament were Presbyterian and wanted no other system of religion. The extreme Puritans in the new Model Army had won the war and were now using their power harshly. In secret, the Presbyterians began to negotiate with the king. Cromwell promptly seized Charles and put to him proposals for a compromise which would allow him to remain king in return for certain limitations to his power. The king appeared to agree but went on plotting secretly with the Scots and English Presbyterians.

The army chiefs met and condemned the king as 'that man of blood', and the second bitter part of the war began. The Scots were beaten by Cromwell at Preston and the survivors were shipped to the plantations of Barbados. The Presbyterians were forcibly ejected from parliament and only those favourable to the army were left. Cromwell had now decided that the king must die. An attempt was made to prosecute the king legally but the lords threw out the bill. Eventually a grim farce of a trial was held, forced through by Cromwell and the army. On 30th January 1649, the brave and obstinate king was executed. For eleven years thereafter England was a Commonwealth, held together largely by the iron will of Cromwell and his soldiers.

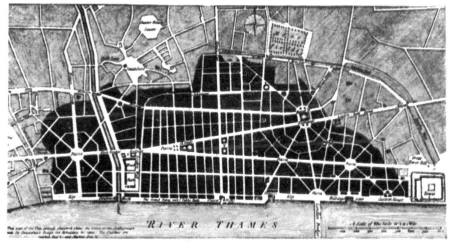
Christopher Wren's plan for rebuilding London after the Great Fire, 1666.

The Dutch Republic

The Netherlands, or the Low Countries as they are sometimes called, were often the scene of heavy fighting when the surrounding great powers went to war. During feudal times the Netherlands were divided into many small political units of no particular importance. But as their favourable trading position, on the coast and at the delta of the Rhine, increased their prosperity, in 1384 they came under the control of the Dukes of Burgundy. A century later they were part of that enormous inheritance which made Charles V the most powerful monarch in Europe.

The Netherlands fall into two natural divisions. The southern half, which has become modern Belgium, remained mainly Catholic after the Reformation. The northern half, which is now Holland, became fiercely Protestant. Its territory is quite unlike the wooded, hilly south. In the north the sea and land inter-penetrate to such an extent that the country is a network of rivers and canals. In early times the northern part was far less important and developed much later. The great city of Amsterdam began as a fishing village based on the herring trade. But in 1532 Amsterdam founded the first stock exchange in Europe and by the time of Philip II, the Netherlands were the richest part of his wide dominions.

Philip was a devout and dedicated man. As he toiled away at governing his empire, his chief ambition was to make his lands safe for the Catholic Church. Spain was the power house of the Counter-Reformation. The Inquisition and the Jesuits both started there.

In Spain the Inquisition had been outstandingly successful. Now Philip found stiff heresy in the rebellious provinces which he ruled as the Spanish Netherlands. He determined to crush the heretics and this decision reactivated the long struggle in which the heroic Dutch gained their freedom and became a nation.

The Spanish Army

In the sixteenth century, Spain, trained in the Italian wars, had the finest army in Europe. But at sea, despite the need for efficient communications between the colonies of America and Europe, the Spanish could not match the Dutch or the English. Spain had a long coastline both on the Atlantic and the Mediterranean. Against Turkish pirates at Lepanto in the Mediterranean Don John had scored a resounding victory with galleys. But the galleys employed in the Mediterranean were already hopelessly out of date.

Ship design lagged behind in Spain, as the crushing defeat of the Armada demonstrated. The Dutch, by contrast, lived in a land which made men into sailors in order to survive. In search of trade rather than colonies, the Dutch fleets sailed the oceans of the world.

The densely populated cities of the Netherlands were the most precious part of Philip's dominions. True wealth is based on sound trade and the Netherlands were more valuable than the mines of America. So, for the two reasons of heresy and income, the Netherlands needed to be brought under strict control.

Seventeen Provinces

Charles V, himself a native of Flanders, had organised the Netherlands into seventeen provinces with Brussels as the federal capital. He respected the self-government of the prosperous cities and his rule was deservedly popular. However he introduced the Inquisition and fiercely persecuted the Protestants, who lived mainly in the north and represented every shade of Protestant thought.

When Philip II succeeded, there was no popular feeling for him and the States General were not willing to vote him money as they had to his father. From distant Madrid outrageous demands were made upon the liberties and wealth of the Netherlands. Three nobles joined together to oppose these demands, Prince William of Orange, Count Egmont and Count Hoorn. The quartering of Spanish troops on the cities and the presence of the Inquisition stiffened the general discontent. This protest was mild, but lesser rebels awoke the extreme Protestants who came out of hiding to burn and destroy churches.

Philip sent the Duke of Alva, his best and most pitiless general, to settle the rebels. His infamous Council of Blood became notorious. Hoorn and Egmont, although Catholics and men of long public service, were executed publicly in Brussels. William of Orange fled to Germany and organised resistance from there. William was a Catholic who believed

William III, King of England

in toleration, an attitude which made him unique in that age. By degrees he went over to Calvinism as he found that all his support was in the Protestant north.

William sacrificed his whole life to resisting Spain. He frequently met with defeat but he never gave up and his obstinate courage inspired the Dutch to final victory. Fortunately for them, Alva proved to be so harsh that even the Catholics turned against him. Also, the 'beggars of the sea', pirates working in the Dutch interest, seized the port of Brill in 1572. Several other towns were freed in response and William was elected Stadtholder, or governor, of the province of Holland, which contained all the main cities. The province of Zeeland linked with Holland to become the hard core of Dutch resistance.

The revenge of Alva was terrible, but the Dutch ability to endure long sieges was so costly that Alva was recalled. An attack on Leyden was relieved when the Dutch opened the dykes, or sea walls, and the Spanish had to flee or drown.

So far only the seven northern provinces had revolted. Now the unpaid Spanish soldiers broke loose and ravaged the whole country. This 'Spanish Fury' brought all the seventeen provinces together to resist Spain. But the Duke of Parma arrived and managed to woo the Catholics away from the Protestants by granting concessions. In reply, the seven provinces united to become the Dutch republic, with William as their acknowledged leader. Recognising his importance, Philip had him assassinated in 1584.

Twelve Years' Truce
Deliverance came unexpectedly to the Dutch when Philip decided to attack France and England. In this breathing space, Jan van Oldenbarneveldt, who represented the cities, and the young Prince Maurice, the gifted soldier son of William, began to defeat the Spanish. Eventually, proud

Spain was compelled to seek the Twelve Years' Truce with the Dutch in 1609. The ten southern provinces remained in Habsburg hands and later became modern Belgium. After the truce the fighting was renewed but in the Peace of Westphalia in 1648 the independence of the Dutch republic was recognised.

This typical scene in old Amsterdam shows the merchants' houses along a quayside. During the seventeenth century the city of Amsterdam was the financial capital of the world.

Summary of key dates
1632 Gustavus Adolphus killed at Battle of Lutzen
1642 Outbreak of civil war in England
1648 Peace of Westphalia
1649 Charles I executed
1651 Louis XIV comes of age
1653 Cromwell Lord Protector of United Kingdom
1660 Restoration of Charles II
1689 William and Mary crowned joint sovereigns of United Kingdom

The Northern Lands

As the Middle Ages ended and the modern world began, the pattern of the future nations in western Europe was fairly clear. But in the north it was a time of great change, and national boundaries altered dramatically as first one country and then another won a brief ascendancy over its rivals.

Religion divided the northern lands even more than those in the rest of Europe. After some hesitation, the Scandinavian people became resolute Lutheran Protestants. Poland, owing to intense work by the Jesuits, remained a Catholic outpost in eastern Europe. After the fall of Constantinople to the Turks, Russia became the acknowledged head of the Greek Orthodox Church. Thus religion increased the tensions caused by the barriers of race and language.

The kingdoms of Scandinavia had a special relationship with each other but all efforts to join them together into an effective combination failed. The Hanseatic League now fades out of the picture. The Dutch had taken over much of their trade and only the Baltic remained. At first Denmark, because of her control of the narrow straits at the mouth of the Baltic Sea, dominated the position. But during the seventeenth century the military

power of the brilliant Swedish kings was too much for her.

Awakening of Russia

Russia, the slumbering giant, was gradually awakening. She began to seek a window to the west and ice-free ports for foreign trade. Brandenburg and Prussia were united in 1618 and the foundations of future German power began to be laid.

At the end of the Middle Ages, Russia became a united country under the princes of Moscow, who now began to call themselves Tsars. They could make no advance westwards but the Cossack settlements were started in the south and the long colonisation of Siberia went steadily ahead. In 1613, Michael Romanov came to the throne, his dynasty of emperors lasting until the revolutions of 1917.

It was Peter the Great who brought the Russian people into contact with the western world and made Russia a European power. He reorganised the administration of the country in

Some years later, Catherine the Great continued Peter's work and the Ukraine and Crimea were added to the empire. The conquest of the Crimea, which Count Suvorov gained from the Turks, gave Russia a port in the south.

Gustavus Adolphus

During the later Middle Ages, Denmark had been the most important country in Scandinavia and her kings ruled for a time over Sweden. But in the seventeenth century Sweden rose to her greatest height under brilliant soldier kings. The first of these was Gustavus Adolphus, who suddenly

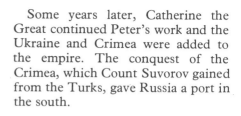

Maria Theresa was empress of Austria and mother of Marie Antoinette. When the male line of the Habsburgs failed, her father, Charles VI, appointed her as his heir to the throne. She married her cousin Francis of Lorraine and when her father died in 1740 became queen of Hungary and Bohemia and archduchess of Austria. In the general warfare which followed her accession, Prussia seized Silesia and the foreign policy of Maria Theresa was dominated by her efforts to regain it. The able Kaunitz was her chief minister. Her husband, and later her son Joseph, shared the responsibilities of government with her. She died in 1780.

every area and made the nobles take a full share in running the state. Realising that Russia was behind in technical knowledge, Peter himself travelled to England and Holland, working as a carpenter in the shipyards to learn the art of shipbuilding. He started Russia's first newspaper and abandoned the old calendar. Russians were compelled to adopt western customs and to shave their beards. After a war with Sweden, Peter gained control of a long stretch of the Baltic coastline and built his new capital at St Petersburg (now Leningrad). This act gave Russia a port in the west.

and dramatically appeared out of the north to save the Protestant cause in the Thirty Years War. Charles X and Charles XII followed. The Swedish ambition was to make the Baltic a Swedish lake, but their land was poor in resources and had only a small population. The supreme effort which their great kings asked of them produced a temporary success but by the end of the century the country was left weak and impoverished.

Poland had been united with Lithuania for two centuries under the great Jagellon dynasty and became a great power. They were often in a position to dominate and interfere in

Russian affairs and hatred between the two countries has lasted until modern times. During the eighteenth century, however, the surrounding great powers of Russia, Austria and Prussia step by step divided and absorbed Poland until the country disappeared.

The Habsburg power was now permanently divided between the Spanish and Austrian branches of the family. Yet the expansion of Austria in central Europe made the Vienna Habsburgs almost as formidable as in

During the eighteenth century military costume reflected the spirit of the new professional soldier. Prussia led the way by providing its armies with smart and colourful uniforms. Seen here are two Prussian grenadiers.

Peter the Great possessed enormous energy and ability which he used to compel his country to adopt the technical methods of the western world.

Eventually, and at a terrible cost, Frederick reduced his enemies to Austria and Russia. At the moment of exhaustion, he was saved by the death of Elizabeth in 1762, which took Russia out of the fighting. Yet in a few years all three powers were working together to divide up Poland and to destroy her as a nation.

When Frederick the Great died in

St Basil's Cathedral in Red Square, Moscow, was begun by Ivan the Terrible in 1554.

the greatest days of the past. Yet the Austrian empire was weaker than it seemed, for these subject lands were very independent and often hated each other. There was no real unity. The Emperor, Charles VI, had no son to succeed him, so in 1713 he altered the law to arrange for his daughter Maria Theresa to succeed him, and bound almost every European power to respect her claim. But immediately upon his death in 1740, these promises were broken and Frederick the Great of Prussia, supported by France and Spain, seized Silesia. In the long war which followed, Maria Theresa proved her worth and rallied her

forces, with the help of England and Holland, to establish her rights. But Prussia had to be bought off with Silesia in 1745.

Prussia Attacks

Maria Theresa, who had a personal friendship with Elizabeth, Empress of Russia, meditated her revenge against Prussia. Her minister, Kaunitz, even achieved a league with France, her old enemy, to contain the rising power of Prussia. Frederick realised the need for instant action and attacked his enemies piecemeal before they could steamroller him out of existence.

1786 he left behind him a strong and vital state unlike any other among the Germans. Austria was still officially the heir to the Holy Roman Empire and by tradition the head of the German states. But in practice Prussia was every bit as strong as Austria. The two powers watched every move made by the other. Each sought to win the petty German states to its own side. Whatever the outcome was to be, either Prussia or Austria would be the leader of Germany in the years ahead. But over the whole of Europe the Napoleonic storm was to break and throw many of the old national patterns into the melting pot.

Rebels and Colonists

Spain and Portugal were already well established in their colonies when the other seagoing nations decided to carve out new lands for themselves. In the seventeenth century, France, Holland and England followed in their footsteps. The rivalry between the five powers and troubles with their overseas subjects make up European colonial history for the next two centuries.

Colonisation made English a world language although French is still spoken in eastern Canada. The old Spanish lands have retained Spanish as their language and Brazil still speaks Portuguese.

The different nature of the European colonies is explained by the attitudes of those taking part. The Spanish and many of the first adventurers were in search of easy wealth, and their tropical lands could

Seal of the Council of Virginia, the first permanent English settlement in America. The colony was named after Queen Elizabeth, the 'Virgin Queen', and was founded in 1607.

be worked only by slave labour on a plantation basis. After the first great extraction of wealth, the Spanish colonies did not flourish to any great extent. The Dutch were traders rather than settlers and they established a network of good ports throughout the world. As explorers, the French were brave and successful but they were not at first natural colonisers or seafarers and their effort was driven on by official decrees from France. But the English had two types of willing settlers, superior to the adventurers and political colonists of other nations.

English Colonists

In England the custom of primogeniture (from the Latin, meaning 'first born') decreed that the whole of the father's land must descend to the eldest son. The idea was to keep the large estates intact and of a worthwhile size. But it did mean that all the

younger sons were left without any inheritance. Normally they entered the army, the professions or the church. But many of these younger sons, ambitious, educated and self-confident, were eager to go abroad and establish estates for themselves in the empty new lands of the west. They maintained their links with home and became a transplanted aristocracy.

The other good colonists, mainly drawn from the middle classes, were the religious refugees who left England in anger because they could not worship God in their own way. In a moment of despair Oliver Cromwell all but went with them. These religious colonists were principally Puritans, Quakers and Catholics. They were consciously starting a new life abroad and their links with home were much weaker. After the Civil War the number of British settlers was greatly increased by Royalist officers who had been dispossessed.

The French exploration of North America began when Jacques Cartier, a Breton, discovered the St Lawrence river and renamed an Indian village by calling it Montreal. The French penetrated into the heart of the continent via the Great Lakes and by 1612 Champlain had founded Quebec and had been made the lieutenant-governor of French Canada. Later the great French explorer, Robert La Salle, travelled right down the Mississippi river system to the Gulf of Mexico, where he founded the state of Louisiana in honour of Louis XIV.

The English were obliged to settle on the Atlantic seaboard between the hostile French in the north and the hostile Spanish in the south. The Indians and the Appalachian mountains stopped them from venturing too far to the west. In this somewhat confined area the original thirteen

The establishment of the Hudson's Bay Company gave England the opportunity to compete with French Canadians for a share in the valuable fur trade.

Early Puritan settlers in America built their first homes near the seashore.

colonies were set up during a period of just over a hundred years.

New England

The first English colonies fell into natural groups of quite distinct types. In the north the four colonies were Massachusetts, Rhode Island, Connecticut and New Hampshire. These colonies were known collectively as New England. They were founded by Puritan settlers. The first wave came with the *Mayflower* in 1620 but thousands more soon followed.

In the south were five plantation colonies. The first successful colony was Virginia, founded in 1607, which had its own Assembly. Maryland was founded by Lord Baltimore for English Catholics. The new colony

Settlements and exploration in North America.

HUDSON BAY

QUEBEC

NEW ENGLAND

PENNSYLVANIA

APPALACHIAN MTS.

VIRGINIA

Mississippi River

British

French

French Exploration

was remarkable for its religious toleration. North and South Carolina were an aristocratic venture and the last to be founded was Georgia. Originally it was intended as a refuge for debtors but it soon became rich. The plantation lands of the southern colonies had to be worked by slave labour, but there was little need for slave labour on the farms of the north. The contrast between the Puritan north and the aristocrat south was laid down from the beginning.

Between the north and south groups of colonies lay settlements which had been made by the Dutch and the Swedes. The Dutch easily conquered the small Swedish settlement at the mouth of the Delaware. Soon afterwards, in similar fashion, the British attacked the Dutch settlement, called the New Netherlands, and took it over. It became two new states, New York and New Jersey. The name of the chief port was changed from New Amsterdam to New York. Delaware made a third separate colony and William Penn, the great Quaker, came out from England to found Pennsylvania. By gentle persuasion, he achieved the hitherto unknown feat of living peacefully with the Indians.

The Caribbean

Settlements were also made in the smaller islands of the Caribbean Sea by both French and English colonists. Jamaica was the only large island in England's hands. It had been seized in Cromwell's day by an English force actually sent against Cuba. Finding Cuba impossible to take, the almost unoccupied island of Jamaica was taken as compensation. Little was made of it for many years until sugar growing was developed. Barbados was the most important small island in English possession. But after some experiment with poor whites and criminals, the plantations had to be worked by slaves.

In the eighteenth century the French and the English were often in conflict where their interests clashed in Nova Scotia and in the Ohio valley. George Washington was engaged in some of this fighting on behalf of the colony of Virginia. Eventually the two countries went into full-scale colonial war both in Canada and India. The result was the utter loss of Canada by the French. In the fighting over the key city of Quebec, both commanders, Montcalm and Wolfe, were killed.

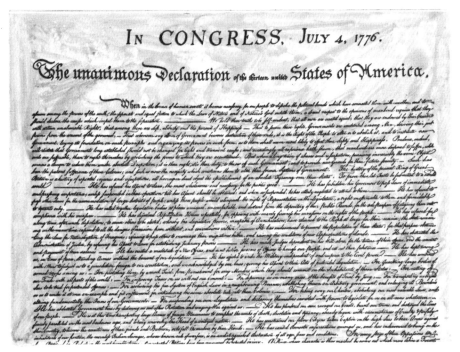

The American Revolution

The North American colonies had been started in a period when the mercantile system was the basis of colonial trade. The idea was to promote trade strictly in the interests of the home country. Products which could not be obtained at home were required from the colonies. In exchange the colonies had to buy their manufactured goods from the home country and no other. Further, trade goods had to be carried in the ships of the home country. The American colonies suffered from this dog-in-the-manger attitude of mercantile trade although conditions imposed by Britain were less harsh than most.

There was very little emigration from England in the eighteenth century, so the bulk of the colonists were descended from the first settlers. By now their lives had developed along different lines from those of English people. Also, the width of the Atlantic made contact with England slow and difficult. The thirteen states had separate governments and were very jealous of each other. The New England states, by their nature, were more hostile to England than the southern plantation states. The main centre of opposition was Boston.

One of the benefits the colonists did receive from England was defence by the home army and navy against any common enemy. While the French were in Canada, the danger of invasion made this privilege very real. But once the English had defeated the French and the danger was removed, the colonists felt much bolder. Then the burden of helping to pay for forces which they did not control and no longer needed, became a very bitter question.

Boston Tea Party

In the period immediately before the outbreak of rebellion, there were various taxation acts, passed by the English parliament, which the colonists rejected. Then in 1773 a new Tea Act allowed the East India Company to export tea direct to America, thus crushing private traders. Actually the tea was cheaper, but the act was high-handed and was resented. A party of American colonists, dressed up as Red Indians, boarded English ships in Boston Harbour and dumped their £18,000 cargoes of tea overboard. This was the famous Boston 'tea party'. In reply, Lord North's government in London closed the port of Boston. This act led to the calling of the first Congress of all thirteen American states at Philadelphia in 1774. At this stage there was no cry for independence at all. But fighting broke out at Lexington and Concord in 1775 between British troops and Massachusetts volunteers.

The first phase of the war was between the British forces and the colonists without outside interference. However, the war was never popular in England with the ordinary people, so many of the troops used by the British were German mercenaries, called 'Hessians'. The British held the command of the sea which enabled them to transport troops at will. At this stage the colonists were very badly organised, but they chose the right leader in George Washington. He was from Virginia and his personal influence did much to bring the southern states into the struggle. As a field commander he lost many battles but he had a will of iron and unbreakable determination. Supplies of money, food and clothing were always short on the American side and great suffering caused continuous desertion. But Washington never wavered. The British commanders, in this first phase, won many battles but had no overall plan to unite their efforts.

Colonists Attack Canada

At first the fighting centred around Boston which the British were finally obliged to quit. The troops were withdrawn to Halifax in Nova Scotia. Thinking that Canada was equally unhappy under British rule, the colonists decided to attack Montreal and Quebec in order to link up with the Canadians. But General Burgoyne, who had come out from England with reinforcements, easily repulsed the attacks, and Canada was safe for the rest of the war. General Howe now successfully took New York and it remained in British hands until the peace treaty.

The lack of overall command in the English army now showed itself. Burgoyne planned to come down from Canada and join forces with Howe who was to march inland from New York. This meeting would have cut the states in two. New England would have been isolated and could have been defeated. But there was poor communication between the two commanders. Howe took his forces off by sea and captured Philadelphia to the south, unbeknown to Burgoyne. With weak forces and dwindling supplies of food, Burgoyne was trapped at Saratoga and compelled to surrender. This exciting victory persuaded the French to come into the war on the side of the colonists, and in 1778 an alliance was made. The Americans not only gained naval support but also some skilled and experienced officers.

Cornwallis Surrenders

Britain now found herself at war with France and Spain as well. Several nations joined together to resist her demands that neutral shipping should be searched in order to prevent them carrying war supplies to the colonists. The British had now lost the command of the sea. They pulled out of Philadelphia and returned to New York, from where they launched a campaign against the south, managing to take Charleston. Washington pursued the British in the south and the French navy blockaded the coast. General Cornwallis was thus compelled to surrender at Yorktown and the war was virtually over.

Lord North's government fell, and the Whigs, who had always been sympathetic to the colonists, came into power. The war had started out with no idea of independence. At the end generous conditions were offered for peace which had they been offered sooner, would probably have been accepted. On the world scene, Britain quickly recovered her naval supremacy and both countries began to prosper. The old colonial system was now dead. From then on, the British Empire was to follow a very different pattern.

The thirteen states had made their Declaration of Independence at Philadelphia on 4th July 1776. Now they had to work out a constitution. Each state was jealous of the others' authority and the task was long and difficult.

Ironically, the help which the French gave to the American rebels recoiled on their own heads. Revolutionaries in France were encouraged by the success of the American colonists. Their example had shown that, if they were determined enough, ordinary people with little resources could overthrow a powerful government.

American soldier

George Washington was born in the English colony of Virginia in 1732 and became the first president of the United States. He was first noticed as a young colonel in the fighting between the English and the French on the Ohio river. In the War of Independence he was the only outstanding leader acceptable to all the American colonists. The war was a triumph for Washington's character and determination not to yield. After the war he returned home to Mount Vernon for a time. He was elected president in 1789.

British grenadier

Summary of key dates
1607 First British colony founded in Virginia
1620 Voyage of the *Mayflower*
1686 League of Ausberg formed
1689 Peter the Great czar of Russia
1713 Treaty of Utrecht
1740 Frederick the Great king of Prussia
1746 Battle of Culloden
1775 American Revolution begins
1776 Declaration of Independence of the United States

British Imperialism

A painting in the Mogul style which reflects the Indian view of a typical English settler.

Vasco da Gama discovered the sea route to India for Portugal in 1497. The voyage was many thousands of kilometres long and took several months by sail. But the Portuguese had built up a chain of ports along the African coast which gave them a great advantage.

English explorers tried for some time to find an alternative route but finally it was decided to challenge the Portuguese along their valuable African route. As a result the East India Company was founded in 1600 and the Dutch followed with their own company three years later.

The Dutch company was better organised and backed with more capital. The Portuguese were soon ousted from their possessions in Ceylon, the East Indies and India. Soon they were confined to a small area around Goa on the coast of India. In the East Indies the Dutch proved stronger than the English and ejected them from the Spice Islands.

Trading Profits

At first each voyage to India was financed as a separate undertaking but by 1657 the British Company was financed on a permanent basis. It then had the resources to build ships, create stocks of goods, and to employ permanent servants overseas. There was both criticism and jealousy of the company but matters were allowed to take their course.

When the British began to trade with India, the rule of the great Mogul emperors was coming to an end. These Mohammedan invaders from Central Asia had developed a fine civilisation, but after the death of Arungzebe in 1707, the empire quickly shrank to a small area around Delhi. Bands of marauding horsemen from the south, called Mahrattas, were looting and raiding at will. Trade was suffering and the situation had to be faced.

The French India Company had not been founded until 1664 but had the benefit of a halfway house at Mauritius. At first there was no conflict between the European traders until a new governor, Joseph Dupleix, arrived at Pondicherry in 1741. Dupleix could see that the chaotic political situation could be exploited for the benefit of France. He created a well-drilled army of native troops, called sepoys, and dabbled in native politics. He started to support puppet rulers in the native states and soon the whole of south India was going over to the French.

Robert Clive

At this point a young man named Robert Clive came out to India in the service of the English company. He had been trained as a soldier, and he immediately proved at the Siege of Arcot that the French could be beaten. Dupleix was recalled to France and disgraced. He died in poverty yet Clive was to follow his policy and lay the foundation of the British power in India.

In Bengal, the British, Dutch and French had trading stations very close together. But they lived in peace until Surajah Dowlah, who violently hated the British, became the ruler. He took Calcutta and shut up his prisoners in a small guard room where nearly all died from thirst or suffocation. This was the infamous 'Black Hole of Calcutta'. When Madras heard about this atrocity, Clive was sent to Bengal. He won a great

victory over a huge native army at Plassey, and Bengal became British.

France was now at war with Britain all over the world. The Comte de Lally raised rebellion again in southeast India in the French interest, but Sir Eyre Coote defeated him at Wandewash in 1760. This was the end of French rule in India. Thereafter they were allowed only to have unarmed trading posts.

Corruption and profiteering were very bad at this time. When Clive came home he was challenged and barely excused himself. But he returned to India and introduced a number of reforms. The truth was that the task of ruling India was now beyond the scope of a private company. Consequently, Lord North, whose ministry did so much to lose the American colonies, passed an act appointing a governor-general, to be advised by a council of four. Warren Hastings, already the governor of Bengal, was chosen to be the first governor-general. He proved to be

worthy of the long line of distinguished men who followed him. Unfortunately, three of the council of four were his personal enemies and there was serious friction. His chief critic, Philip Francis, on his return to England campaigned against him. During the American Revolution when British resources were stretched to the limit, the French made one more attempt to regain their position. But Sir Eyre Coote was again equal to the task and Bombay was saved.

In 1785 Warren Hastings was recalled to answer charges of corruption and false dealing. His trial dragged on for seven years but he was at last acquitted. The outcome, however, was excellent, for Pitt caused the trading and governing sides of the company to be separated. The British cabinet now took full charge of India through the governor-general and this system lasted until the mutiny of 1857.

Robert Clive, the founder of the British Empire in India, began as a clerk with the East India Company. After victories over the allies of the French, he was rapidly promoted until he became governor of Bengal.

William Wilberforce was the member of the British parliament who led the movement to abolish slavery. He roused the nation's conscience to end slavery in the British Empire. The drawing above shows the way slaves were stowed on ships.

The new governor-general was Lord Cornwallis, who had surrendered to the American colonists at Yorktown. In Bengal, Cornwallis organised justice and taxation so well that it became a model for other provinces.

The Wellesley Brothers

Two brothers next made a considerable mark on India. At the time when Napoleon was on his great campaign in Egypt the Marquis of Wellesley arrived in India as there was a serious threat to her security. Mysore again became troublesome. Its ruler declared himself in favour of the French revolution and called himself 'Citizen Tippoo'. The military campaign against Mysore was fought by the Marquis's younger brother, Sir Arthur Wellesley, the future Duke of Wellington. He easily defeated Tippoo who was killed in the fighting. All south India passed into British control. The two brothers realised that satisfactory control of India could only be achieved by a power that governed the whole country. By force and by alliance, they expanded the British possessions until half India was under British control. The Mahratta lands were now ringed round on three sides. Alarmed by so aggressive a policy and by its cost, the government recalled Wellesley. But his work had brought peace to India by eliminating the military states. A more humane spirit was abroad and William Wilberforce was freeing the slaves. Peace was now to bring its blessings to India.

Australia and the Far East

Even though their home countries might be locked in desperate wars, the traders and seamen of Europe went on with their work of exploration. Year by year the unknown world shrank as the tiny ships ventured into uncharted seas and made contact with fresh lands. In the sixteenth century the Far East was brought into the area of European trade by sea.

The Portuguese led the way, following their discovery of the route to India. They had trading stations everywhere on the African and Asiatic coasts. As early as 1517, in the days of the great Ming dynasty, they founded a post at Canton. They were the first in Japan but were closely followed by the Spanish and the Dutch. However, over-aggressive missionary activity forced on by the Inquisition caused the Portuguese and Spanish to be expelled. For a time the Dutch were permitted some limited access but then Japan closed her doors to the foreigners for centuries. They were not reopened until 1853 when Perry compelled entry on behalf of the United States.

Ferdinand Magellan was a Portuguese sailing in the service of Spain. He was killed in the Philippines but the few remaining members of his crew brought their ship safely home and thus were the first men to sail round the world.

Captain Cook commanded three scientific voyages which mapped the Pacific Ocean and Australasia.

One outcome of this feat was that the thousands of islands which make up the Philippines were occupied for Spain in the days of Philip II and given his name. They remained Spanish until the United States took them over in 1898.

In 1652 the Dutch established a useful port of call at the Cape of Good Hope on the southern tip of Africa. The Dutch were always more interested in trade than in the founding of colonies. Consequently they advanced their eastern exploration considerably while the French and English were fighting each other.

Abel Tasman

The early makers of maps believed that there was a large undiscovered continent in the waters of the southern hemisphere. They called it *Terra Australis Incognita* or 'the unknown land of the south'. From this Latin label, Australia received its name. As the early seamen found landfall in the southern Pacific, they thought they had discovered this unknown territory. The Dutch cruised along the coast of north and

west Australia. The most famous of them, Abel Tasman, landed on the island which is named after him. He also found New Zealand which he named after a Dutch province.

The man who brought Australasia on to the world map was Captain James Cook of the British Royal Navy. Cook had been with Wolfe at Quebec and, in fact, made the chart of the St Lawrence which was used in the attack. He was chosen in 1768 to take command of a scientific expedition to the South Seas. With him sailed Sir Joseph Banks, a president of the Royal Society. He was also the chief founder of the Botanical Gardens at Kew which have ever since been concerned with the study of the world's plants.

Cook was a fine professional sailor. He sailed to Tahiti and from there made for New Zealand where he explored both the North and South Islands and carefully charted the coasts. He then discovered the eastern coast of Australia and sailed the whole length of the Great Barrier Reef. This hazardous voyage without charts

showed Cook's amazing skill as a navigator. Later Cook was to be killed at Hawaii by natives.

The most promising part of the newly discovered Australian coastline was named New South Wales by Cook who thought the country looked similar to Wales. Sir Joseph Banks was particularly struck by the wealth of vegetation and gave the name of Botany Bay to the place where they landed. The area seemed very suitable for colonisation and the expedition reported back favourably to England. But the home country was having its bitter experiences with its American colonists and further colonisation was not an attractive idea.

Port Jackson

The home government, however, did have one use for New South Wales. The loss of America had deprived them of a dumping ground for criminals not wanted in Britain. A penal settlement was therefore founded at Port Jackson and run on the harshest military lines. The port was renamed Sydney in honour of the Home Secretary of the time. Since English penalties for petty offences were the most severe in Europe at that time, some very good men and women found themselves in the Australian penal settlements. These vigorous, enterprising people made very hardy colonists when they were freed.

A small number of free emigrants also went out to Australia from the first, but progress was slow. Then in 1813 the Bathurst Gap was discovered in the Blue Mountains behind Sydney and the wonderful grassy plains beyond were revealed. To this superb grazing ground, English sheep were introduced, some from the herds of that excellent farmer,

The first explorers found native peoples in both Australia and New Zealand. The Aborigines of Australia (left) were a primitive hunting people but the Maoris of New Zealand were far more advanced.

George III. The free immigrants rapidly increased in number and the future of that great country now lay in the hands of farmers and explorers.

Gibbon Wakefield was a great man to whom both Australia and New Zealand owe much. He wished to remove the convict stigma from the new lands. When Charles Sturt traced the Murray River to Encounter Bay, Wakefield formed the South Australia Company. Adelaide was founded and the idea of assisted passages to help willing but poor colonists to come from England was begun.

Self Government

The discovery of gold in Victoria increased that state's population four times in five years. About the same time the new Australian states were given self government by Britain.

The Aborigines of Australia gave no trouble to the colonists but the Maoris of New Zealand were a different matter. They were fierce, warlike and intelligent. There was a good deal of fighting but once again Gibbon Wakefield formed a new company to regulate New Zealand affairs. Sir George Grey had two excellent periods of service as governor-general and the problem was overcome. The Maoris were bought out and now live peaceably with the other colonists with whom they are becoming absorbed.

Maori wood sculpture

159

The Revolutionary Age

By comparison with the rest of Europe, Britain was a fortunate country in the eighteenth century. Serfdom had long been extinct and parliamentary government was well established. No class of people was excused responsibility to the country. England and Scotland were joined together, giving each other mutual strength, and the nation was successful abroad and growing quickly in prosperity at home. English institutions were held up as a model by French writers in contrast to their own unfortunate country.

The situation in Europe was desperate by comparison and led to the outbreak of the revolution in France in 1789 which completely changed the political face of the world.

Throughout the eighteenth century France had been declining from the high peak of Louis XIV's reign. The well-merited discontent of her people was fanned to danger point by the scorn and indignation of her able writers. Also, in the neighbouring countries to France, there was an audience of underprivileged peoples ready to respond to the thrilling cry of 'Liberty, Equality and Fraternity' which was the republican slogan of the revolution.

A Master of War

At first the brilliant military achievements of Napoleon, a master of war, might seem to have been as superficial and disastrous as so many of the conquests of great soldiers in aggressive wars. But to many of the suffering peoples of Europe Napoleon came as a saviour. His reorganisation of France has also proved permanent. He laid the foundations of German and Italian unity, an end which had been desired for centuries.

The settlement of 1815 which ended the Napoleonic Wars was, however, a resounding setback for liberty and democratic progress. Prince Metternich of Austria easily persuaded the frightened rulers of western Europe that the correct policy was to put the clock back to the eighteenth century. Thus the Holy Alliance attempted to ignore the revolution and to re-assert the traditional control of Church and Crown. The forces of nationalism were given as little encouragement by Metternich as were the forces of liberalism. Small countries were placed under the rule of larger ones without reference to their wishes.

Socialist Ideas

Yet the changes going on in Britain, where the population was surging upwards and the cities growing like mushrooms, was to be the pattern for all western Europe in the years ahead. New problems were emerging which demanded new solutions. Much thought was being given, particularly in France, to the effects of industrialisation. Liberal and socialist ideas were being spread among the men and women of the overcrowded towns. Nationalism, by which people prefer to be governed by men of their own race, was also very powerful. Sometimes these two forces worked together and sometimes against each other but they were both opposed to the old order. All this ferment gave rise to two general outbreaks of revolution in 1830 and 1848.

In 1830 France changed the powers of the monarchy to those of a constitutional king, and the Belgians broke away from the Dutch. The revolutionary movements of 1848 were more general and affected France, Italy, Austria and Germany. The reign of Metternich came to an end in Austria and feudalism was over. There was an unsuccessful attempt at representative government in Germany and the Second Republic

The ideas of philosophers and writers, such as Kant (above) and Rousseau (below), encouraged the French Revolution.

The word *sansculottes*, meaning 'without knee breeches', was the name given to the Paris mob by the aristocrats.

lasted only four years in France. Italy was in turmoil but the King of Sardinia emerged as the leader of the campaign for a united country. The setback was only temporary. By 1871 Germany and Italy had achieved unity and the Third Republic of France had been firmly founded.

Summary of key dates
1789	Beginning of French Revolution
1798	Battle of the Nile
1804	Napoleon Bonaparte emperor of France
1805	Battle of Trafalgar
1806	Holy Roman Empire dissolved
1808	The Peninsular War begins
1812	French retreat from Moscow
1815	Battle of Waterloo. Holy Alliance of Russia, Prussia and Austria

The storming of the Bastille in Paris showed that violence could succeed. The poster demands that the Revolution's ideas must be accepted on pain of death.

The French Revolution

France's power declined rapidly in the eighteenth century, and the monarchy became distrusted. Richelieu and his successors had built up the central power of the throne until every petty decision had to be taken by the king's Council at Versailles. The nobles, despite their arrogance and endless privileges, had no power. Both in Church and State, France was in the grip of the past.

Taxation, which hardly touched the nobility, was increased to breaking point upon the unfortunate peasants. The village mill, the wine-press, slaughterhouse and oven all belonged to the local lord and he charged for their use. The peasants alone endured compulsory military service. Agriculture, by which they lived, was backward in technique. Tithes had to be paid to a Church which was corrupt and unpopular. Not only were taxes murderously unequal but they were collected inefficiently. At last the situation became so desperate that the king resolved to call the States-General, an old form of parliament which had not met for nearly two hundred years.

Louis XVI attempted reforms but received no help from his Austrian wife, Marie Antoinette, whose influence upon him was harmful. The States-General met in May 1789 with the intention of producing a programme of reform. The delegates represented three groups: the nobles, the clergy and the common people, called the third estate. But the government had no plan to put before this assembly, and the delegates quarrelled about whether the three groups should meet together or separately. The third estate won the argument and the united body became known as the National Assembly. A step towards reform had been taken.

Storming the Bastille

The Paris mob, which played a leading part in the revolution, was increased dangerously at this time by the failure of the preceding year's harvest, which caused starvation and great hardship to the people. Impatient of delay, on 14th July they stormed the Bastille prison and released the handful of prisoners they found inside. That act became a symbol and the day is still a national holiday in France. A citizen army was formed to prevent looting and placed under the command of Lafayette, who had distinguished himself in the American War.

The Assembly at Versailles declared an end to serfdom and the privileges of the nobles. The starving mob compelled the king and queen to move to Paris. The Assembly followed and continued to make sweeping reforms. The Church was made a department of the state and its property sold. The king decided to

The French writer Voltaire helped to destroy the old order in France by his ridicule of its absurdities.

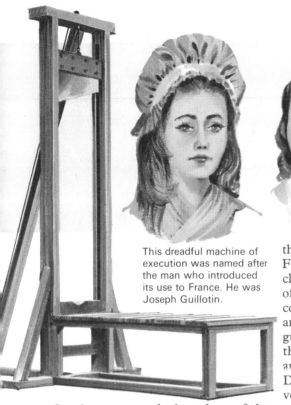

This dreadful machine of execution was named after the man who introduced its use to France. He was Joseph Guillotin.

Louis XVI and Marie Antoinette, his Austrian wife, were executed on the guillotine during the Revolution.

flee, but was caught just short of the frontier at Varennes. On his return to Paris the king had to accept a new constitution.

The Assembly which met in October 1791 still had a majority of moderate members but the mood was changing, driven on by the mob. Friction grew between the king and the Assembly. Many of the leading nobles, including the king's two brothers, had fled the country but were waiting just across the frontiers to return and overthrow the revolution. Naturally, the Assembly wished to punish them but the king refused to co-operate. War now broke out with Austria and Prussia, and eastern France was invaded. There was a massacre of royalist prisoners in Paris, the king was deposed, and the new Convention declared France a republic.

The Reign of Terror
The ugly side of the French Revolution was now to come, with power moving swiftly from the moderates to the extremists. There was little difference in principle between the two parties, but the moderate Girondins had their main support deep in provincial France. The extremist Jacobins were tougher, cruder and better organised, and they had the support of the Paris council and the mob. The king was tried and put to death. The Jacobins had triumphed and the Reign of Terror began.

The Terror was justified because in

the perilous emergency in which France found herself, the Jacobins claimed that all treachery was worthy of death. It made a fifth column or counter-revolution impossible. Priests and aristocrats were hurried to the guillotine, Marie Antoinette among them. Wealthy men followed next, and finally the leaders of the Terror, Danton and Robespierre, were devoured by the monster they had created. Then the pendulum began to swing back. France was no longer in serious danger and the remaining aristocrats were of little importance. Trials became fewer and fairer.

The Convention, which had meanwhile been doing excellent work in reorganising France, recovered control of the country. To prevent small

groups seizing power a new constitution, called the Directory, was introduced, so arranged that royalists could never gain a majority. This new body was unpopular and the real power was with the army. The mob attacked the Directory in the Tuileries but were easily dispersed by the artillery under the command of General Bonaparte. This small action, known as 'the whiff of grapeshot', finished the power of the mob. With their disappearance, the disorders of the revolution were over. Constitutional government was restored and a great man of destiny took a soldier's hand in solving the political difficulties of his country.

Yet the Directory was weak and inefficient. French defeats in war made its position impossible. The Directory was overthrown in favour of the Consulate. Napoleon Bonaparte, who had by then won his laurels in Italy, became the First Consul. In the course of a mere ten years, France passed from monarchy, through the Revolution, and back again to a situation where power was given to one man. But it was a different France which Napoleon was to lead. The worst evils of the past had gone for good.

The eighteenth century was a time of great cultural activity and no one better illustrated its elegance and good taste than the composer Mozart. In his short life he produced an amazing quantity of music of superlative quality. With his sister Maria Anna, he toured the courts of western Europe giving public concerts as a child prodigy. Also he began to compose when six years of age and the unceasing flow of invention never failed, despite chronic ill health, until his early death at thirty-five. Mozart had no gift for business and was always very poor.

Wolfgang Amadeus Mozart (1756–91)

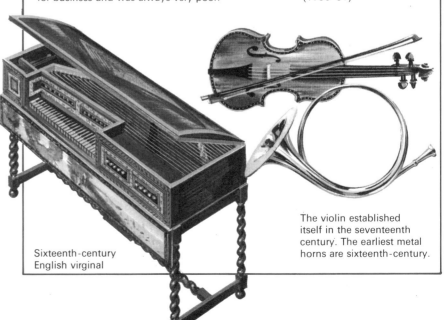

Sixteenth-century English virginal

The violin established itself in the seventeenth century. The earliest metal horns are sixteenth-century.

Napoleon and Nationalism

At the time of the French Revolution the general opinion among the European powers was that France was no longer a military menace to other countries. No one could have foreseen that France's greatest soldier was about to lead her on a brilliant career of conquest.

The Convention asked for trouble by appealing directly to the oppressed peoples of Europe to overthrow their masters with the co-operation of republican France. They promised to abolish feudalism and establish republics wherever their forces were successful. Consequently, all the leading powers joined a coalition against France. Despite the odds being greatly against them, the recently freed people of France rose to the occasion and defeated their enemies. French armies were successful everywhere and France and Spain entered into an alliance. Only Austria, Great Britain and Sardinia were left in the ring.

The young General Napoleon, who had already ably defended Toulon and routed the Paris mob, was now sent to Italy. Here he at once displayed his military genius. His speed and efficiency, backed by good artillery, demoralised his enemies. He had also the ability to pick outstanding officers. He soon split the Austrians and the Sardinians and defeated them separately. The treaty of Campo Formio, which ended the war, gave France great benefits. The left bank of the Rhine and the Austrian Netherlands became French. The Venetian Republic ceased and across the whole of northern Italy, republics favourable to France were created.

Command of the Sea

The year 1797 was critical for Great Britain. She now stood alone against France who had the fleets of Spain and Holland at her service. Invasion became possible. But the English admirals secured command of the sea and the long struggle between the whale (Great Britain) and the elephant (France) began. Partly because a sea-power and a land-power find it difficult to come to grips, the struggle was drawn out until 1815.

In 1798 Napoleon made his famous expedition to Egypt and met his first serious defeat. The English admiral Nelson at last caught the French fleet and destroyed it at the Battle of the Nile. Napoleon was called back to France to deal with troubles nearer

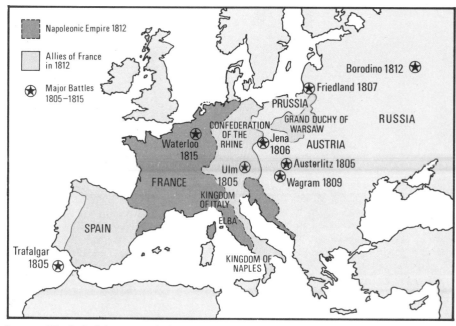

Napoleon's Empire and the scene of his battles.

home. He left his army behind and eventually it was compelled to surrender. Napoleon made no more sorties out of Europe.

A second coalition was formed against France, which had some success in Italy. When Napoleon was sent there, he won the battle of Marengo and Austria had to accept again the terms of the earlier treaty. But, in addition, the German states began to be reorganised according to French ideas. Once again Great Britain stood alone against Napoleon. The sea-going nations formed a league to prevent the British controlling neutral shipping, but it was defeated. Stalemate between the British, successful at sea, and the French, successful on land, produced the Peace of Amiens in 1802. France kept many of her gains while the British remained safe behind the Channel.

The Consulate, with Napoleon at the head, restored centralised government which the Revolution had weakened by dispersing the old royal power too thoroughly. Napoleon was beyond question the real ruler of the state and the monarchy was well on the way to being restored. Taxation was improved and the revenues collected with a new efficiency. In

imitation of the Bank of England, the Bank of France was established and French credit improved abroad. By trying to outlaw religion the Revolution had lost much support, but now a Concordat, or agreement, was made by Napoleon with the pope. The Catholic religion was again recognised as the official religion of France, and in return a substantial measure of state control of the Church was agreed upon.

Napoleon as Emperor

Napoleon's own position as consul was first confirmed for life and then, by a special vote, he was made emperor. He placed the crown on his own head in the presence of the pope in 1804. Napoleon liked to think that there was a great similarity between his new empire and the mighty Roman empire. Both were born out of a republic and grew to rule many nations. Napoleon copied both the

In 1813 patriotic Prussian women gave up their jewels to raise money for a war with France. They received iron copies which bore the words 'I gave gold for iron'.

This impression of Napoleon is based on Vernat's painting of the victorious French leader at the battle of Jena in 1806.

An incident at the Battle of Waterloo in 1815 when the French cavalry charged the British line.

Roman style and the days of Charlemagne. When his son was born, he was called the 'King of Rome'. The French nation had chosen glory rather than liberty.

Napoleon's new rule was harsh and dictatorial but extremely efficient. The prefects and mayors who ruled local government were appointed from Paris and not elected. The government was reasonable to the émigrés (refugee aristocrats living abroad) and its old political opponents, giving them the chance to change their minds and to settle peaceably in the new France.

Magnificence was the keynote of the emperor's court. But there was one great contrast with the splendour of the old kings. The men in high honour at Napoleon's court were all there because of merit, because of outstanding service to France. Ability was the only path to promotion.

Napoleon was a gifted organiser and a man of high intelligence, apart from his military genius. He was responsible for the organisation of French law and had the famous Civil Code drawn up. Not only was it a permanent influence on French life but the French armies carried it into foreign countries. Napoleon's conquests may have disappeared but his organisation of France remains today.

France steadily increased her power and was hailed as a liberator in many countries. But although she received efficient government from the change, it became increasingly clear that Napoleon was becoming a tyrant. He began to mobilise his power for an invasion of Britain, who had again declared war. Britain also made extensive preparations. The French and Spanish fleets attempted to shake off Nelson's blockade but the English were always superior and brought the

French fleets to Trafalgar where they were destroyed. Britain was safe again at sea but mourned Nelson, her greatest sailor, who was killed at Trafalgar. Russia and Austria now joined Britain, but Napoleon was equal to the threat and defeated the combined armies of Russia and Austria at Austerlitz.

Napoleon Supreme

Prussia organised a north German confederation on her own account and linked forces with Russia. Before the Russians could help, the Prussians were destroyed at Jena and Napoleon entered Berlin as a conqueror. The Russians later met defeat. The Peace of Tilsit followed in 1807. Napoleon was supreme in western and central Europe. This was the highest point of Napoleon's power.

Napoleon now devised the Continental System, a total blockade, which sought to destroy British trade. Britain was in much the stronger trading position and took similar measures which fell hardest on the neutrals. Portugal, an old ally of Britain, refused to join the blockade and Napoleon invaded the Spanish peninsula. He upset the Spanish at the same time by the dictatorial act of placing his brother on the throne of Spain. Using Portugal as a base, Britain waged the long Peninsular

War against the French with the help of Spanish patriots. By 1814 General Wellesley (later the Duke of Wellington) had cleared Spain of the French and invaded France itself.

Finding that Napoleon was heavily engaged in Spain, eastern Europe rose against him. When he attacked the Russians retreated skilfully into their own country. They lured him on and he reached Moscow to find it in ruins, having lost 200,000 men on the march. The Russians played at surrender until the winter set in. Napoleon's disastrous retreat began. Despite Marshal Ney's heroic rearguard action, the Grand Army was cut down from 600,000 to less than 50,000.

At last, in 1814, Napoleon was deposed. He was allowed to keep the title of emperor and to retire to Elba. France was treated very leniently in view of all the suffering she had caused.

The Hundred Days

Watching the victors quarrelling in Vienna, Napoleon left Elba and began the famous 'hundred days', his last attempt to regain power. He was hysterically welcomed in France and the veterans, released prisoners of war, flocked to his standard. All his enemies united against him. Fearing the joint power of the British and the Prussians most, he advanced swiftly to strike before they could combine. At Waterloo, Wellington held on grimly until the Prussians came up and together they slaughtered the last of Napoleon's armies. This time Napoleon was confined on the lonely island of St Helena until he died in 1821.

Wellington, 'the Iron Duke', was a brilliant general and Napoleon's great adversary on land.

Nelson

The dominant figure of the war at sea was Horatio Nelson who went to sea as captain's servant at thirteen and died in the hour of his supreme triumph on the quarterdeck of the *Victory* at Trafalgar. When Britain stood alone, the fleets of Spain and Holland were added to the French fleet. But they were beaten by the British Navy. An attempt to make the Mediterranean a French lake, when Bonaparte invaded Egypt, was foiled by Nelson's destruction of the French fleet in the Battle of the Nile. The action then moved from the Mediterranean to the Baltic, where the northern nations had united to resist the British search for neutral shipping. The Battle of Copenhagen destroyed the Danish navy and Russia collapsed because of troubles at home. Napoleon realised that the invasion of England was the only answer and he schemed to clear the Channel of English ships. The French and Spanish fleets ran for the West Indies. Nelson followed but suspected a ruse—as it was. Finally he brought the enemy to Trafalgar and British naval supremacy was established for a hundred years.

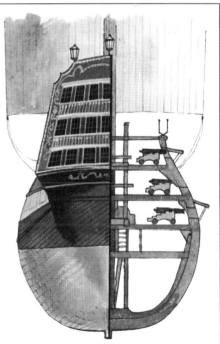

Cross section of an English man-of-war.

Germany and Italy

The forces which so many countries had raised in order to fight Napoleon left Europe an armed camp. By her revolution France had taught the suffering peoples of Europe and the colonies that liberty was possible. Napoleon had shown the dizzy heights to which national pride can raise a country. All over Europe, peasants and work people who had no voice in their government, agitated for a new constitution. The national groups, who were under the rule of a foreigner or sadly disunited, prepared to assert their nationality. As a counter to these hopes stood the figure of Prince Metternich of Austria. He believed that all change was bad, that a return to the past was the only safe course. He had the ear of the crowned heads of Europe and for thirty years his influence was supreme.

Austria and Prussia

There had long been a struggle between Austria and Prussia for the leadership of the German peoples. Austria was established as the greatest German-speaking power but only a part of her empire was German. German unity would weaken her so she was only lukewarm in the cause. On the other hand, the separate German states would never agree until they felt the hand of a master. The prosperity of Germany was rising as its engineering industry expanded, but German unity had to wait for Prussia.

In 1861, a soldier-king, William I, came to the throne of Prussia. He chose as his minister Prince Otto von Bismarck who believed in 'blood and iron' and victory by any methods in order to unite Germany. Bismarck

saw that Austria must be replaced as the leading German power. The Prussian fighting machine was brought to a new peak of efficiency and three key wars against Denmark, Austria and France were won decisively. Bismarck used the Danish war as a trial run. He then lured France into remaining neutral while he dealt with Austria. The efficiency of the Prussian forces, armed with the new breech-loading rifles, easily defeated Austria and all the German states who supported her. Having isolated France, Bismarck arranged a quarrel and crushed her with ease. In 1871 the triumphant Prussian king was crowned German Emperor.

Italian Patriots

For centuries, Italy was the cockpit for wars between the French, Spanish, Austrians and Germans. Among the ever-changing pattern of petty states, only Italy's large cities achieved an outstanding position. Despite this ceaseless unrest, the Italians never lost their sense of race and remained united by their language and religion. Under Napoleon's domination, the divisions of Italy had been reduced to three. But Metternich restored absolute rule and hope of Italian unity appeared to be lost again. The chief difficulties were Austria and the pope, whose lands lay like a barrier across the centre of the country.

Secret societies and revolutionary attempts were organised, but with little success. Then the vision of the Italian patriot Mazzini founded the Young Italy Association and the movement for liberty had a voice. However, the first military attempts against Austria were crushed by

Emperor Francis Joseph came to the throne of Austria in 1848 and ruled for sixty-eight years, dying in 1916. He tried at first to rule absolutely but failure in war caused him to accept a parliament.

Radetsky. But when the fortunes of Italian patriots were at their lowest ebb, Victor Emmanuel came to the throne of Piedmont. He chose as his prime minister the great Count Cavour who began to expand the economy and build a large and efficient army. By allying himself with France, he was able to defy Austria and soon gained most of northern Italy in return for Savoy and Nice, which went to France.

When revolt broke out in Sicily, the daring Garibaldi dashed to the rescue and soon mastered the island. With his famous 'thousand' men he invaded the mainland, overcoming hopeless odds by his enthusiastic bravery. He linked with Cavour at Rome and in 1861 Victor Emmanuel was proclaimed King of Italy. There was still a good deal to do but for once fortune smiled on Italy. In the next ten years, the ambitions of Bismarck shielded Italy from both France and Austria and made her unity permanent.

Garibaldi was the great fighting leader of the Italian patriots. He became a soldier of fortune when he was exiled. His greatest feat was to conquer Sicily with his 'redshirts'.

South American Nations

In the early eighteenth century, the successful revolutions of the American colonists and of the French people encouraged the badly governed Spanish colonies to attempt to gain their freedom. When Wellington waged his long campaign against the French in Spain, he had Portugal and the Spanish patriots for allies. Portugal served as a base for supplies and reinforcements, and the help of the Spanish patriots was most valuable when fighting in a difficult country.

Ferdinand VII, whom Napoleon deposed in order to put his own brother on the throne of Spain, was not beloved by the Spanish people. However, all Spaniards joined together to resist the French and the king made many promises of more liberal ways when the hour of victory arrived. After the downfall of Napoleon, Ferdinand VII again became king under the shadow of Metternich and showed his true intentions by re-introducing press censorship and the Inquisition. When the people rose in revolt, the Holy Alliance encouraged the French to come in and crush them. At this point the South American colonies revolted.

Fortunately, at this dangerous time the colonists in South America found two powerful friends in the United States and Britain. The British government contained men like Canning and Huskisson who were not in favour of repression and wanted the British Empire to be run for the common good of the people at home and abroad. Their foreign policy favoured nations being free to run their own countries without interference. Since the British were the undisputed rulers of the sea, Canning's support was worth having.

Similarly, the United States did not intend to witness an invasion of South America by the reactionary powers of Europe. Canning tried to get the United States to act with him in this matter but they preferred to act on their own account. In 1823 President Monroe made his famous declaration, known as the Monroe Doctrine, to which the United States has adhered ever since. He declared that 'the American continents . . . are henceforth not to be considered as subjects for future colonisation by any European powers'.

Simon Bolivar

In this atmosphere of encouraging hope, the man appeared to meet the hour—Simon Bolivar, 'the Liberator'. He was born in Caracas, Venezuela, in 1783 to a distinguished family. He was educated in European universities, and as a boy was in Paris at the tail end of the Revolution. He joined the liberation movement in his own country, and for the next ten years was its inspiration. Often he had to run for his life but always returned to renew the struggle.

Ten years' hard fighting followed until the Spanish were finally beaten in 1821. Bolivar became the first president of Venezuela and Colombia.

Ecuador was soon added to the republic. The Peruvians now called on Bolivar to help them and, after hard fighting, the upper part of Peru was formed into Bolivia and named in his honour. But despite his great services Bolivar proved too autocratic and he was finally required to resign on a pension, having spent his life and wealth on the cause of freedom. Nevertheless, the victory was won.

During the campaign in Chile and Peru, José de San Martin took his forces across the Andes.

Simon Bolivar, 'the Liberator'.

The American Civil War

The thirteen colonies who won their independence from Britain were never all of one mind and when the fighting ended, the domestic quarrels began. Great differences existed between the New England states, founded by the Puritans, and the plantation states of the South, founded by English aristocrats. As time passed the differences deepened rather than healed.

There were really two Americas. New England and the middle Atlantic states were developing as modern manufacturing centres. The railway system was well developed and the McCormick reaper had mechanised the harvesting of wheat in the mid-west with revolutionary results.

Southern Slaves

The South had all its main wealth in cotton. The way of life was almost feudal. There was little desire to make any changes at all. Cotton made up nearly half of the exports of the United States and it was also manufactured into cloth in the factories of the North. But cotton meant plantations worked by slaves. The handwork involved in picking cotton gave employment to men, women and children and was suitable to a slave economy. The original slaves had been brought to America many years before and their descendants were inherited by the plantation owners. By the middle of the nineteenth century the number of negroes in the South was about half of the white population; there were few in the North where they were not needed.

No one, however, could successfully pretend that slavery was consistent with the principles set out by Thomas Jefferson in the Declaration of Independence. That fine document clearly proclaimed equality, liberty and 'the pursuit of happiness' to be the birthright of all Americans. In the early years of independence the problem of slavery was played down, because it was hoped that with wise handling it would disappear in time. Before about 1830 most of the plantations were run on paternalistic lines and the lives of the slaves were not too hard. But as the demand for cotton increased by leaps and bounds,

The northern troops shown here in battle are commanded by the officer with the sword held aloft. At first neither side was prepared for war. The Federal regular army was very small and the Confederates relied on willing volunteers. Most of the experienced men had served in the Mexican war or against the Indians.

the plantations were organised differently. They were increased in size and supervised by harsh overseers whose job was to make as much profit as possible. Then oppression, cruelty and real suffering resulted. Feeling began to run very high as the North demanded freedom for the negroes in the South.

In 1849 the Californian gold strike sent thousands of Americans racing westwards in search of an easy fortune. The normal development of the West was given an artificial boost. Texas was acquired in 1845 and there was more opportunity for the southern states to move westwards. Most of the North could accept that the southern slaves had always been there and that this to some extent excused the present owners, but now new territories were being opened up in the West. The old evil must not be allowed to start all over again. Here was an opportunity for a fresh start. The new territories must not support slaves. On the other hand, the owners in the South naturally wanted to take their slaves with them when they moved west.

At this point a book was written which became a world bestseller. It was *Uncle Tom's Cabin* by Harriet Beecher Stowe. It demonstrated that slavery and cruelty were inseparable. One could not be had without the other. The book aroused widespread indignation and pity.

Abraham Lincoln

Abraham Lincoln now came forward as an opponent of slavery and when he was chosen as Republican candidate and later made president, some of the southern states left the Union. They formed a Confederacy under their own president, Jefferson Davis. Eventually there were twenty-three northern states with a population of twenty-two million against eleven southern states with nine million. The North had good railways which they knew how to use. Their factories were able to supply their forces with all the necessary supplies and ammunition. The South was blockaded from the start and was starved throughout of essential supplies. There were two issues at stake: the right to leave the Union of the United States, and the right to own slaves. These issues were now to be settled by war. Lincoln firmly declared that a house that was divided against itself could not hope to stand.

The war was not expected to last very long but it went on for four bloody years and resulted in very heavy losses, solely between Americans. Immediately upon the outbreak of war, the North instituted a naval blockade upon the South's ports. A naval force took New Orleans and, moving up the Mississippi, also took Memphis. Thus a great blow was struck in the very heart of Confederate country. But in the east, the South were far more successful. The North could not capture Richmond, the southern capital, and there were severe losses on both sides. The South had two magnificent generals in Robert E. Lee and Stonewall Jackson. Then, while defeats in the east went on, the North appointed Ulysses S. Grant to a command. He moved down the Mississippi system from the north and linked up with northern troops in the south. Texas and Arkansas were cut off from each other.

The South Surrenders

Time was now running out for the South. Battles were still won at a heavy cost and in one of them Stonewall Jackson was killed. Robert E. Lee led a despairing attack into Pennsylvania and was heavily defeated at Gettysburg. This was the occasion of Lincoln's historic speech on democracy: 'government of the people, by the people, for the people'. The Union forces closed in on Richmond from all sides, led by Grant and Sherman. On 9th April, 1865, Lee was obliged to surrender to the North at Appomattox. Lee was deservedly the hero of the lost cause of the South. Lincoln was equally the hero of the North and the champion of democracy.

The terms of the peace were mild: 'with malice towards none; with charity to all'. Hardly had Lincoln won the war than he was struck down by an assassin's hand. But the thirteenth amendment abolishing slavery was added to the Constitution. Peace was not easy and there was military occupation of the South for many years. The South was broken by the war and badly needed reconstruction. Leadership of the now firmly consolidated United States passed permanently to the North.

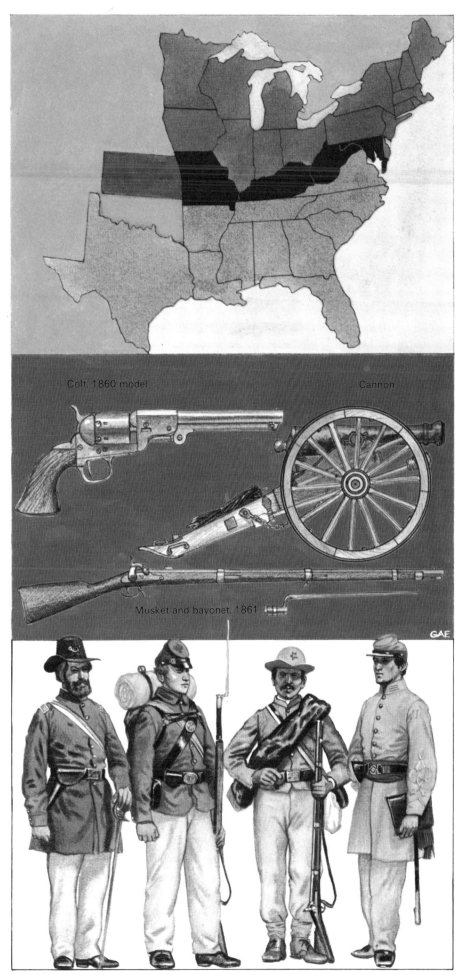

Colt, 1860 model

Cannon

Musket and bayonet, 1861

GAF

Infantry lieutenant and private of the Federal army

Infantry captain and private of the Confederate army

169

The American West

The opening up of the West by the daring American pioneers is the most thrilling part of the American story.

During the British period, the early colonies were shut between the ranges of the Appalachian mountains and the Atlantic coast. But with the coming of independence the cry went up, 'Go West, young man!' It was an ideal situation for the brave who had initiative and could be self-sufficient. Wealth, education and social position counted for nothing in the wilderness. Those who pushed the frontier westwards were judged solely as men and women for what they were and what they could do. Living in log cabins and defying the Indians, the pioneers moved farther and farther west. Farmers in New England found that the prairies of the Mississippi valley offered easier crops than the tougher ground at home. Land quickly increased in value and there could be a big profit as a reward for daring.

Thomas Jefferson, that most gifted leader of early America, bought Louisiana from France for fifteen million dollars and a few years later Florida was bought from Spain. Only the south-west territories remained in Mexican hands. They were eventually acquired by warfare. There was rivalry between Britain and the United States for the desirable Pacific coast but this was settled peaceably by the Oregon Treaty of 1846. Canada and the United States agreed to recognise the 49th parallel of latitude as an unguarded frontier. The Gold Rush of 1849 drew thousands to California in a frantic search for wealth and revealed that there were precious metals in the mountains. In this way the last unclaimed territory was taken up by the miners.

Between the Civil War and the First World War the United States experienced an industrial revolution which transformed her into a modern manufacturing nation. The romantic stagecoach was now replaced by the railways. The first trans-continental line was completed in 1869.

The Buffalo

A step was now taken which proved fatal to the Indians' way of life. It was found that the roaming herds of buffalo were a serious danger to the safety of trains speeding along the tracks which crossed the great plains. The order was therefore given to destroy the buffaloes. This meant economic death to the already badly harassed Indians. The buffalo was the source of all their supplies. They ate its flesh and used its skins for their wigwams and every article of clothing. After bitter fighting in a lost cause, the Indians were reduced in numbers and compelled to go into special reservations. The expansion of America was now complete.

American Indians were living in Old Stone Age ways by hunting when the Europeans first arrived. Their way of life required wide hunting grounds and constant movement. From the Spanish settlers they inherited wild horses and from traders they acquired guns. The new colonists who came to settle on farms cut up their hunting grounds and the railway drew an iron line across their lands. In Pennsylvania there was peace with the Quaker settlers at first but later there was fierce fighting. The Indians' skill with the horse, which they rode bareback, and with the rifle made them dangerous foes.

The construction of the railroad was the key to the unification of the United States. The continent was spanned by rapid transport, linking settlers and cities.

Industry and Agriculture

In Britain during the eighteenth century, startling developments took place in agriculture and industry, which rapidly changed the character of the community. These developments are conveniently known as the agricultural and industrial revolutions. They brought great wealth to Britain and gave her a long lead in commercial enterprise. Previously Britain had been an agricultural country made up of villages with very few large towns outside London. The only important industry was woollen cloth-making and the work was based on the cottages of the workers. This peaceful scene was to be transformed to the modern one of mechanised agriculture and the great factory towns in which most British people live today. What happened then in industrial Britain was followed in the rest of Europe and America during the next century.

In order to bring the benefits of the new farming methods to the countryside, the old ways of land ownership had to be revised. Sometimes it was arranged by mutual consent but mainly it was brought about by Enclosure Acts which fell heavily on the poor. A great deal of Britain was still farmed on the old three-field system which worked two fields and left one fallow for a year to recover its goodness. Thus a third of British ploughland was not being used. Strip farming was wasteful of time and effort. The land of good cultivators was spoilt by that of the idle. But the smallest farmers had independence, helped by common grazing rights and other benefits. These men wanted to continue in the traditional way, as their fathers and grandfathers had done before them, but the Enclosure Acts compelled them to obey. As they could rarely afford to fence their land or were unable to prove legally their age-old rights, the free peasants became servants of other men or drifted to the towns. Apart from this human failure, the enclosures benefited the whole nation by forming large modern farms.

Improving the Land

A general interest in the improvement of land was awakened. In the early eighteenth century Jethro Tull, the English agriculturist, taught farmers to drill their seed in rows, instead of broadcasting it in all directions. This simple principle meant that all plants

Population growth in Britain between 1751 and 1901.

Great care was given to scientific breeding of animals in the nineteenth century. Sheep were bred for their flesh as well as for their wool.

A new breed of shorthorn cattle was developed.

Rotation of crops growing in different soil levels allowed better use of land.

grown in regular rows could be hoed without damage to the plant. At this stage the motive power was the horse but the principle was to hold good for all later farm machinery.

Land owners began to take an intelligent interest in their estates with the idea of improving both their appearance and their usefulness. Many of the better ideas of cultivation came from Holland, but great progress was made in the county of Norfolk where Viscount Townshend, or 'Turnip' Townshend, as he came to be called, and Squire Coke demonstrated the value of rotation. It was not necessary, they proved, to leave the land fallow if the crops were changed round. In fact, if the crops grown were clearly balanced, such as

roots and grasses, the soil benefited from the mixture. In this way all the land could be used and the harvests were larger. This great improvement of crops helped to feed the growing towns and to produce better animals.

The Industrial Revolution transformed Britain from an agricultural country to the leading manufacturing nation in the world. Machinery began to be applied in all sorts of ways. Slowly, the British people were changed from being farmworkers and village craftsmen to factory hands working in large groups in the towns. The process once begun never ceased and has spread out from Britain throughout the civilised world.

The Textile Industry

The first inventions were made to help the textile industry which handled the weaving of wool and cotton. Lancashire was not so set in its ways as the older wool-weaving centres and attempted to use the new material, cotton. Labour was scarce and employers offered rewards for labour-saving inventions. In 1733 John Kay of Bury made the first mechanical shuttle. This invention made the power loom possible and handweaving began to die. For a brief period, water worked the first power looms. Consequently these looms were situated on the slopes of the Pennines to harness the water power. Hence they were called 'mills'. The spinners were hard pressed to provide yarn for these mechanical looms and it took thirty years for the balance to be restored. Eventually a machine which could spin yarn rapidly enough was developed by the work of Hargreaves, Arkwright and Crompton. Soon after, one of Watt's steam engines took over the driving power and the mills moved back to the coalfields. Because of several advantages of situation and opportunity, the Lancashire cotton trade raced ahead to clothe the world.

Iron Ore

With a sharply growing demand for machinery, a plentiful supply of iron became necessary. For centuries iron had been made by burning iron ore with charcoal. The important centres, therefore, grew up where iron ore and large forests were found together. The early British iron centres were the Forest of Dean, the Weald of Sussex, and Sheffield, near Sherwood

Forest. But the demands of iron-makers and shipbuilders had seriously deforested the iron areas and a new fuel became increasingly desirable. Coal had been tried but its impurities resulted in poor quality pig iron. A father and son, both named Abraham Darby, worked at improving the use of coal and produced coke, which they used in a special furnace. This process transformed iron-making and production leapt ahead, particularly in the areas near the coalfields which also contained iron ore.

The new iron ore was soon made into cast steel by Huntsman in Sheffield, and Henry Cort invented the puddling process to make it purer. The time-consuming task of hammering the metal, used in the old method, was reduced to a fraction by the invention of the rolling mill, which achieved the same end mechanically.

Thought was now given to the power that drives machinery and how that power could be increased or improved. The first steam engines were stationary. They were used in the Cornish tin mines for pumping because the great depth of the mines gave trouble with water. James Watt greatly improved the steam engine by inventing a condenser which increased the power output considerably. His inventions were taken up and organised by Matthew Boulton and the steam engine became the driving power of the new factories.

Organisation now left the small cottage units far behind. Large factories employing several hundred workers were the order of the day. Raw materials were drawn from distant countries and the products, after manufacture, were despatched throughout the world. The increased trade, much of it in heavy goods, put a tremendous strain on Britain's primitive transport and communications system. The roads had been neglected and merely patched for centuries. Turnpike Trusts, which constructed better roads and charged passengers tolls for using them, began in the seventeenth century but became really effective in the eighteenth.

Roadbuilding
Three great roadbuilders transformed Britain's roads in the eighteenth century—Metcalf, Telford and McAdam. Metcalf was blind but built many of the roads in northern England. Telford was a Scot who built thousands of miles of road and hundreds of bridges. His greatest achievement was the iron suspension bridge over the Menai Strait. The 'macadamising' process of grading stones which were crushed by pressure and made into a strong smooth bonded surface, has done as much for the modern motorcar as it did for the flying horse-drawn coaches which gave the first thrill of speed on the improved roads.

Eighteenth-century industry, however, made brilliant use of water transport. Canals were constructed to link the rivers into a national system so that goods could be moved gently all over the country without off-loading. Wedgwood's famous pottery travelled by this route. Telford was equally busy with canals and cut the Caledonian Canal across Scotland. There was a fever of canal building and most of the products of the early factories were transported by water to their destination. But with the coming of the steam locomotive, the canals were undeservedly neglected as the railway mania swept everything before it. Much of the technique of tunnelling and making cuttings, which was necessary for the canals, paved the way for the railway network which followed.

Industrial Towns
For reasons that are far from clear, the population of Britain expanded rapidly at this time, almost doubling during the reign of George III. The old textile areas, which were not on coalfields, became unimportant and today are part of the more charming countryside. On the coalfields the new towns grew at an alarming pace. There was little planning. The towns grew to serve industry and were ugly and unpleasant to live in. Except for London, which remained the largest city, the biggest towns were in the Midlands and the North and there was an exodus of the population to them. The drift to the towns increased as their prosperity drew in the dispossessed countrymen.

The slums which were then created in ignorance have haunted the major cities ever since. In the new towns

Farming was studied by many progressive British landowners in the eighteenth century. Technical books were read and many new methods tried out. Here are the Rotherham horse plough of this period (above) and the title page of a book on farming written in 1669 on a new system of agriculture.

Diagrams showing the new conversion of open strip fields to enclosed fields. Jethro Tull's drill (left) made mechanical hoeing possible and created modern farming.

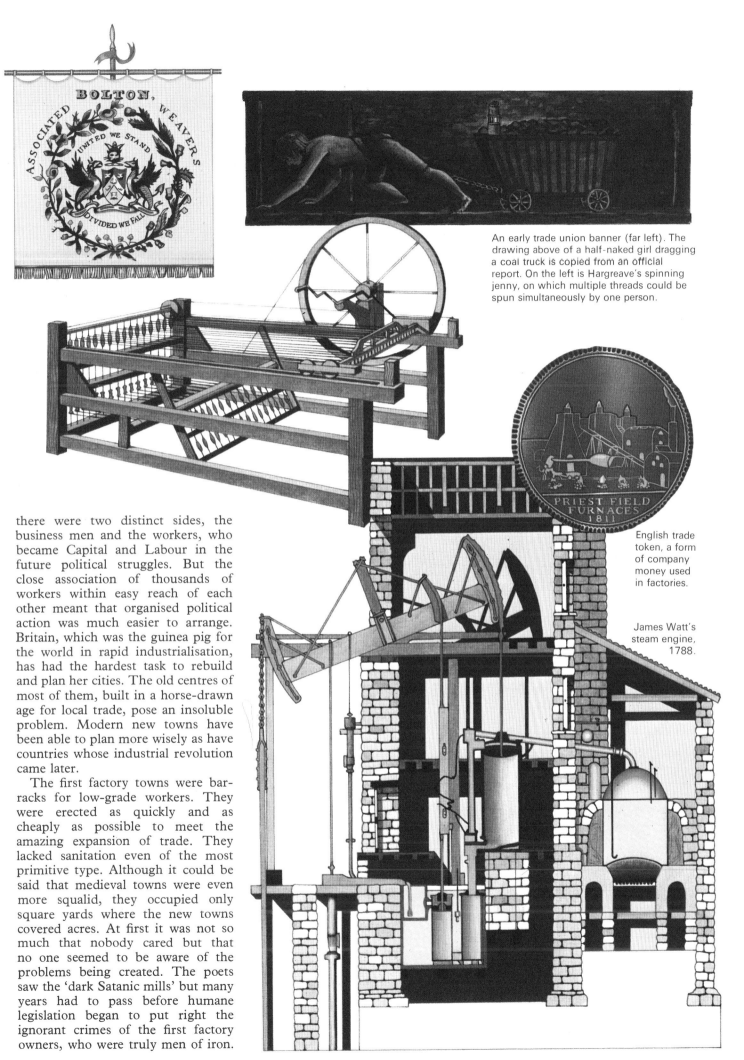

An early trade union banner (far left). The drawing above of a half-naked girl dragging a coal truck is copied from an official report. On the left is Hargreave's spinning jenny, on which multiple threads could be spun simultaneously by one person.

English trade token, a form of company money used in factories.

James Watt's steam engine, 1788.

there were two distinct sides, the business men and the workers, who became Capital and Labour in the future political struggles. But the close association of thousands of workers within easy reach of each other meant that organised political action was much easier to arrange. Britain, which was the guinea pig for the world in rapid industrialisation, has had the hardest task to rebuild and plan her cities. The old centres of most of them, built in a horse-drawn age for local trade, pose an insoluble problem. Modern new towns have been able to plan more wisely as have countries whose industrial revolution came later.

The first factory towns were barracks for low-grade workers. They were erected as quickly and as cheaply as possible to meet the amazing expansion of trade. They lacked sanitation even of the most primitive type. Although it could be said that medieval towns were even more squalid, they occupied only square yards where the new towns covered acres. At first it was not so much that nobody cared but that no one seemed to be aware of the problems being created. The poets saw the 'dark Satanic mills' but many years had to pass before humane legislation began to put right the ignorant crimes of the first factory owners, who were truly men of iron.

The Nineteenth Century

From the battle of Waterloo in 1815 to the outbreak of the First World War in 1914, Great Britain enjoyed a century of comparative peace. Her navy ruled the seas and there was nothing to hinder the development of her world trade. By the end of the century, Germany and the United States were important competitors but for many years Britain could build on her long lead in the machine industry. Meanwhile, on the continent of Europe there were serious wars and revolutions. Germany and Italy emerged as proud nations. In the east of Europe, Turkey continued to decline and shrink back towards Asia. As she withdrew, the Balkan nations fought for their national independence and Russia crept ever southwards towards the Black Sea and the warm Mediterranean. The Civil War tore the United States apart in the middle of the century, but by the end her industrial power was beginning to make itself felt.

There was a tremendous advance in all practical fields. Inventors, engineers and scientists were very active and successful. The British Empire came to its highest point of power and glory. In the first part of the century the human problems created by these lightning advances were either ignored or not appreciated. But there were also tremendous political advances during the century; the lone voices of conscience were eventually heard and the evils they revealed dealt with.

The trickle of discoveries made by invention and research in the eighteenth century broadened into a river in the nineteenth century. It has continued in ever-increasing volume until the present day. By harnessing the power of steam, gas and electricity to its machines, the nineteenth century created a new type of civilisation. The mass production of goods at low prices revolutionised the ordinary person's way of life throughout the world.

Steam Power

Steam power which had been used in the early factories was now applied to transport. In 1802 William Symington had a steamship, the *Charlotte Dundas*, sailing in Scotland on the Clyde; five years later Robert Fulton ran a passenger service in America on the Hudson. The first Atlantic steamship used sails as well as steam, but by the 1830s ships were crossing the ocean entirely by steam. The process of shrinking the world by modern transport had begun.

Steam locomotives require track to run on and took a little longer to develop. All the experimental work was done in the mines where George Stephenson learned his trade. He became the engineer in charge of building the first two railways in the world. In 1830, on the opening day of the Liverpool and Manchester railway, his prize engine, the *Rocket*, ran at nearly fifty kilometres (over thirty miles) an hour. Unfortunately, Huskisson, Canning's enlightened colleague, became the first railway accident victim when he was run down while crossing the line to greet the Duke of Wellington. The *Rocket* carried him, mortally injured, to hospital. There was a mania for railway building, sometimes with two or three competing lines between the same places. Men of the stature of Brunel built the great tracks of the nineteenth century, and all the advanced countries hastened to equip themselves with railways after the British pattern.

Distance was annihilated in other ways as well as travel. Galvani and Volta in Italy and Faraday in Britain

The American inventor Thomas Edison started as a railroad newsboy. Perhaps the most prolific of all inventors, his chief work was with the telegraph and the gramophone.

Electricity was coming into its own in the nineteenth century as inventors discovered its potential. Marconi was the pioneer of early radio and sent the first signals around the world.

A family of emigrants set off for the New World. During the late nineteenth century over 55 million people left Europe, mostly to settle in America.

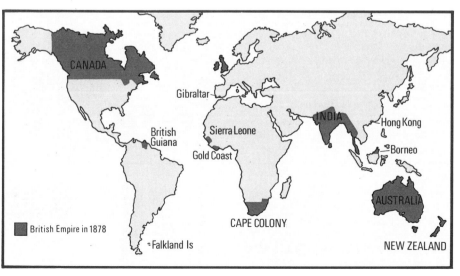

The British Empire at the height of its power.

discovered many of the secrets of electricity, which was destined to outstrip steam in the next century. The invention of the Morse Code and the electric telegraph meant that messages could be sent over long distances in a flash. The first cable between Britain and France was laid in 1851. Reuter's newsagency was founded the same year and the era of instant press coverage had begun. A little earlier, in 1840, Rowland Hill had begun the Penny Post which broadened out to become the Universal Postal Union of 1878. At a remarkably low cost everyone could send and receive letters from all over the world. By the end of the century Bell had invented the telephone and global conversation was made possible. The communication network was now complete for the modern world.

Applied Science

Science took a more practical turn in the nineteenth century. The demands of industry made scientists think more about applied science to assist the new machine production. Chemistry, which investigated how substances

The Great Exhibition of 1851 was the first of the great trade fairs which now regularly promote world trade. It was held in London in Joseph Paxton's Crystal Palace.

were made up, became more important. John Dalton, the English chemist, was able to show by his atomic theory that substances were put together by fixed rules and their behaviour could be controlled. A whole new world of materials for human use was revealed.

The greatest boon to communication for the poor was the introduction of the Penny Post by Rowland Hill in 1840. Previously, the cost of a letter was calculated on distance and the money collected on delivery. Hill proposed a small pre-paid flat charge for letters, regardless of distance, and the volume of business would average out the cost. The early penny stamps were black (see above) and they are greatly treasured by stamp collectors.

The health of the new towns gave great cause for concern. The basic squalor produced outbreaks of typhoid and other dangerous diseases. The virtues of cleanliness and good sanitation were realised and gave rise to much research on the transmission of disease. The work of Louis Pasteur in France on germs and bacteria inspired Lister to produce antiseptics to protect wounds from infection. Surgery was also enormously improved by Simpson's discovery of chloroform which began the control of pain by drugs and anaesthetics. Near the end of the century, Ross discovered that malaria was due to the mosquito; it is said that a quarter of the globe was made habitable by his work. One encouraging new development at this time was that the world of science became international, and knowledge began to be exchanged as a duty to mankind, regardless of the barriers of nation and religion.

Origin of Species

The sciences connected with nature were not left behind, and their work had a revolutionary effect on religious thinking. For centuries thoughtful men had been intrigued by fossils found in rocks. In 1830 Charles Lyell wrote his great work, *Principles of Geology*. It was clear that the earth was much older by millions of years than had been popularly supposed. One of the finest naturalists who ever lived, Charles Darwin, accepted the great age of the animals and wrote *The Origin of Species* in 1859. The human race, he thought, had been produced by a long process known as the survival of the fittest. Nature selected the best types for survival. Later he suggested that man was nearest to the apes. The gentle Darwin took no part in the storm which broke out from literal believers in the Bible. The sturdy Huxley acted as Darwin's bulldog to protect him. A modified version of Darwin's views is accepted by most educated people today, and religious thinking has never been quite the same.

The mechanisation of Britain which took place in the nineteenth century also revolutionised the social lives of the men, women and children who took part in it. Profit-making ran ahead of public welfare in all directions. Gradually the lonely voices of people with a conscience were heard, and parliamentary action was taken. Children did simple jobs minding the early machines. The first acts to control their work sought to make sure that they did no more than

twelve hours work and were at least nine years old! But since factory inspectors were not yet appointed, these harsh mercies were rarely carried out.

The Royal Commission on the Mines revealed unknown horrors. Young girls of twelve, stripped to the waist, were hauling small trucks on hands and knees along narrow galleries. Much better acts were passed and the government at last intervened to see that they were carried out. Yet there was fierce opposition to these measures. The 'good Earl' Shaftesbury was the driving force who saved children from the mines and the climbing boys from death in the old winding chimneys.

The Slave Trade

The slave trade had disturbed the consciences of good men and women for years. At the end of the eighteenth century, a committee was formed, mostly of Quakers, to suppress the slave trade. William Wilberforce led this movement but it took twenty years to pass the necessary Act in 1807. But in 1833 slavery was

abolished throughout the British Empire. Another lone figure to achieve success was Florence Nightingale who went out to care for the wounded soldiers suffering piteously in the Crimean War. She was a woman of ferocious determination, and from the filth and neglect of the primitive military hospitals, she organised modern nursing. The high ideals of the nursing profession date from her day.

The Working Classes

Although single figures of high character could accomplish miracles in a narrow field, the barbarous condition of the whole country demanded state action. The basis of government also had to change. Successive reform acts gave the vote first to the middle class and then to the working class but not to women. Local government was organised to carry out public health acts, and local as well as national pride in a well-run country was born.

The workers themselves began to organise. The case of the Tolpuddle Martyrs shows how hard it was for them. Six farm labourers were sent as convicts to Australia for taking an oath of loyalty to their union. The bitterness between capital and labour which was sown in those days can still make working in harmony difficult in modern times. Public education was now provided in England, and by 1900 the working class had its own Labour Party. Meanwhile, a refugee German Jew, Karl Marx, was quietly writing *Das Kapital* in London, providing the explosive communist message for the next century.

Karl Marx is one of the key names in modern history because of his association with communism. He was a German Jew who spent the greater part of his life in exile in England, and was buried at Highgate, London. With his friend Engels he developed his ideas of socialism. They wrote the Communist Manifesto and Marx was foremost in educating working people to understand the nature of their economic problems. His great work was *Das Kapital* which was finished from his notes by Engels. His writings have become the bible of modern communism. Marx was an intellectual and a scholar but Lenin brilliantly set his ideas to work in modern Russia whence they have spread throughout the world.

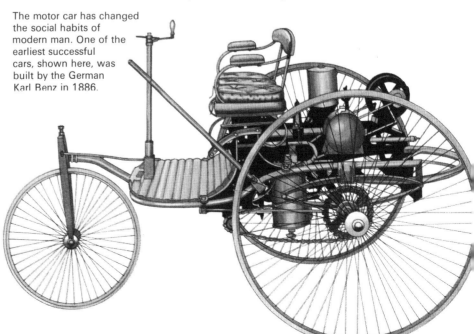

The motor car has changed the social habits of modern man. One of the earliest successful cars, shown here, was built by the German Karl Benz in 1886.

Russia was breaking down under the rule of the last of the Czars. In 1905 there was intense unrest and street barricades were erected in Moscow.

The World at War

When the Prussian king became the Emperor of Germany in 1871, it was soon seen that the new Germany was the greatest military power in Europe. For the next twenty years Bismarck used his considerable diplomatic skill to keep Germany supreme. France was the main danger but she needed allies. Russia's weakness had been exposed in the Crimea, and Austria was having serious trouble with the mixture of races she attempted to rule in the Balkans. Bismarck favoured the Third Republic of France because republics upset the crowned heads of the nations that could become France's allies.

Balance of Power

This balance of Europe in Germany's favour was kept going by Bismarck until he fell from favour. With the coming of the rash William II to the throne of Germany, German policy became openly aggressive. Then the Great Powers began to move towards the groupings which they formed in the First World War. Austria, Germany and Italy made a solid block across Central Europe, keeping France and Russia apart. But these two powers drew closer together by treaty, and Britain, although nearer to Germany in many ways, was

compelled to work with them. The careful and hesitant steps by which this was accomplished unfortunately made the German block feel that British determination was half-hearted and their arrogance increased.

Tension grew and an international armaments race broke out. Germany set out deliberately to outbuild the British Navy. In reply Britain designed the heavily gunned dread-noughts. Germany also began her 'drive to the East'. Rulers of German origin came on to the thrones of

Edwardian England was peaceful and, for some, prosperous. But the elegance and calm of European society was to be shattered by the First World War.

Bulgaria, Rumania and Greece. Of the Balkan powers, only Serbia, which was Slav and looked to Russia, was not under German influence. Then the Balkan Wars broke out and Serbia's success awoke the national pride of the other Slav groups in south-east Europe. Austria resolved to crush her rebellious subjects in Serbia and thereby set world war in motion.

The First World War

Preparations for war were intensifying on every hand when the crisis suddenly came in June 1914. The heir to the Austrian throne, the Archduke Ferdinand, was assassinated by a Slav while on an official visit to Sarajevo. Austria seized the opportunity of forcing an unconditional ultimatum on Serbia, whom she blamed for the crime. Austria attacked Serbia and Russia and France were drawn in to support her, while Germany supported Austria. The First World War had begun. Italy stayed neutral until 1915 when she joined the Allies. In an attempt to halt conflict, Britain had asked France and Germany to respect the treaty which required them not to violate Belgium. France agreed but Germany refused to answer and invaded Belgium. Britain declared war the following day, 4th August 1914.

Attempts were made to maintain the volunteer system during the war by the use of forceful recruiting posters.

War on Two Fronts

The German Central Powers had long been prepared for war on two fronts, against France and Russia. They assumed that Russia would be slow to mobilise, so they threw their main forces against France and turned the French flank by invading Belgium. The French and British armies were driven back but they managed not to be encircled, and saved Paris. Then the two lines of trenches were constructed from Switzerland to the North Sea which were to be the grim front line for the next four bloody years. Russia was quicker in the field than expected and invaded both Germany and Austria. Hindenburg crushed them at Tannenberg with terrible losses, but they fared better

against the Austrians. Germany switched much of her effort to getting the Austrians out of trouble and Russia had to retire badly mauled.

At this point Turkey threw in her lot with the Central Powers. This was a bitter blow as Russia could no longer be supplied by sea. The ill-fated Gallipoli expedition was an attempt to break this blockade. In the Near East, however, the Turks were gradually beaten.

The seas still belonged to Britain and the blockade against Germany was tightened mercilessly. At last the Germans decided to commit their fleet to battle. On 31st May 1916, the two mighty fleets met at the Battle of Jutland. The fighting was very severe

and losses were extremely heavy on both sides. Although the success of the battle is debated, the Germans retired to their home ports, not to emerge again until Germany surrendered at the end of the war.

The next German attempt to break the blockade took place under the water and was nearly successful. The German U-boats, or submarines, began to sink merchant ships as well as naval craft with apparent ease. Eventually the convoy system was devised which gave merchant ships some degree of protection and the position improved. But when, without warning, Germany declared unrestricted submarine warfare against passenger ships it did much to sway the United States to join the side of Britain and France. The arrival of the new ally in April 1917 was the signal of eventual victory for the Allies, although much hard fighting remained to be done.

The collapse of Russia after appalling losses was hastened on by internal revolution. When the USSR was established, the Russians withdrew from the war and signed a peace treaty with the Germans. Germany and Austria hurriedly

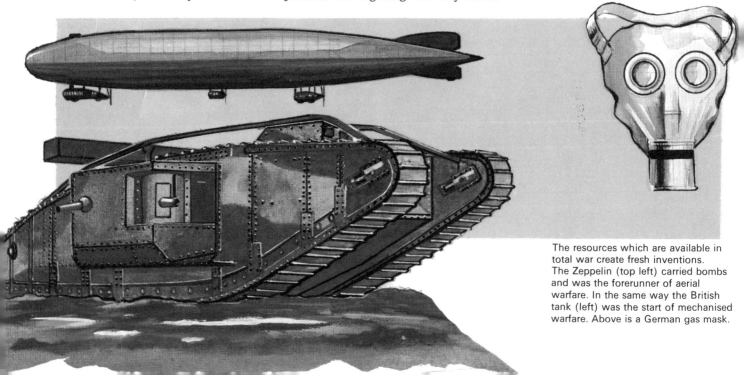

The resources which are available in total war create fresh inventions. The Zeppelin (top left) carried bombs and was the forerunner of aerial warfare. In the same way the British tank (left) was the start of mechanised warfare. Above is a German gas mask.

switched troops to the western front and mounted a last great spring offensive in 1918. By the end of the year the German forces were forced back to their own frontiers. The German emperor fled to neutral Holland and a republic was set up in Germany, which sued for peace.

This was the world's first experience of total war and the loss of life was sickening, running into many millions. Such casualties had never been known before, or foreseen, and the care of the wounded was often primitive. All the great powers of the world were involved at some point in the struggle.

Mechanical Weapons

The nations who went to war were the new industrial nations of the machine age and they drew on all their resources to manufacture new mechanical weapons. The weight of artillery and the reckless use of ammunition made trenches and underground shelters necessary. Troops wore clumsy gas masks but gas proved unreliable as a form of attack and was used very little. The machine gun and the tank proved their deadly worth. Simple human courage was no longer enough to face the mechanical odds. Gradually, understanding grew of the horror which had been released.

In the air, bombing began from airships, known as Zeppelins, and there were the first encounters between single-seater aeroplanes. The very first dogfights were fought out with pistols! Yet aviation leapt forward during the four testing years of war and made amazing progress. On the ground the recently discovered petrol engine had displaced the horse by the end of the war.

Treaty of Versailles

The Treaty of Versailles in 1919, which drew up the conditions of peace, was based on Fourteen Points

Trench warfare was a permanent feature of the soldier's life in the First World War.

put forward by President Woodrow Wilson of the United States. Wilson was an idealist and the Fourteenth Point made provision for a League of Nations which should prevent further outbreaks of world war. The three dominating figures at the conference were Wilson, Lloyd George from Britain and 'Tiger' Clemenceau of France. Russia was not asked to the conference as she had withdrawn from the war much earlier. But this discourtesy to the new Soviet government boded ill for the future. Also, Clemenceau would not allow the defeated nations to become members of the League. Lloyd George and Clemenceau had brought their nations through the crucible of war and could not be persuaded to soften their attitude to Germany. No one at the peace conference could imagine the extent of the social and industrial breakdown which the war would bring in its train.

Submarine warfare

Until the present day the submarine has been strictly a naval craft, except for special diving 'bells' designed for scientific research. Shipbuilders attempted for many years to construct an underwater ship but practical success did not come until the end of the nineteenth century. John P. Holland, who emigrated from Ireland to the United States, built a submarine which was adopted by the American and British navies. In the First World War, the U-boats of Germany proved their value in attacks on Allied merchant ships. A basic type of craft was developed which could be cheaply and quickly produced in bulk. Modern navies have been reduced in size because of the vulnerability of surface ships to air or missile attacks, but submarines have increased in number and they are the warships of the future. Seen on the right is a decoy ship used by Britain during the war to counter enemy submarine attacks. Usually called Q-ships they were merchant ships manned by trained crews and armed with carefully concealed guns which could be brought into action when a submarine approached.

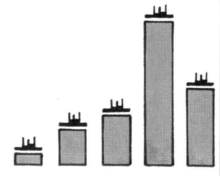

This chart shows the total tonnage of British merchant vessels sunk by enemy submarines during the war.

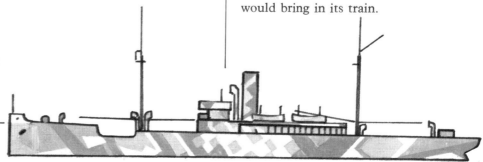

Between the Wars

The tremendous efforts of nations of Europe in the First World War made the return to peace very difficult. The switch back to peace-time production after total war was a long and testing process. The soldiers of the victorious armies had been promised a home fit for heroes to live in, but what they returned to was widespread unemployment and a long period of rationing and shortages. The past was shattered and a new world was painfully born. Lines of kings, who had been famous in the history of Europe for centuries, disappeared. Republics were set up and a new type of ruler, the dictator, appeared. The dictator was head of a one-party government with unlimited power. He offered swift, decisive solutions to urgent problems but his authority could rarely be checked once it was established.

The League of Nations
After the First World War, the League of Nations carried the hopes of all high-minded people. It was felt that the leading nations must have learned wisdom and were eager to beat their swords into ploughshares. But the League was based on the Treaty of Versailles, which contained many seeds of future trouble. The reparations forced on Germany and the harsh treatment of Austria were revealed as hopelessly severe in the sick economic conditions which followed the war. The League enjoyed some success and in the first ten years prevented many minor wars which could have spread dangerously.

Although Woodrow Wilson formed the League, the United States, despite being helpful, did not join it. Republican Germany was admitted in 1926 but Hitler took her out contemptuously in 1933. Russia was then admitted in 1934 but it was too late. Against large-scale aggression, sanctions were applied weakly and with no real effect. Italy invaded Abyssinia and Japan invaded Manchuria in defiance of the League. As France and Britain were the only effective members trying to work the League, it was looked on with some truth as a Franco-British organisation formed to promote the interests of the two countries. Only in the more peaceful sphere of world health, labour conditions and drugs did the League

The depression in the United States in the 1930s threw many men out of work and forced them into bread lines to obtain food.

achieve some success. This work has been continued and built into the United Nations Organisation.

Changes in Russia
The swiftest and most violent changes occurred in Russia. The massacre of her hopelessly under-equipped armies forced her out of the war and gave the revolutionary movements, which had been going on for years, their chance. The opportunity was brilliantly seized by Lenin who had been plotting the revolution from exile outside Russia. Lenin believed in Karl Marx's teaching that all production and wealth should belong to the people of a country as a whole.

In a nation as sunk in the past as Russia, these changes required the most drastic measures. The small, dedicated Communist Party, or Bolsheviks, with Lenin at their head, set out ruthlessly to achieve state socialism. Lenin brought order out of chaos and the effort cost him his life. Under Stalin, the USSR paid less attention to world revolution and by mighty five-year plans dragged Russia to the forefront of modern industrial nations. The suffering involved was enormous but the practical success was clear. Turkey was also transformed from a backward eastern state to a modern power by her dictator, Kemal Ataturk. Dictatorship was seen to get results.

The breakdown of parliamentary government in Italy resulted in the two extreme parties, the Communists and Fascists, fighting for supremacy. Mussolini with his black-shirted Fascists won. The intense hatred

A bus protected against attack during the 1926 General Strike in Britain.

the financial system collapsed. Hitler, with his brown-shirted storm troopers, began his meteoric rise to power. He promised to make Germany strong again and to unite one victorious Reich. The blazing hysterical patriotism of Hitler won the humiliated Germans over to adoring support. He declared himself the avowed enemy of the Treaty of Versailles which he proposed to destroy. Following Mussolini's example of impressive public works, he improved Germany at home and began to take over neighbouring territories which had once belonged to Germany by gambling on the threat of war.

His success was adroitly advertised by a most efficient propaganda machine which won him increasing power and support. The methods by which this success was gained were vicious and without principle but none more so than his treatment of the Jews. The Jewish community in

A day of emotional excitement and patriotism at a Nuremberg Rally in Nazi Germany.

Germany was very powerful and influential, particularly in the professions. Hitler set out to persecute them and to make them the scapegoats for all Germany's failures. The resulting death camps and gas chambers, begun in the cool times of peace, have left an indelible blot of shame on the German people. As Hitler's ambition grew and his self-control dwindled, war grew ever nearer. His insane hatred for Communists made a contest with the Soviet Union inevitable.

Economic Unrest
Economic troubles caused most of the political unrest and experiment after the First World War. The cycle of trade had got out of hand due to the war, and economic booms were followed by slumps with disturbing regularity. The worst slump began in the United States with the Wall Street crash. Unbelievably, wealthy America collapsed economically. Fortunes were lost in a few hours as hundreds of firms failed. Unemployment began to be reckoned in millions and the repercussions swiftly spread from country to country.

Britain also had unwisely tried to maintain a pre-war gold standard, which was impossible. A General Strike of the whole country's work force followed. The effects of the American crash caused Britain to resort to a coalition government in order to fight the problem on a war basis. Germany had the worst experience of slump and inflation. But for her economic suffering, Hitler may well have not come to power.

shown by Fascists and Communists for each other boded ill for the future peace of Europe. Mussolini began to organise his stricken country and promoted large-scale public works to create employment. The great Italian motor highways became a feature of Europe. But ideas of grandeur led to war in order to expand the country's territory and to distract the people from any failures at home. Abyssinia was invaded successfully.

The Rise of Hitler
Germany suffered most from the effects of the war. The early republican governments had no chance and

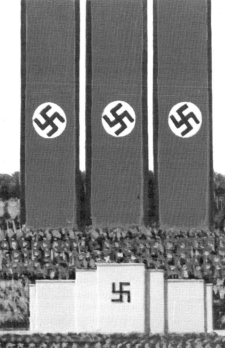

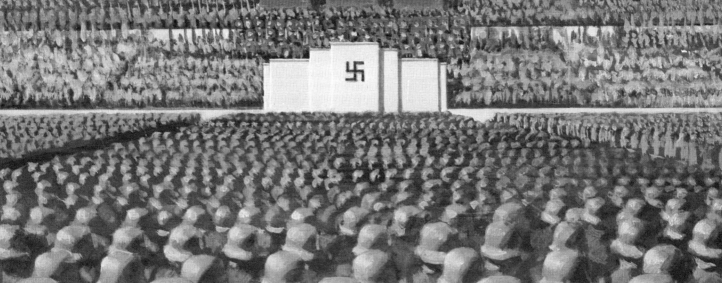

The Second World War

St Paul's Cathedral, London, in the blitz of 1940 when British cities were the prime target of the German offensive.

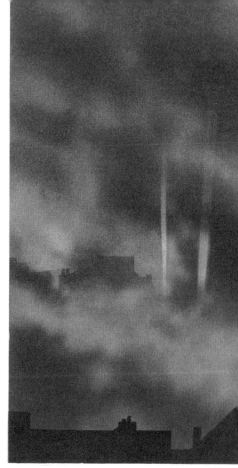

Most European statesmen just before the Second World War had experienced the first 'Great War' between nations. They were anxious to prevent such a thing happening again. Adolf Hitler exploited their unwillingness. He shrewdly concealed his long-range ambitions and proclaimed that he wished only to restore the former Germany. There was some sympathy for this ambition but Hitler was the master of the big lie. He gambled on the general desire for peace and grew bolder and bolder. The Rhineland and Austria were brought safely back into the Reich. Then Hitler revealed himself over Czechoslovakia. Just inside her frontier was an area with many Germans. Hitler wanted them back in the homeland. Czechoslovakia refused and war loomed up.

A hurried meeting between Germany, Italy, France and Britain was arranged at Munich. Great pressure was put on Czechoslovakia to accept occupation of a small area of her country in order to avoid war. Back in Britain, Chamberlain claimed that he had achieved 'peace with honour'. He had obtained neither. Hitler marched in and by various means took the whole of Czechoslovakia. There was a general feeling of shame and the western nations raced to rearm. Britain and France then decided to contain Hitler. If he invaded Poland, as he was preparing to do, they would fight. Hitler gambled and invaded, and Britain and France immediately declared war, on 3rd September 1939.

A month before the outbreak of war, Hitler had unexpectedly signed a treaty of neutrality with Soviet Russia. Certainly, neither side was deceived. Russia obtained a period to prepare and Germany was assured of fighting on one front only. Poland collapsed before the might of Germany, and Russia moved in from the east to occupy her old provinces. In the west, the first stage was a repetition of 1914. Belgium was invaded and the Maginot Line was turned. The British were flung back on Dunkirk and sacrificed all their equipment. But the 'little ships' came over from the south coast of England in swarms and rescued the soldiers of the professional army, who were to be the spearhead of all the later campaigns. Italy now decided to come into the war on the German side, and France surrendered. Germany occupied all the coastal zones and ruled France through a puppet government at Vichy.

Britain Alone

It was a black hour for Britain, alone and facing invasion, but the crisis brought to power Churchill, who roused a united nation. As a preparation for invasion, the Germans launched a massive daylight air attack on Britain. Unexpectedly, the small professional Royal Air Force, the famous 'few', destroyed them because of the very high quality of the pilots and the machines. Germany switched to bombing at night and the British cities had a long hard winter but did not break. Then Hitler made his colossal mistake. He decided to attack Russia. Already their arrogant treatment of the conquered compelled Germany to maintain large armies to hold down occupied countries. Now there was war on two fronts.

The dropping of two atom bombs on Japan abruptly halted the war in the Far East. It fell to President Truman to make the decision to let loose this terrible bomb which could destroy a whole city. Since that time conventional weapons have had to be regarded as relatively unimportant. The cost of atomic weapons has made the richest nations more powerful still but simpler methods of manufacture are now increasing the number of atomic powers. Fear of the consequences has prevented the full use of atomic power in war but all men today live under the bomb's shadow.

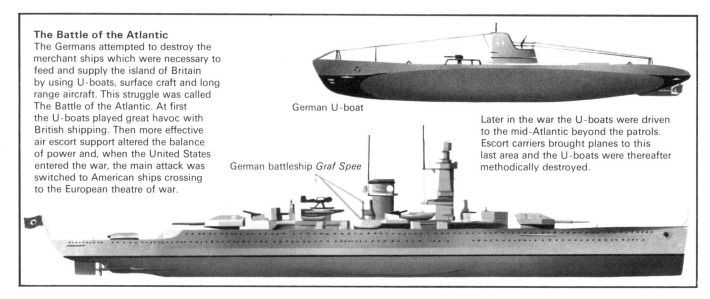

The Battle of the Atlantic
The Germans attempted to destroy the merchant ships which were necessary to feed and supply the island of Britain by using U-boats, surface craft and long range aircraft. This struggle was called The Battle of the Atlantic. At first the U-boats played great havoc with British shipping. Then more effective air escort support altered the balance of power and, when the United States entered the war, the main attack was switched to American ships crossing to the European theatre of war.

German U-boat

German battleship *Graf Spee*

Later in the war the U-boats were driven to the mid-Atlantic beyond the patrols. Escort carriers brought planes to this last area and the U-boats were thereafter methodically destroyed.

The first German onslaught reached the outskirts of Moscow and Leningrad but the Russian winter offensive threw them back. But in June 1942 the Germans drove to the south-east in a bid for Russian oil and reached Stalingrad. The defence of Stalingrad, street by street, ranks with the Battle of Britain in the air as an heroic turning point of the war. The German army was trapped, and its long sad retreat from Russia was similar to the rout experienced by Napoleon.

During the winter of 1941, Japan without warning attacked the American fleet at Pearl Harbour in Hawaii. The United States came into the war on the side of Britain and Russia, and both the Atlantic and the Pacific became theatres of war. China, who had been fighting the Japanese for years, automatically became an ally. Like the Germans, the Japanese were well prepared and the lightning speed of their offensive across south-east Asia took everyone by surprise and brought them to the borders of India.

Meanwhile there had been fighting in North Africa. The Italians had a brief success by attacking Egypt but were soon hurled back by Wavell. Then Rommel, with superior German forces, pinned the British back in Egypt again. Eventually, after a long build-up, Montgomery decisively won at El Alamein and the German army had to surrender.

Invasion of Europe

The time had now come for the counter-invasion of Europe. American supplies were flowing to her allies. Throughout the war the United States was not bombed and her factories could work unmolested night and day. The bombing of Germany, however, grew to be a terrible punishment for her crimes. The Anglo-American forces landed and overran Sicily. Italy was invaded and Mussolini overthrown. Its new government declared war on Germany. In reply, large German forces entered Italy and a long bitter struggle began which lasted to the end of the war.

The invasion of Normandy began on D-day, 6th June 1944, under the command of Eisenhower. The preparations had been stupendous. Artificial harbours had been made which were towed across the English Channel and a fuel pipeline was laid under the water. After much hard fighting, France was liberated and Germany herself attacked. The Germans made a desperate last stand but the spring offensive defeated them and there was a race between Russia and the Allies for Berlin. Hitler committed suicide and the war in the west was over.

The Allies now turned on Japan. The new atom bomb was available and Truman decided to use it to save American lives. The first bomb destroyed Hiroshima. No surrender followed and the second bomb destroyed Nagasaki. Japan then decided to give in, and six years of global war came to an end.

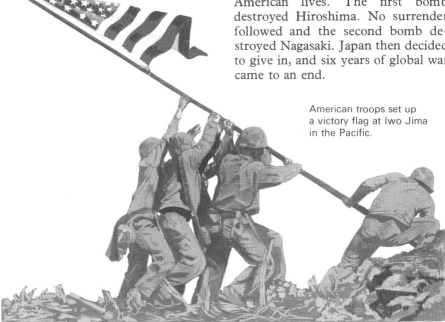

American troops set up a victory flag at Iwo Jima in the Pacific.

The Modern World

After the defeat of Hitler's Germany, the victorious nations immediately split into two groups. The Communist nations were led by Russia, and the democratic free-enterprise nations by the United States. At that time only the Americans had the atomic bomb, the power of which had been demonstrated in Japan. The new nuclear weapons, which further research made more deadly every day, held the great powers back from a major war. Instead of actual fighting, a Cold War began, in which everything short of actual war was used to persuade the smaller nations to come under the Russian or American umbrella. This creation of eastern and western power blocs has ruled international politics ever since.

Russia increased her hold in southeast Europe and created a wall of buffer Communist states between her country and western Europe. There was some evidence of independence in one or two of these countries, but the immediate suppression of risings in Hungary and Czechoslovakia has shown how little liberty of expression Russia will tolerate. In China the Communists triumphed. They were aided by Russia but more recently the Chinese have shown marked independence and support a harder Communist line than Russia.

Economic Aid

After the war, the Americans gave enormous economic help to neutral and undeveloped countries. The results have been mixed. Many of those receiving aid wanted no strings attached and many have played off Russia against America and obtained help from both sides. Generally speaking, the poorer countries tend towards Communist sympathy despite lavish American aid.

Defeated Germany was divided into zones under each of the Allies. The Russian zone in the east was by far the largest. Free elections were not held there and Russia wanted East Germany to be recognised as an independent Communist state. Isolated far to the east was Berlin, the German capital. This city was also divided into four zones and the Russians and the Allies constantly bickered. Eventually the Russians blockaded the rail and road routes into Berlin in 1949, cutting off supplies from the west. The Allies could not accept this and mounted a huge airlift which kept the city supplied for some months until the Russians removed the blockade. In 1961 the Russians built their famous wall right through the heart of Berlin, and also sealed off East Germany. Millions of refugees had escaped to West Germany since the war, but now their route was blocked.

A more promising development arose from a conference in San Francisco in 1945. At this conference, the United Nations Organisation was begun, to promote security and international co-operation and to defend peace. It was founded on a broader basis than the old League and has since admitted several new independent states. Despite its failures, there have been no major wars for nearly thirty years and many disputes have been talked out at the United Nations headquarters.

Two great weaknesses, however, have beset the organisation. Communist China was not at first allowed to be a member although a quarter of the world's population was under her rule. The other weakness was the veto. The five great powers each had the right of veto to stop United Nations decisions and Russia made excessive use of this dangerous privilege. Another growing weakness is the large number of new small states who have an equal voice in the General Assembly with the major powers. Under its present constitution, by a majority vote these new undeveloped countries can dictate to the United Nations Organisation.

No adequate method of disarmament has yet been found between East and West because there is no true basis of trust between them. Thus the arsenals of the world are

The Berlin airlift was planned as a military operation. Transport planes and lorries maintained a shuttle service bringing tons of essential goods to the surrounded city.

full of nuclear weapons, waiting to be used in anger. Rockets and sub-marines are now equipped with nuclear power and surprise attack is easy. Extensive early-warning systems, costing millions of pounds, surround the world in a nervous network. There have been very dangerous confrontations in territories belonging to small nations. But the conflicts are really backed by Russia, or China, or the United States. Korea, Cuba and Vietnam have all been scenes of conflict but so far the action has been localised and nuclear weapons have not been released.

Another great movement of the post-war years is the wholesale re-treat of the European colonising powers from Asia and Africa. The British Empire has almost entirely disappeared, although most of the newly created countries have decided to stay in the loose association known as the Commonwealth. The Dutch have left Indonesia and the French have left Algeria and Indo-China. The new independent countries have rarely had a smooth beginning and obviously a long period of time must elapse while they develop and plot their future course. Very often their need for urgent action causes them to choose undemocratic methods.

Problems of Peace

After the last war, the nations had the experience of 1918 to guide them in preparing economic recovery. In some cases the transition back to peace was introduced before the fighting stopped. Bombing had made so much repair work to the cities necessary that there was no lack of work. Yet severe economic difficulties still harass all the industrial nations. The control of production in order to avoid inflation is a constant worry. The most successful industrial nations of peacetime have been the defeated countries of Japan and Germany. Japan, in particular, is becoming the United States of the Far East.

To offset the domination of Russia and America, Western Europe has founded the Common Market. Starting with trade agreements, a full political unity is eventually hoped for. This expanding organisation is a recognition by the old European

The United Nations buildings (right) are situated on Manhattan Island, New York. The blue flag of the United Nations is shown and below it the symbols of FAO (Food and Agricultural Organization) and WHO (World Health Organization).

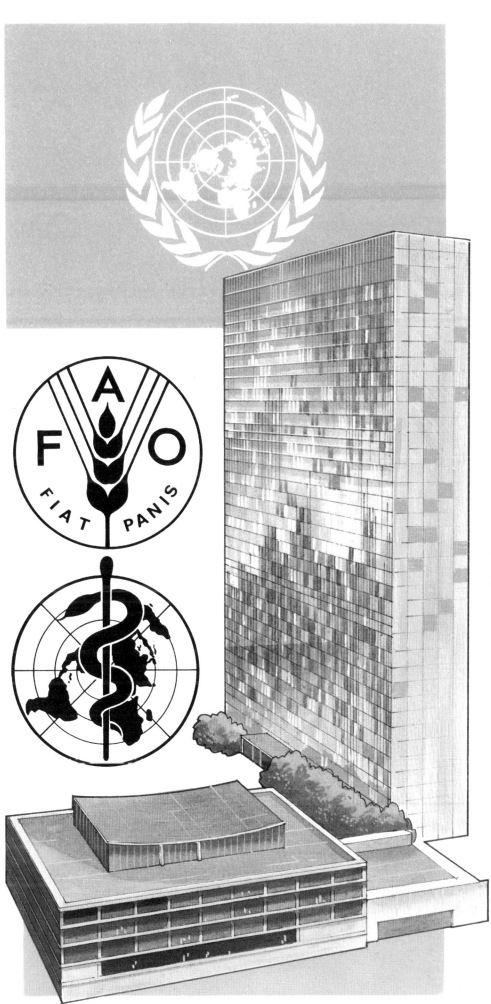

powers of the West that small countries can no longer 'go it alone' but must unite.

Protest and Concern

The post-war period abounded with difficult problems. The cities and communication systems which were in ruins had to be repaired or rebuilt from scratch. Population steadily increased and the pressure on new housing was severe, particularly as higher wages brought a demand for better accommodation. Gradually the camps for displaced persons helped the stateless refugees and half-wild children to return to normal life.

The generation born under the shadow of the bomb would not accept the quiet restraints of the traditional well-ordered life which their parents knew as peace. Throughout the world there has been student unrest. A voice of protest has arisen on every side, often without any clear plan of action but determined not to accept tamely what is wrong. Thousands marched to protest against the atomic bomb tests. Negroes fought openly for civil rights in the United

Refugees displaced from their homes by war are one of the most terrible features of the modern world.

States and there was widespread public reaction against the horrors of the Vietnam war. In Ireland, Catholics and Protestants fought street battles over old religious differences made worse by economic worries. Colonists rejected European rule. Violence has been a rising feature of politics and crime. The American president, John Kennedy, was assassinated and public figures can no longer be sure of protection against bomb or bullet.

Despite all the difficulties of the modern world, however, governments have brought in many improvements in social care and welfare. There is more concern by the majority for the unfortunate and underprivileged. But disturbing factors are the shortage of world food and the growing gulf between the 'haves' and the 'have-nots'. Modern technical production continually increases the wealth of the fortunate industrial nations while the underdeveloped countries lag farther and farther behind.

One extraordinary outcome of the rising prosperity of the industrial working class is tourism. The poorer countries are mainly in the warmer parts of the world and they have found that sunshine is their most valuable possession. The modern jet plane can transport the jaded city-dwellers of colder lands to warm sunlit beaches in a matter of hours. Thus all the Mediterranean areas and many of the sub-tropical lands have organised tourism to support their poverty-stricken economies. Skyscraper hotels with all the apparatus of amusement have been built in their hundreds in little fishing villages whose names are now well known throughout the world. All this new prosperity depends on the arrival of

In 1961 the Berlin Wall was built through the heart of the city and still remains as a barrier between East and West. Check Point Charlie is the famous control point which links the two halves of the city.

the tourists from industrial countries far away. It is rooted only in the climate of the host countries and should a war or a slump cause a major breakdown, it would immediately collapse as swiftly as it has grown. Meanwhile it has become a world business of great importance.

Man on the Moon

The technical advance since the war has leapt ahead and increases daily. The Russians and the Americans competed to conquer space with the result that men have been placed on the moon, the greatest engineering feat of all time. In 1957 the Russians launched Sputnik I, the first satellite to travel round the earth. Four years later, Yuri Gagarin of the Red Army became the first man to travel in a satellite and he thereafter toured the world as Russia's most precious propaganda figure. The Americans concentrated the full power of their scientific and engineering resources on surpassing the Russians, and succeeded in landing men on the moon. These men transmitted television pictures back to earth and amazed mankind, who watched this scientific miracle in the safety of their own homes. Man had not only conquered his environment on earth but he had defeated gravity and visited the moon.

Many technical benefits have resulted to man from these attempts, although the colossal cost is difficult to justify. Television, first in black and white and then in colour, is available in the homes of all civilised countries. By 'bouncing' pictures off a specially equipped satellite, 'live' transmission throughout the world of any event can take place as it happens. Today the whole world is in touch by sight and sound at a second's notice. The communication system has been established for world government.

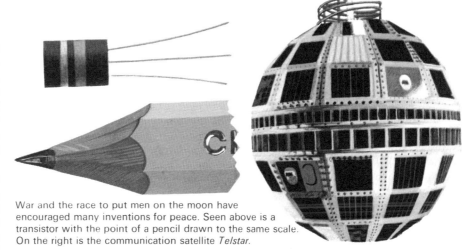

War and the race to put men on the moon have encouraged many inventions for peace. Seen above is a transistor with the point of a pencil drawn to the same scale. On the right is the communication satellite *Telstar*.

Life in the Home
The individual home in the industrial countries is now marvellously equipped. Central heating, radio, television, telephones, refrigerators, vacuum cleaners and waste disposal arrangements make the ordinary householder able to endure all that the climate can do. Life is secure, hygienic, comfortable and entertaining by virtue of technical excellence. The motor car also ministers to man's restlessness and dominates his leisure. But modern man is perhaps more unhappy and discontented in his mechanical palace than he was in his poorer days. Religion has lost much of its force and man's spirit is often sadly depressed in the midst of plenty and comfort.

The young people of the leading industrial nations have begun to show an international pattern in their behaviour. They reject authority more firmly than authority has been rejected before. Travel is part of their education and they often work for a time on the opposite side of the world to their homes. Barriers of society and race constantly weaken. The old classes based on custom and privilege are being disregarded. Promotion through merit alone has spread wider and wider. But because of the enormous profits to be made from commodities which everyone wants on a world market, it is still possible to make astronomic fortunes. The business man, dealing in property, and the star performer providing mass entertainment, are examples. But the young today are more aware of the problems of living and are better prepared to meet them, as change follows change with bewildering speed. It is part of the strength and glory of the human spirit that each age produces the leaders to surmount the problems which face mankind.

The modern age is above all one of protest. Every possible subject and grievance has its active protesters. The movement not to endure in silence appears to be worldwide and growing.

Index

192